THE BAMANA EMPIRE BY THE NIGER
Kingdom, Jihad and Colonization 1712-1920

To the Sisters:

Ollie
Idella
Teasie
Mary
Nora

THE BAMANA EMPIRE BY THE NIGER
Kingdom, Jihad and Colonization 1712–1920

by
SUNDIATA A. DJATA

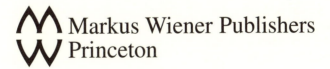
Markus Wiener Publishers
Princeton

Cover photo: The house of Fatima, daughter of Fama Ali, at Yamina. Abon E. Mage, Voyage dans le Soudan Occidental (Paris: Hachette, 1868), p. 179

For information write to: Markus Wiener Publishers
114 Jefferson Road, Princeton, NJ 08540

Library of Congress Cataloging-in-Publication Data

Djata, Sundiata A.
    The Bamana empire by the Niger: kingdom, jihad, and colonization, 1712–1920/Sundiata A. Djata.
    Includes bibliographical references.
    ISBN 1-55876-131-4 hardcover
    ISBN 1-55876-132-2 paperback
    1. Ségu (Mali: Région)—Politics and government.
    2. Bambara (African people)—Politics and government—Mali—Ségou (Région) I. Title.
    DT551.9.S44D53 1996
    966.23'01—dc20   96-11512
                                                                       CIP

Printed in the United States of America on acid-free paper.

Contents

Acknowledgements

I would like to thank my advisor, Dr. Charles C. Stewart, for all his assistance, including the sharing of his research experiences and historical perception which were very helpful to me in every phase of this project. In addition, I am thankful to the other committee members, Dr. Donald Crummey, and Dr. Juliet E. K. Walker for their advice and assistance. Moreover, I extend thanks to the professors in my minor fields, Dr. Nils Jacobsen, Dr. Joseph Love and Dr. Daniel Littlefield.

This work was made possible by the cooperation of many people of the Republic of Mali. I extend thanks Dr. Aly Yero Maïga, the Director General Adjoint of the Centre National de la Recherche Scientifique et Technologie, for granting permission for this study to be done in Mali. I am very grateful to Ali Onquiba, the director of the Archives Nationales, and the staff, Timothée Saye, Abdoulaye Traore, and Alyadjidi Almouctar for all their assistance. I spent so much time in the archives, people thought that I worked there.

I am indebted to several people at the Institut de Sciences Humaines who adopted me as one of the family, including Klena Sanogo, director; Mohammed Erless, Traditions Orales; Kiadiatu Dembele, librarian; and, Seydou Camara, Head of History and Archeology. Moreover, I thank Sasa Dramane, Director of the Office du Niger, and Mohamed Sissoko, Reneothypiste Documentation de l'Office du Niger for all their help. I am also grateful to Salim Touré, the director of Voisins Mondiaux, and his secretary, Assitan Diakite, for their hospitality.

I express my appreciation to several people for their technical advice, including Mr. Balla Moussa Keïta, Radio et Television Mali; the late Mr. Moulaye O. Kida, historian; Prof. Bill Kelleher, anthropologist; Dr. Seydou Theiro, Malian government minister and historian; and Prof. Adam Ba Konare, historian and First Lady of Mali.

A long list of people have been instrumental in other ways, including Tarik Abdel-Halim, Metwalli Abdelsalam, Nazir Chahin, Martin and Calpurnia Compton, Mamadou Coulibaly, Balla Diawara, Eric Dreyer, Matthew Green, Ibrahim Jara, Amadou Jirè, Rosa de Jorio, Adja Keïta, Bassidiki Keïta, Ina Keïta, Modiba S. Keïta, Salif Keïta, Felix Konè, Ibrahim Konè, Byron Lawson, Bob Newton, Marilyn Poole, the late George Randle, Patrick and Kathy Royer, Ismail Safieh, Gaoussou Samake, Kaba Sangare, Sissoko Sidi, Aminata Soumare, Raymond Taylor, Ibrahima Wade, Gaye Wong, and the staff of the University of Illinois Inter-Library Loans. I also thank the real, supreme Supreme, Mary Wilson, for her encouragement; touch! We were both working to complete major projects at the time. Morevoer, Rod Jones of the Cincinnati Bengals was willing to help just when I needed him. Rod, keep making interceptions, and you will wear a Superbowl ring! In addition, I appreciate the enrouraging words of poet Gwendolyn Brooks, a mother to many of us.

I extend special thanks to Sekou Berté for all of his hospitality, assistance, advise, guidance, and sacrifices. I doubt if this dissertation would have ever been written without his help. I would like to thank my research assistant in Segu, Alpha Diallo, who was very instrumental in many phases of the field work in Segu. In addition, general assistants Marco Tirado, Joey Crowder and Aliamane Sa´id, have also contributed to this effort in special ways. Furthermore, I acknowledge field liasons Marouph Jara, Bakaramogo Jirè and Dedeor Simaga, all of Segu. Also, I enjoyed the hospitality of Ba Daby Fofana and family of Segu.

There are no words to express my gratitude to several individuals. First, Makan B. Keïta has worked diligently for the success of this project. Most importantly, I extend a very special recognition to three peerless women who have made every stage of my academic career possible, Ms. Idella M. Madison-Djata, Ms. Ollie B. Perkins-Madison, and Ms. Idella Perkins-Page. To these three, my gratitude is eternal.

Spelling Conventions and Caveats

I have used a spelling system which follows the phonic structure in conformity with the real pronunciation in the Bamana circle for names and places in the Middle Niger. However, I have retained the French or Arabic spelling which appears in the citations of sources written in those languages. The following list includes the different spellings of terms most often used in the text:

Bamana Usage	French Usage
Bamana	Bambara
Bozo	Boso
Jara	Diarra
Kulubali	Coulibaly
Sinzani	Sansanding
Gwènka	Gueniekalari

I have also used different terms for several names and places.

Fula	Peulh
Futaka,	'Umarian Toucouleur
	(also Tokolor)

For many names, only the spelling differs. For instance, I have used '*u*' instead of the '*ou*' in French, '*j*' instead of '*di*,' and '*c*' instead of '*ti*.' In addition, I have avoided apostrophes which French writers have inserted in Bamana names where there are consecutive consonants. Moreover, the plural of Bamana words is formed by adding a '*w*.'

There are a number of Arabic, Bamana and French terms, and most have been italicized. However, I have used a few of them throughout this study, and they appear in regular type. They are: *Tòn, Tònden, Tònjòn, Fama, kafo, talibe and Tirailleur.*[1]

In the seventies, a student[2] of African history coined the term *Atair* to represent "African Traditional Religion." I have adopted this structure to represent Bamana Religion as *Batair.* I have avoided certain terms because of their racial connotations. When the words appear, they do so in the context of the statements by other authors. The word '*warrior*' is a good example. Claude Welch Jr. explains, "the image conjured up by the word warrior is one of the valiant, intrepid individual, courageous and bold in his actions."[3] However, the image is often condescending. In many French archival records and French publications, the men in the African military are called '*warriors*,' but after these same men are conscripted in the French army, they are then called '*soldiers*.' Therefore, I have attempted to avoid certain terms unless they are used in quoting sources, or to avoid confusion. In addition, I have used other terms which more adequately express the concepts in Bamana society than western terms use in the literature. These include:

This study	*Standard Literature*
Population, or specific name of group	Race, tribe, ethnic group
Fama	King
Military leader, lieutenant, general	Chief, warlord
Non-Muslim	Pagan, kaffir
Soldier	Warrior
Leader, head	Chief (of village or province)
Our era	A.D.
Saharan	Moorish, Berber

The term *slavery* is also problematic because too often the word creates images from the institution as it existed in the Americas. Therefore, it is better to use *captive* in most instances. However, I use *slavery* when I cite other informers.

Several oral histories have been translated and published. These works are listed under the name of the oral historian in the footnotes and the bibliography. I also use the name of the translator in parenthesis in the footnote so that the work is more easily identified.

e.g. Banbera (Conrad), p. 25.

However, if the information is found in the introduction or in the footnote supplied by the translator, the translator's name appears first in the footnotes, and the oral historian's name follows in parenthesis.

e.g. Conrad (Banbera), p. 25.

The Bamana Fanga of Segu
c. 1808–1836*

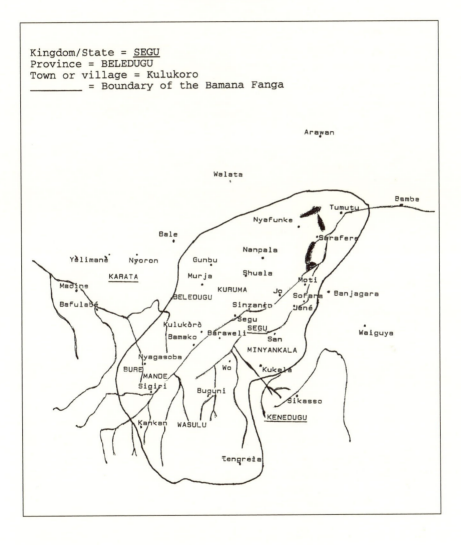

Kingdom/State = <u>SEGU</u>
Province = BELEDUGU
Town or village = Kulukoro
_____ = Boundary of the Bamana Fanga

* Seydou Thiero, "Les Ngolosiw et la decadence du Fanga de Segou, 1818–1893." Unpublished thesis. Ecoloe Normale Superieure de Bamako, 1985, p. 7.

The Sphere of Shaikh Hamad of Masina*

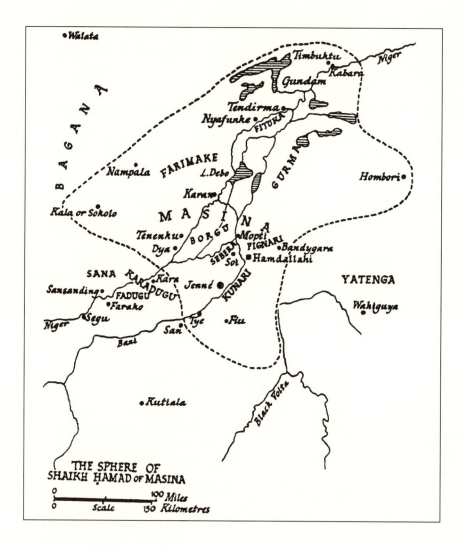

* J. Spencer Trimingham, A History of Islam in West Africa (London: Oxford University, 1970), p. 178.

The 'Umarian State
1861–1890*

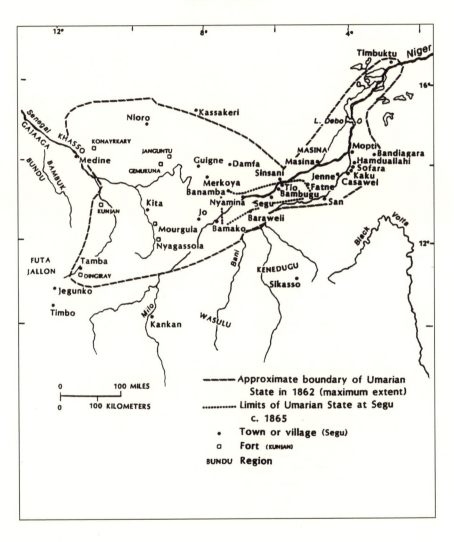

Actual Political Structure
1861–1890*

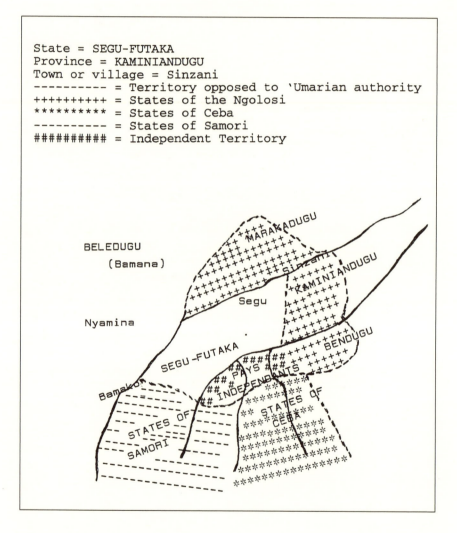

State = SEGU-FUTAKA
Province = KAMINIANDUGU
Town or village = Sinzani
---------- = Territory opposed to 'Umarian authority
++++++++++ = States of the Ngolosi
********** = States of Ceba
---------- = States of Samori
########## = Independent Territory

MARAKADUGU

BELEDUGU

(Bamana)

Sinzani

KAMINIANDUGU

Segu

Nyamina

SEGU-FUTAKA

BENDUGU

Bamako

PAYS INDEPENDANTS

STATES OF CEBA

STATES OF SAMORI

---

* Based on Thiero, p. 74; Notice sur le Royaume Bambara de Segou, Mage-Barth et a Farako, 1889; Abdourhamane Dramane Sissoko, "Segou sous l'occupation Toucouleure, 1860–1890," Unpublished thesis, Ecole des Haute Etudes en Sciences Sociales, 1990, pp. 42-3; Abon Eugene Mage, Voyage dans le Soudan Occidental (Paris: Hachette, 1968), p. 156.

The Cercle of Segu
March 1896*

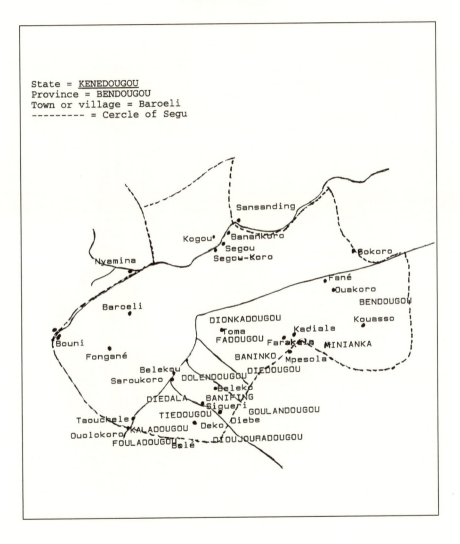

State = <u>KENEDOUGOU</u>
Province = BENDOUGOU
Town or village = Baroeli
--------- = Cercle of Segu

* ANM 1E 71 Rapport politique de Capitaine Commandant de Cercle, mois de mars 1896.

Chi wara, the antelope
headdress of the Bamana.

Introduction

This study is about the history of the people known as the Bamana. There are three major focal points of this study which will be important to the historiography of West Africa and to the study of political hegemony. First, this history is approached from the Bamana point of view. Second, the Bamana *Fanga* is an example of ways in which state unity was formed by ideologies other than religion. The third focus of this study is a comparison between African and European occupation of the same African society. These political activities take place in the Middle Niger Valley.

The Middle Niger region in the West African Sudanic belt has a long history as a buffer between the Mediterranean world and West Africa. From their archeological findings around Jenné and Ja, the McIntoshes have described the entire Upper Niger Delta at the end of the first millennium of our era as a "culture area," a vast region of cultural interaction and integration.[1] The Niger River served as the major axis of communication and transmission of cultural elements.[2] The trade system that developed along the Niger connected a vast West African commerce to the major entrepôts of the Maghrib as well as to the West African coast to the South, and had long been integrated into both Mediterranean and South Atlantic maritime economies.

The Middle Niger is close to the geographical center of West Africa, and is included in the Savanna (dry plains) belt which stretches from the Atlantic Coast to Lake Chad. The northern territory under the political hegemony of the Segu empire stretched through the Sahel into the fringes of the Sahara desert. The Savanna has alternating wet and dry seasons with an annual rainfall ranging from 500 to 1,000 mm a year between May and November. As we will see, the rains affected agriculture, transportation and warfare.

The Niger River (*Joliba* in Bamana) is the dominant geographic fea-
ture in the Middle Niger Valley. First, it provided fish, important to the
local diet, and it supported an important occupational activity. Second, it
facilitated long-distance trade. Third, it was a major form of transportation for travellers, merchants and armies. It connects with the Bani River
north of Mopti; the two rivers were vital to development in the region.

Because of this, the Middle Niger became the heartland of several
states from at least the eighth century, including Ghana and its successors,
Mali and Songhai. The Bamana state of Segu emerged in 1712 as a heri-
tor of the political and economic power centered on the Middle Niger
which ended when the Moroccans invaded the Songhai Empire in 1591.
Exploiting this strategic agricultural and commercial location between
the Niger and Bani Rivers, the Bamana extended their sphere of influence
from Timbuktu in the North to Odienne in the South, and from Bure
Guinea in the West to the frontiers of present-day Burkina Faso in the
East.

Most of the inhabitants of the Middle Niger Valley are Bamana, and
Bamana is the principal language, spoken from the Gambia River in the
West to the Volta River in the East. The other populations are the Maraka
(Marka or Soninke), Fula (FulBe), Bozo, and Sòmònò. Each group spe-
cialized in (but was not limited to) an economic activity: the Fula tended
to be herders; the Maraka traders (and plantation agriculturalists); the
Bozo and Sòmònò, fishermen, and the Bamana, farmers (but animal hus-
bandry was gradually adopted).[3]

The Bamana welded an empire based on a strong, professional army
which developed from the Tòn (den), an age association, under Mamari
Kulibali, called Bitòn. Roberts explains:

> The emergence of the state gave coherence to the, social formation
> in the Middle Niger Valley, home to diverse groups. The state pro-
> vided the conditions for, the reproduction of each group not as an
> individual, community, but as a set of interpenetrated units.[4]

The Bamana farmers produced surplus grain, and the Bamana soldiers
produced slaves and booty.

The Bamana social hierarchy consisted of the *hòrònw*, the nobles; the
nyamakalaw, casted groups;[5] and *jònw*, slaves.[6] It is the Tòn association

which changed its role in the Bamana community itself, and transformed politics in the Middle Niger Valley. Bamana religion, *Batair*, is based on belief of a supreme creator and lesser divinities. *Batair* is expressed through rituals associated with occupational and other institutions, i.e. age sets, secret societies, and religious associations. The secret societies were village organizations whose members performed important duties such as preserving agricultural knowledge, and religious association members who served as intermediaries between the spiritual and the temporal worlds. A ritual object, called the *boliw*, was necessary to carry out these duties. The *boli* served as a place of sacrifice which was performed to call on the spiritual force, the *nyama*.[7]

The Bamana Fanga of Segu was itself conquered by two foreign powers in a thirty-year period; the first was African, led by al-Hajj 'Umar Tal (1861) in the name of religious reform, and the second was European (1890) for the cause of French imperial expansion. The objectives of the two conquests were similar: to dominate the rich agricultural lands and commercial routes in the Middle Niger.

The problems faced by each occupying force were also similar: 1) to consolidate their occupation over the Middle Niger Valley, 2) to protect the trade routes, and 3) to integrate local economies of the various populations into the institutions of the governing regime. The Bamana state of Segu had succeeded in consolidating political control over the Middle Niger Valley through a series of military campaigns, and it secured the trade routes with a standing professional army. In addition, they integrated local economic activities in a contractual system which benefited the Bamana regime and the other participants in the economy (Sòmònòs, Marakas, Fulas, etc.). On the other hand, the Bamana regime allowed smaller political units, particularly on the periphery of the state, a high degree of autonomy.

The 'Umarians had less success in their political quest during their short-lived occupation (1860 to 1890). Al-Hajj 'Umar Tal and his son, Ahmadu, never fully consolidated their political occupation, hampered by a thirty-year war with the Bamana dynasty that refused to submit, internal problems after the death of 'Umar, and the imperial expansion of the French. If war boosted the economy in the Bamana period, it seriously disrupted the economy during the 'Umarian phase. In addition, the

'Umarians were unable to protect the trade routes, thereby stifling the trade which had flourished until 1860. Moreover, unlike the Bamana, the 'Umarians attempted to force their ideology, Islam, on the non-Islamic populations, especially in nearby urban areas and in the central zone of the capital.

The French regime falls between these poles set by the Bamana and the 'Umarians. The French attempted to re-create the atmosphere for economic activity which had existed under the Bamana regime, but transformed certain features of the political system in order to integrate their interests into these economic activities. Although the populations, particularly those in the villages, maintained some autonomy, the French attempted to spread another ideology, the French language and culture, through various institutions (schools, military, missions, etc.)

This is a story of those two conquests and efforts by two alien powers to assert hegemony over the Bamana. In contrast to most of the accounts written from the viewpoint of the occupying forces, this one attempts to examine events from the perspective of the Bamana themselves. The themes I will focus upon are: how oppressed populations respond to hegemonic regimes, how the culture and politics of the oppressed influence subsequent occupations, and how their actions affect the decision-making processes of the occupying regime.

A common theme in the historiography of foreign occupation is how it transforms societies. Equally important is how the oppressed respond to the occupation, and the degree to which the colonized affect the colonizer. The French regime in the Middle Niger attempted to use various established political, social, and economic institutions to their advantage. This required the need to investigate and understand those institutions. Meanwhile, the colonized population also studied the occupying forces to better understand them and to design their responses.

In this study, we will focus on the region of Segu, one of two principal kingdoms (the other being Kaarta) that the Bamana ruled. The Bamana kingdom of Segu offers an excellent opportunity for this type of study because of the proximity in time of the two foreign occupations. I selected the Segu kingdom over Kaarta for two principal reasons. One, the Segu state was at the core of the Middle Niger commercial network, and each alien force used Segu as a major power base. Two, Bamana control in

Segu was stronger than in Kaarta, and the Bamana regime was better able to fend off these foreign forces.

There is a small amount of monographic literature on the Bamana. The earliest studies are ethnographies written by French anthropologists, including Abbé Joseph Henry (1910), Charles Monteil (1924), Louis Tauxier (1927), Germaine Dieterlen (1951), and Viviana Paques (1954). These ethnographers attempted to explain the cultural, religious, and political organization of the Bamana society, presumably in order to better serve the needs of the colonial administration.

More recent studies have given new insights to Bamana political, economic, and cultural structures. For example, Richard Roberts' economic history (1987) assesses the Bamana, 'Umarian, and French domination of the Middle Niger and the effects on the economy by each regime. He focuses on the major commercial activities of the Middle Niger, but gives slight attention to the social history of the Bamana.

Lilyan Kesteloot (1978) and David Conrad (1990) have translated the oral history of Tayiru Banbera, a local historian, and have added their analysis to the text.[8] The monograph by Conrad offers a more extensive text by Banbera. Banbera cites many examples of the Bamana social, judicial, and political systems. Serge Sauvageot (1965) and G. Dumestre (1974) have provided additional translations of oral texts. These translations and the ethnographies include versions of the historical legends about the arrival of the Kulubali family to Segu, and the emergence of the two dynasties which ruled Segu, the Kulubali and Jara dynasties.

The conquest of al-Hajj 'Umar and the propagation of Islam in the Middle Niger has been well documented. Martin Klein (1972) and Marion Johnson (1976) have both treated social and economic motives in Islamic expansion. Several 'Umarian chronicles and documents have been translated into French and/or English, and three are quite extensive. Mohammadou Tyam's work on the life of 'Umar has been translated from Fula by Henri Gadsen (1935). In addition, Sidi Mohamed Mahibou and Jean Louis Triaud (1983) have translated several documents which discuss the military career of 'Umar and the reign of Ahmadu. On the other hand, John Hanson and David Robinson (1991) have translated and analyzed documents which focus mainly on the reign of Ahmadu in Segu and

Nioro. David Robinson's monograph on 'Umarian political history (1985) chronicles 'Umar's conquest and subsequent rule. These latter works provide important working chronologies for the region.

Likewise, the French occupation of the Middle Niger has also been treated by French administrators who explain the goals of French colonialism, and the actors in the field. These include Joseph Gallieni (1885), Camille Pietri (1885), Henri Frey (1888), Louis Archinard (1890), and Lt. Hourst (1899). These works, however, are written from the French point of view.

Others in the military have written works on the Africans in the French African army, including Hippolyte-Victor Marceau (1911), and General Duboc (1939). Lassalle-Séré's monograph appeared in 1929. Recently, Shelby Davis (1970) and Myron Echenberg (1991) have written more objective syntheses of the African soldier experience in the French African army.

The 'Umarian chronicles and the works by the French have described, from the perspective of the conquerors, the economic, political, and social transformations they attempted to set in motion. What remains unanswered from these studies is the participation in this period of the majority population in the Middle Niger, the Bamana.

I have made minor use of the standard ethnographies written during the period of French occupation; however, many secondary works have been grounded in the literary tradition of these ethnographies. C. Tsehloane Keto has expressed a growing concern of African historiography:

> The Africa of the 1900s presents a haunting global paradox. African reality represents the long-term effects of a system of decision-making about culture, economics and politics, to name a few areas, in the hands of people based outside the continent itself from the colonial and neocolonial contexts.[9]

This study relies heavily upon oral histories and archival reports. I have conducted a series of interviews identified as the Maksun Collection in the bibliography. Most of the informers were elder members of families instead of professional oral historians, but the latter were not precluded. Most of the interviews were conducted in Bamana. I have also used oral testimony collected by other scholars, especially that of Seydou Theiro. The oral informants tend to focus on the political history of the region although they make references to other institutions. These oral histories, and those which have been published provide a strong basis for a history of a region from the Bamana point of view.[10]

I also made extensive use of the National Archives in Bamako. The archival reports often reveal how the Bamana responded to the foreign occupation, and how they helped shape the decision-making processes of these administrations, especially during the French occupation. It is important to note that the information in the archives on the early history of the Bamana and the Middle Niger and on the 'Umarian period were based on interviews by early French administrators and travel reports. Particularly helpful are the few letters written to and from African functionaries.

This study is divided into seven chapters. The first is a brief overview of the Bamana state of Segu, focusing on oral tradition relating to the emergence of the two Bamana dynasties, Kulubali and Jara. In addition, the relationship between the Bamana and the other populations in the region is crucial to understand economic prosperity of the Middle Niger, and how the Bamana were able to hold political power (in Segu itself) for 148 years.

The second chapter concerns al-Hajj 'Umar Tal and the 'Umarian occupation of Segu. After a brief biographical background on al-Hajj, I discuss the inability of the 'Umarians to occupy the entire Middle Niger valley, and the cleavages within the 'Umarian political structure. Economically, the 'Umarians were unable to build upon the structure created by the Bamana, nor were they able to create new economic stategies.

The third focuses on the Bamana thirty-year war against the 'Umarians, how the Ngolosi (the Jara dynasty) maintained its leadership throughout this period, and the Bamana response to 'Umarian occupation. The 'Umarian attempt to Islamize the Bamana was hampered by the Bamana who fought to maintain their cultural and political heritage. The role of the Tòn continued to be essential in the Bamana struggle to maintain independence.

The fourth chapter describes the third major set of actors in the Middle Niger; the French. Until the 1890s, the French used negotiation (treaties, alliances and paper claims) as their primary method to expand their imperialist goals. In promotion of their own cause, the French attempted to take advantage of the anti-'Umarian forces, internally and externally.

In the fifth chapter, we see how the French made the transition to the militant phase of imperial occupation. One of the major themes in this chapter is the role of the Africans in the European occupation of Africa. The main focus is the Bamana role in retaking Segu from the 'Umarians, and the ultimate defeat of Ahmadu.

The sixth chapter discusses the attempt of the French to re-establish the political economy of Segu created by the Bamana during the pre-'Umarian period, and place the French administration atop that structure. However, the Bamana leaders opposed the overlordship of French administration. The war against the French was a continuation of the effort by the Ngolosi and other Bamana leaders to maintain independence.

The seventh chapter returns to the Bamana responses to alien rule, and their influence upon the early years of French occupation, culminating with the beginning of World War I. Our focus here is on French attempts to spread their culture among the local populations through religion, systems of justice, education, impressed colonial service, and language.

In conclusion, I have returned to the general themes of alien or colonial occupations as seen from beneath, by the colonized, to compare the effects of African overule and European colonization. To this end, I have tried to respond to particular questions that have been put to the Middle Niger populations, e.g. the "emergence" of the Bamana as an "ethnic" identity by contemporary anthropologists, the significance of the vocabulary in the historiography of political hegemony, and the inclusion of the "African voice" in the history of Africa.

CHAPTER 1

THE BAMANA FANGA OF SEGU

The Bamana were able to build an empire with one of their major social institutions. The development of a professional army enabled the Bamana rulers to develop a military state, but one where the military was intricately tied to politics. The Bamana use of war and peace parties was essential in the expansion and cohesion of the state, and in the promotion of the rich commercial activities generally in the hands of other populations.

Although the Bamana state of Segu has been assumed to have emerged around 1712, the Bamana presence in the Middle Niger dates to a much earlier time. It is believed that the Bamana migrated to the region in the mid-seventeenth century. Pottery collection identified as Late Assemblage has been found in an excavation on small, low-mounded habitation sites, mostly located within the longitudinal dune system. This site produced numerous tobacco pipes which are believed to have been introduced in the Western Sudan in 1591 by the Moroccans when they invaded the Songhai Empire. Based on oral accounts in Nampala, founded by the Bamana during the seventeenth century, the Bamana, probably millet farmers, settled on the light sandy soil of the longitudinal dunes, or its contact with the degraded dunes.[1]

Barth (based on Mage's finding) asserted that the Bamana came from the south at the end of the seventeenth century, and settled in the country without opposition from older settlers, mainly Markas. "The two groups never confused themselves (he reported), and today, still, the differences are clearly marked."[2] Elsewhere, French ethnographers reported that the Bamana came from the mountains of Kong in the East;[3] when this migration occurred is unknown.

Abderrahman b. Abdallah b.'Imran b. 'Amir Es-Sa'di in his *Tarikh Es-Sudan* gives some indication of Bamana presence as early as the mid-sixteenth century around Jenné.[4] In the summer of 1559 El-Amir of Jenné is reported to have said to Askia Daud on the latter's arrival:

> We have placed you at the head of a district and you do not keep watch on it because the Bamana are here now in very great numbers, and they have succeeded in assuring some advantages.[5]

Later, when Masina battled the Moroccans in 1600, many Bamana mercenaries fought with the Prince of Masina, Hammedi-Amina who "took flight with his companions, leaving only the Pagans [viz. Bamana] to the seizures with El-Mastafa."[6] The Moroccans eventually punished the city of Chininku because Cha'a-ma ku, who headed a troop of Bamana soldiers, raided Jenné.[7]

By the end of the sixteenth century the Bamana had already built a reputation for being great soldiers, and their hire as mercenaries attested to the esteem in which they were held by their neighbors. In addition to fighting with the Prince of Masina, Bamana mercenaries fought with Fondoko Hammedi-Amina in 1599, and fought against Jenné at Ti (or Tiya) where all the riflemen of the Moroccan column perished except for two.

Until 1645 the non-Islamic masses still followed a political system stemming from the Mali Empire. That year the Bamana revolted against the Sanakoi and Farko-Koe. Apparently little came of the revolt since Es-Sa'di writes, "God, the Most High by His Power and force, calmed the fire of that insurrection."[8] Despite this, Person argues that the Bamana, in fact, destroyed Sana and Faraku, and Es-Sa'di agrees that the Bamana did return and destroy the latter. That same year the Bamana went to Chibla, and found that the entire population had evacuated; nevertheless, they are reported to have destroyed the city, "stone by stone," except the mosque and the home of Es-Sa'di.[9]

In the early eighteenth century, the Bamana opposed the hegemony of

Kong. Person argues that the literature includes "racist myths," created by French ethnographers who asserts that the initiative of this opposition was due to an invasion of a "superior race," the Fula. However, Person asserts that this theory is indefensible, and it was the internal evolution of the Manding society which produced the new political features. Moreover, Bazin maintains that the revolt of the Fula (of Masina) against Timbuktu in 1645 was the decisive factor. Since the Bamana soldiers were mercenaries for Masina, that campaign produced a strong military organization. As a result, the Bamana, a group at the bottom of an urban and Islamized society, began to emerge as a powerful force.[10]

Regional oral literature traces the origin of Segu to four settlements. The first was Sikòrò, founded by Usumani Jirè, a distinguished Muslim who came from the East.[11] The second, Sekòrò, was named for Seku Marifu Kari Kusi (also known as Seku Kòròba), another Marabout.[12] Eventually, Seku Kòròba assembled students, built the village of Se, and called it Sebugu. When the population increased, Sekura was founded.[13] Thereafter, Segu was composed of four villages, Segukòrò (Sekòrò), Segu Bugu (Sebugu), Segukura (Sekura), and Segu Sikòrò.[14] Segu was known as the city of the balanzas (trees), the balanza being the symbol of royal treason, and treason was an important ingredient in the political history of Segu.

According to oral tradition, there was no king in Segu before the rise of the Bamana. Instead, the villages were founded and led by village leaders. At that time, armies encircled the village and raided them, taking riches, animals, and slaves in order to sell them. As a result, the village leaders assembled in order to find a solution, and each leader agreed to send men to their neighbors when raiders came to attack them. The village leaders met once a week, and recruited the young men to defend the villages. This is how the elders created the Tòn (the association of young men). Each time the young men heard the drums signaling an attack, the Tòn went to fight.[15] The Bamana state would be built upon the institution of the Tòn, and two of the early great leaders came to power via their relationship to the Tòn while changing the relationship between the Tòn and the developing state.

Three legends are very important in the history of Segu: 1) the founding of Segu and Kaarta by two brothers, 2) the emergence of Bitòn, and

3) the triumph of Ngolo. These are essentially historical legends because, while many of the developments involved actual events, they are intermingled with supernatural occurrences. The supernatural elements were significant for the emergence of rulers because the Bamana Fama, as Person explains, was connected to supernatural forces which assured the order of the world.[16] The great leaders of Segu had divine intervention, protecting them so that they could attain their destinies. In addition, Kesteloot argues that nearly all great kings and heroes have a legendary origin, justifying *a posteriori* their importance in their respective societies, i.e. Sunjata, Chaka, Achille, Silamaka, Charlemagne, etc.[17] Moreover, Monteil asserts that "The Blacks do not admit that an important man, a powerful leader, could be ordinary or simple. This is why the supernatural facts are in the historic traditions."[18] Furthermore, Mamadou Wane explains that each myth is tied to the problem of power, and concerning Bitòn Kulubali, it is evident that the primary object of the myth is the legitimation of power.[19]

Symbolism connected physical and spiritual worlds. For example, the Niger River or Joliba was the base of the Sudanese empires, serving as a means of transport vital to commerce and for the military, but as also a source of foodstuff, and the corresponding industry. It is understandable that somehow the supernatural forces of the River would be included in the historical legend of Segu which was situated on the Niger River. The Niger (Joliba) plays an important role in all three of the historical legends. Bitòn, and the triumph of Ngolo.

It has been noted that in one version the Bamana came from the mountains of Kong around the end of the seventeenth century, led by two brothers, Niangolo and Baramangolo Kulibali.[20] They are said to have arrived at the Niger, near Nyamina, and were unable to cross the river; however, a fish, offered to aid them. Baramangolo crossed first and warned the fish to not aid his brother. Nevertheless, the fish did aid him, and Niangolo killed the fish. Consequently, Baramangolo refused to stay with his brother, and continued north where his descendants founded Bèlèdugu and Kaarta. Meanwhile, Niangolo installed himself in Segu.[21] It is ironic that the more "ruthless" of the two would lead to the founding of a dynasty which would one day rule the Middle Niger.

Mamari Kulibali, called Bitòn, developed his power base by reorganizing the Tòn, by then an age-grade[22] association, making it the dominant force in Segu society. The Tòn operated on a co-operative basis, hunting and fishing, which reflected the larger Bamana society. As a result, it became a haven for the poor of society, both slave and free. Kesteloot found that of the ten versions recorded of the founding of the state, all had several events involving Bitòn in common: 1) He was a stranger and founder of the empire; 2) he was a hunter in a country populated by fishermen and farmers; 3) he settled at Segu with the consent of the people; 4) Faro, the river spirit, gave him grain and instruction; and 5) the choice of Bitòn as leader of the Tòn was contested.[23] In short, Bitòn was the choice of the Spirits since Faro, the river spirit, aided and advised him.[24] In addition, Bitòn was the choice of men since he was elected to be the leader of the Tòn.

Bitòn Kulibali came from Bèndugu to settle in Segu in the late seventeenth century (around 1689). Persons' oral sources reveal that he came from Fa, a village near Segukòrò (Sikòrò).[25] Bitòn migrated because of the proverb that "when the end of the world comes, one should be in great towns; when the end of the world comes, one should be by the rivers."[26]

Bitòn Kulibali,[27] was born after his father's death. Being an orphan made a child different, thus creating a rupture with his origins, foreshadowing the creation of a new order. On the other hand, the mother, Masunu Sako, was important in mostof the versions collected because she moves with him to the river. However, the father, Fa Sine Kulubali, is "deleted" from the legend although some versions do refer to him.[28] For example, Monteil's informer, Kare Tammura, spoke of Bitòn's father, Fa Sine, who was too poor to pay the fine of eighty heads of beef for Bitòn. In addition, the elders later complained to his father about Bitòn's actions.[29]

After Bitòn and his mother relocated to the river, she planted *ngòyò* (a bitter vegetable similar to a tomato or eggplant), but a water spirit ate the plant. When Bitòn caught the spirit, she took him to her father, Faro. She warned Bitòn to refuse all the things which Faro would offer him except the millet seed. Consequently, he refused the 100 horses, 100 cows, 100 sheep, 100 [gold] *mithqals*, 100 goats, and 100 virgins, and accepted the millet seed. Faro instructed him to plant the millet, but not to harvest it. Instead, the birds would spread the seeds over the region, and as far as they took it would be the extent of Bitòn's power.[30]

Now that Bitòn was the choice of the Spirits, he had to be the choice of men. Bitòn competed with Menkòrò Kulibali and Kassum Boarè, son of the leader of Doua, as leader of the Tòn. The other members of the association were divided according to their allegiance to one of the contenders. Menkòrò's father and other elders complained that the Tòn worked little, and wasted millet (probably making millet beer). The fact that the Tòn refused to work in the fields was a break from the social role of the young men. Although the Tòn had been an institution which reproduced social and economic systems of the Bamana, and were controlled by the elders, Bitòn created new functions for the Tòn. Therefore, Person sees the Tòn as a "rupture with the lineage system" of the Bamana and the "more or less egalitarian ideology of the society."[31] Eventually, Bitòn asked his Tòn followers to build a place where he could live in complete independence at Segukòrò.[32]

Some Tòn members elected Bitòn as their leader because his mother was very kind to them, making *korokoro* beer and honey liquor for them. Unlike the other mothers who made beer for the Tòn members, she did not require that they plough or clear the land. Therefore, they decided to give what they could to Bitòn's mother. This collection for Bitòn's mother became a permanent custom, called *disòngò*, the honey price, and was given to subsequent regimes. However, it later became known as *nisòngò*, or soul price.[33]

Versions differ on the events which led up to the ability of the Tòn to wield control in the vicinity of Segu, but they agree that a big celebration was planned at Dugukura,[34] and free men were invited. The Tònden were told not to drink, and when the people had drank most of the beer, the Tònden attacked them. After they cracked the heads of 100 free men, the rest submitted. Afterwards, the people in the villages within close radius of Segu lived in fear. Dyara notes that the Tòn repeated this episode in order to gain the allegiance of other villages.

Some villages refused to pay the newly-imposed tax which led to events which enabled the Tònden to acquire captives. When Binaba (Big Bina) of Fabugu realized that the tax would be permanent, he refused to pay. The Tòn sent men to destroy Binaba's house and take the village people, dividing the men among the Tòn leaders. These men, whose heads were shaved (two braids were left) became the first captives of the Tòn, or the *Tònjònw*.[35]

According to Charles Monteil, the defeated people of Siguiri were alos taken and made slaves of the Tòn. However, the first slave was an old captive of Mamari's father who asked to be a slave. The first captives of the Tòn performed odd jobs, but their roles changed as they were co-opted into a professional army. Initially, the military leaders were the original members of the Tòn, or the Tònden; these were free men.

Jean Bazin argues that the political model of Bitòn's rule (the "primitive Malinke Mode") was ancient, and that Bitòn was "more of a renewal than an origin." The model was a chieftaincy that exacted by force the surplus and riches of neighboring communities, and formed an association of dependents, voluntary or captured militarily, around a leader.[36]

French archival records note that the Tònjònw were originally slaves of the Fama, being his permanent guard. The Tònjòn executed "raids, murders, revenges and generally all the bad things decided by the Fama."[37] This is unclear because it depends on when the actual title of Fama was taken by Bamana leaders. But, from oral testimony it seems to be the consensus that the Tònjònw were originally slaves of the Tònden. It was Ngolo who would break the control of Tònden, and reduce all Tòn members to Tònjònw status. Perhaps at this point, they became the guards for the Fama. According to Person, the personal slaves were the *sofa*, serving as the Fama's bodyguards.[38]

The number of the Tònjònw augmented rapidly with the addition of war captives. They lived close to the Fama, and did not farm, "possessing only a horse or bow."[39]

G. N. Uzoigwe provides an overview of the soldier's relationship to the ruler, his function in territorial administration, and his impact within the state. He argues that the soldier saw politics as state power. He adds:

> Since a number of African states were conquest states, the integration of the military and politics and the invocation of soldier values in these states was carefully cultivated along with the construction of historic charters with an overlay of the divine right of rulers in order to ensure the survival and viability of these states.[40]

Although Uzoigwe maintains that the ideal king was a great soldier (as could be seen in the military states he described, i.e. Shaka of the Zulu nation), this was no longer the case for the Bamana state of Segu when Ngolo took control. The throne remained within the Jara family, and was no longer given to a Tòn member based on his seniority, or his bravery in battle. As we will see, Ngolo succeeded in attaining this by effectively destroying the power of the Tòn.[41]

Although Richard Roberts insists that the Bamana state was a military state, Uzoigwe explains how, for example, in the Oyo Empire the army, while a very important instrument in the rise and fall of the empire, did not make the Oyo Empire a military state. Similarly, military expeditions created the Bamana state, but the military was fused with politics, mainly as a means to insure tribute. In addition, the military leaders were also administrators, positions which further tied them to politics. Bitòn placed clients (relatives and military leaders) in villages. Later, Ngolo placed sons and other relatives in the provinces.[42] Uzoigwe further explains that the "warrior tradition" manifested itself in socio-cultural and economic relationships in the organization of the state. The individual soldier was first and foremost a citizen, a part of the extended family, subject to social manipulation by the state in the interests of stability.[43] However, the survival of the king depended on the alliance between the king and the soldiers.

Generally, the Tòn members ceased to provide agricultural labor, and under Bitòn became professional soldiers. Soldiers were no longer assembled in an ad hoc manner to respond to specific emergencies. Instead, young men, regardless of origin or artisan castes were obliged to serve in the army.[44] In this sense, the basic egalitarian ideology of the Bamana was preserved. The one exception was the Fama. "Due to a basic solidarity imposed by the Tòn on the common cult of the national *boliw* of Segu, the Fama, first equal to the Tònden, succeeded in imposing himself as master."[45] On the four great boliw the Tòn members took oaths which were impossible to break.

The soldiers were divided into units called *kèlèbolow*, arms of war, under a leader, called Tònjòn *Kuntigi*. The "arms" flanked a central mass called *disi* (chest), composed of the pure Tònjòn. The army also had feet and a head (what Ibrahima Kake calls the anthropomorphisation of the army). Behind the *disi*, was a special reserve, also formed of pure Tònjòn (*Tòn-kòrò-bolo*). The Fama either designated a general or *Kèlè tigi*, or took command himself. Kaké explains that the youngest of the sofa were pages or grooms while the older ones were men of confidence that the Fama charged with missions. Some of the young sofaw were recruited among young prisoners of war, placed under the immediate authority of the sovereign, and required to perform diverse functions.[46] Moreover, garrisons were placed around Segu and on strategic routes between campaigns.

The Bamana elite troops were armed with axes in order to break the walls (around the city). However, the important military leaders carried a copper or silver ax. In addition, spears were also a weapon of distinction because the common soldiers had bows and arrows. The military leaders carried a curved sword (probably of Turkish origin). Gradually, guns were introduced in Segu during Mamari's reign by an army from Kong, according to one account;[47] then flintlock muskets appeared sometime during the seventeenth century.[48] Later, the Marabouts of Ngolo went to Morocco once a year with gold to buy guns. "In order to hide the arms, they wrapped them in cowhides so no one knew how the arms entered the country."[49]

Dyara maintains that the Tònjòn had no social obligations. "They did not even recognize God, only the Fama." Their loyalty to the Fama superseded any other relationship, even with their families because "they had no other occupation than to wait on the Fama." He argues that the Tònjòn did not fear death. On the other hand, they feared humiliation and the shame of defeat, and this is reflected in a popular Bamana proverb, *Saya ka na ka di ka tèmè malo ka na ka,* which means "death is better than shame."[50] The Bamana created a state where "capturing slaves [sic] and conquering territory were the clearest expressions of warfare."[51] Essentially, the Bamana society was twofold: the Bamana farmers provided surplus grain, and the soldiers produced slaves and booty. Some of the booty was distributed to the soldiers, and some was retained by the Fama which over time created a valuable treasure for the Famaw.[52]

Roberts argues that warfare was the principal expression of state power and remained the primary form of enterprise, an expression of the internal cohesion of the state, and acted as an engine of economic growth.[53] The oral history of the Bamana rule seems to base the analysis of the Bamana military campaigns in terms of politics, not economics whereas

The grave of Bitòn Mamari Kulibali at Segu-Sekòrò.
(Photo by Makan B. Keïta)

Roberts describes the importance of the military campaigns to the economy as well as their providing political cohesion and expansion. For instance, in the many oral histories that I have collected, none include information on the sale of captives outside the kingdom of Segu. On the other
hand, they do include discussion of how the captives were used by the
state. Roberts explains that the emergence of the Segu state coincided
with the era of increased slave exports. However, the Segu state avoided
dependency on one primary market, unlike its coastal counterparts, by
exporting slaves into three markets (Atlantic, desert and interior).[54] In
addition, many captives were placed in the Bamana military.

Bitòn placed clients in major villages, his cousin Cèkura at Nango, and
military leaders Tòn Masa at Noi, Kanuba Nyuma at Pelengena, Kafa
Jugu at Gassi, and Nogoli Keba at Sama. This is why Conrad argues that
after Bitòn died, the kingdom only existed by the "episodic collaboration
of these leaders."[55]

After Bitòn's death in 1755, his sons ruled for a short time.[56] At that
time Tòn leaders were powerful and had faithful followers in their districts. Bitòn's first son, Bakari, was a Muslim which made him unaccept-

able to the Tòn leaders. During his reign, the Segu army failed to conquer the villages they attacked which is contrasted in oral narrative to former times when they could easily destroy them. From the day of his coronation, Bakari was in conflict with the Tòn members who were divided among the probable claimants to the throne when Bitòn died.[57] Bakari's rule was further complicated by his having been sent to Jenné for an Islamic education, and that he openly encouraged his subjects to practice Islam.[58] Bakari is reported to have died six months after his father's death.[59]

Bitòn's second son was a leper. A vain individual, he was also very brutal, and his reign was marked by terror because he was powerful enough to oppress the Tonjon.[60] For example, on one occasion he was reported to have executed 450 people. When he refused to live in Segukòrò, he created additional criticisms (instead, he lived in Segubugu). His biggest mistake, however, was his attempt to disempower the Tònjòn, causing the four principal military leaders, Tòn Masa, Kanuba Nyuman, Kafa Jugu and Kolè, to refuse to fight or farm. Eventually, Jekòrò was assassinated. Monteil asserts that Tòn Masa shot him,[61] and most sources agree that most of Bitòn's family was assassinated. Bitòn's last son, Jònkolo, however, was spared by seeking refuge in the house of Ngolo Jara who was married to one of Bitòn's daughters.[62]

The empire was then ruled by three Tòn leaders, Tòn Masa Dembele, a Senufu (1757-60); Kanuba Nyuma, a Fula (1760-63); and Kafa Jugu, perhaps a Kulibali of secondary lineage (1763-65). Tòn Masa of Nguin was not a slave, but a hunter who is said to have come to Segu chasing an elephant; subsequently, he came to hold an important place in the Tòn.[63] In 1740 the Tònjòn initially refused to follow Tòn Masa in a campaign against Konguere, but changed their decision after great deliberation. Tòn Masa, however, was wounded in the battle and later died. It was suspected that one of the Tòn members shot him because the arrow could have only been shot from behind him.

Next, Kanuba Nyuma assumed power. He was also a free man even though people considered him a slave for reasons which are unclear. He was wounded in a battle against Kafa Jugu and was paralyzed on one side, and died after four years of suffering. The last Tònjòn to rule was Kafa Jugu of Gasi. He too was free, but had the name of a slave. Unfortunately, he managed the state affairs poorly. As a result, Ngolo sent an emissary to warn him that he "acted like someone who sought to lose power," but Kafa Jugu ignored this advice, marched against Kolè, and died under mysterious circumstances.[64]

Following Kafa Jugu's death the throne was vacant. The fate of the next Fama, Ngolo, had been intertwined with the life of Bitòn Kulubali. Versions differ on how Ngolo became a slave of Bitòn, but they do agree that he was placed in servitude in lieu of taxes. Monteil asserts that his father was dead, and his uncle, Menkòrò, lost money gambling; therefore, Ngolo was sent to Bitòn in place of the tax. Versions given by Person and Dyara agree that Ngolo's brothers wanted to get rid of him because of the prophecy that he would someday become a king. Ngolo's family promised to purchase him at the end of the year. Again, Ngolo's father is not mentioned in most versions, but Dumestre mentions his father, although not by name, and that the brothers hid their plotting from their father. A final account comes from a French ethnographer in an archival report that asserts that Ngolo's father, Fan Jara, did not have enough to pay the tax, and sent his son instead.[65]

Ngolo was born between 1710 and 1720 at Nyuaba, 100 kilometers southwest of Segu.[66] After an old man predicted that Ngolo would one day be powerful, his brothers decided to remove him from the area, fearing the power he would gain in the future. They did this by deciding to withhold a portion of the tax, and offering to send Ngolo instead, with the promise to come and pay the remainder of the tax within a year.[67]

The brothers failed to purchase Ngolo, and he remained a slave in the house of Bitòn. Bitòn and the elders of Segu became aware of Ngolo's prophesied rise to power. Fearing the prophecy, Bitòn plotted to rid himself of Ngolo. According to Banbera, Bitòn put a mithqal in a pot of porridge and had all the children eat from the same container as instructed by a religious leader; the one who found the mithqal in the ladle would inherit power. Unbeknownst to Bitòn, Bitòn's children had asked Ngolo to eat with them, and Ngolo found the mithqal.[68] Afterwards, Bitòn told Ngolo to keep the gold piece until he asked for it, but if Ngolo would lose it, he would be executed. Bitòn instructed his men to steal the mithqal from Ngolo, who kept it in the sack which young boys carried. The men stole the mithqal while Ngolo was sleeping, and threw it in the river. When

Bitòn requested it, Ngolo realized that he would be executed if he could not produce it. However, Bitòn's favorite wife loved Ngolo, and requested that the execution be postponed until Ngolo went to get fish for her and clean it. Ngolo bought some fish from a Sòmònò fisherman, and when he cleaned one of the fish, he found the mithqal. After Ngolo returned the mithqal when asked, Bitòn could do nothing to him.[69] After the failed attempt to rid himself of Ngolo, Bitòn decided to render favor to Ngolo, installing him at Segukòrò and giving him the name *Jenfa*, priest of the four great *Boliw*. Eventually, Ngolo married one of Bitòn's daughter.

Following the death of Kafa Jugu in 1766, Nankòròba Nzange was the eldest Tòn leader in line, but Ngolo was his rival. After Ngolo killed Nzange, he assembled an army at Segu, and invited the Seguvians to choose a successor. They selected Ngolo, but he declined the nomination, saying, "What I came to do, I did not do it by the desire of power," but to save the country. Nevertheless, Ngolo accepted power three months later.[70] It is Ngolo's family that a formed a dynasty which would last until the end of Bamana state of Segu, and it was called the *Ngolosi*, since after Ngolo, only his sons and grandsons would reign as Fama. However, a Marabout from the Kunta family warned Ngolo not to name any of his descendents "Ali;" otherwise, the Bamana would lose their power in Segu.[71]

After he became Fama, Ngolo reorganized the army, which included a powerful personal guard. First, he took revenge on the village of his birth, and sacrificed his uncles who betrayed him to the Boliw.[72] Then he eliminated the vestiges of the former Tòn, divesting them their armies and domains. When they resisted, they were militarily crushed. Ultimately, under Ngolo, there was unity in the kingdom and after destroying the seven military generals. After the defeat of the last, Toranke, he began the renovation of the kingdom, making war against villages and local rulers closest to the center of Segu.[73] The Kulibali of Sokolo (in Kuruma), and its leader Sidi Baba, wanted revenge for his defeated relatives at Segu. This led to Ngolo's greatest war.

It is known that Ngolo extended the power of Segu to Kènèdugu in the south, the Valley of the Niger and Bani in the east (to Jenné and Masina), and to Kaarta to the west. In 1770 Ngolo led a campaign to Maninyan of Folo (in present day Côte d'Ivoire) and a column was established in

Odienne to help the Malinke against the Senufu of Nafana (also in contemporary Côte d'Ivoire). Moreover, a governor had been installed at Sa by the 1760s, and Bamana mercenaries had been sent to Yatenya to help Naba Kango regain power.[74]

Person also suggests that with the Jara, the court of Segu was in charge of Bamana cultural tradition, and gave it a new dimension. The dialect of Segu exemplified the elegant fashion of speaking Bamana, and eminent families sent their children to be trained in Segu.

The power of Segu reached its apex during the rule of Ngolo's successor, Mònzòn (1782-1808), who extended suzerainty north to Seguela, west to Kangaba, and south to Mpesoba. One historian argues that Mònzòn built 300 villages, and could place a 60,000-man cavalry on the battlefield as he did in a war against Kunari.[75]

The Bamana System of Contract

Dyara argues that the Famaw of Segu did not seek riches for themselves; instead, they sought power. "To acquire riches and have it in abundance, that was a part of power. To choose riches is to diminish power. To renounce riches is to enhance power."[76] Dyara also portrays the four populations of the Segu region—the Bamana, Maraka, Sòmònò and Fula—as living in harmony. "No one considered leaving the Kingdom of Segu to go somewhere else."[77]

It appears that the other populations reacted positively to Bamana power, submitting to the Bamana administration while maintaining their economic and cultural activities. "The other populations did not complain about the Bamana administration even during the reign of Daa (1808-1827) who acquired the greatest power."[78] Instead, the challenges came mostly from the periphery of the empire (Masina, for example).

The central zone of the empire was held by the Tònjòn, and the people submitted to direct administration. Nevertheless, other villages were autonomous. For instance, the Famaw never compelled the Maraka to provide soldiers. However, the Maraka and other populations were required to pay tribute. In return, the Bamana provided the Sòmònò and the Maraka with war captives. In addition to their fishing enterprises, the

Sòmònò, enriched by captives the Fama gave them, constituted a true navy.[79]

Although the other populations were Muslims, religion was not a problem within the Kingdom of Segu (in contrast to their Muslim neighbors in Masina). Islam had been "ejected from the political and military domains," but the religion functioned on the marginality of the commercial minorities.[80] Dyara adds that all the inhabitants, whether Muslim or not, "never got in trouble with their Famaw."[81] Mahibou and Triaud add that the leaders of Segu accepted the presence of the Muslim educated and merchants in their territory, on the condition that they did not challenge the existing social order. Such peaceful cohabitation conformed to an old Sudanese model, embedded in the exchange of services.[82]

Dyara emphasizes that contrary to French reports, neither banditry nor theft was permitted in the state. "Some pretend that the power of Black Africa rested on plunder. That was not the case in the Kingdom of Segu."[83] If a theft/plunder was committed and the guilty party discovered, the head of the two villages were led to Segu to remain until the guilty party was found.

The system of Bamana domination in Segu was flexible since the central power permitted local peripheral powers or small states to govern themselves on the condition that they pay a tribute or tax to Segu. When the central power deemed a ruler to be one of high calibre, the latter was made an ally of the central state and could begin collecting taxes. The new ally could keep troops, contract local alliances and possibly lead military expeditions with the agreement of the Fama.[84] However, if Segu, as any central power, showed signs of weakness, the smaller rulers could profit by revolt, declaring themselves independent.

Kaaba serves as an example of how this contract benefited both the central power of Segu and of the suzerain state of Kaaba. The hegemony of Kaaba extended from Bamako to Siguiri and dated from the eighteenth century when Terena Manbi received military support from the Bamana of Segu.[85] Although an ally, Kaaba did not furnish a contingent of troops to Segu.

The *lisòngò* (honey price) was paid uniquely in gold.[86] The Manden had been a producer of gold for many centuries, and gold was used to pay the annual tax. In principle this tribute which was paid to Segu placed the country under the protection of Segu. An additional tax had to be paid in war time called the *kèlèwelefin* (literally, "things to call the troops") which provided food supplies for the Tònjòn during a campaign.

The political strength of Segu had a major impact on the associated populations. Some villages were raided or destroyed; even some entire populations were transferred to Segu. The localities of Sekòrò (Segukòrò) and Baransen are examples; their inhabitants were led by force to Segu and installed in a place which took the name Segu Sikòrò ni Balanzando (Sekòrò of Segu and the fief of the inhabitants of Balanzan).[87]

Kaké informs us that the more the state developed, the more war was transformed to an ever-complex process less comparable to professional raids. Dyara adds that wars made for political reasons were not viewed as plunder.[88]

In the kingdom of Segu the essential unit of economic and social life remained the village communities. The Ngolosi placed a Tònjòn soldier, called *kuntigi*, over an administrative district, called *kafa*. The villages paid an annual tax in an act of allegiance. Some villages, however, were older than the institution of the Fama itself, and called themselves *hòròn-dugu*, town of the nobles. Others were created by the Fama where the Tònjòn farmed during the cold season.[89]

The Maraka (in Sinzani and Markaduguba) and the Sòmònò played important roles in the economic life of the empire. According to Richard Roberts, the Muslims provided the commercial infrastructure that the made the military state viable.[90] The Marakas maintained their autonomy, and the Famaw never installed soldiers among them. Nevertheless, they paid the disòngò as did the other villages. During the reign of Mònzòn, Roberts suggests that the Muslim community lobbied at the court, suggesting that court politics were dominated by contending war and peace parties represented by military leaders and Muslim merchants. He argues that the duality in state policy between waging war and aiding commercial activity formed part of the structure of the Segu state.[91]

Robert also argues that one of the central paradoxes of the Segu state was how the war economy related to economic growth. The war economy under both dynasties provided long-term security within the context of perpetual warfare, which in turn yielded "slaves." Warfare and slavery were crucial to the expansion of commerce and production of the Maraka.

The state also intervened in the riverine economy, and the Sòmònò owed their origin and their social organization to the Segu Bamana political system.[92]

The Sòmònò exchanged goods and services for state support and protection. The Sòmònò paid a special tax directly to the Fama, provided transportation, manufactured gunpowder, and repaired and built the walls of the palace.

Much of the state structure in place at the time of the 'Umarian invasion seemed to have been put in place during the reign of Mònzòn. Twelve of Mònzòn's thirty-five children ruled as Famaw.[93] Da, or Fama Da (1808-1827), was the most popular. It was during the reign of Nyènèmba, who ruled only nine months in 1839, that Masina tried to subjugate Segu, but Bakari, son of Jan, took authority of over the Tònjòn and killed the leader of the Masina forces. After 1850, the Tònjòn emerged with new military strength under Torokòrò Mari, and Segu re-established itself on the northern fringes of present-day Côte d'Ivoire.[94]

At the time of the 'Umarian invasion, the Bamana empire was economically and politically stable. The Bamana were able to secure the trade routes, and to promote the economic activities of the Marka, Sòmònò, and Bozo through a series of contracts.

Unable to exploit internal weaknesses (as the French did to the 'Umarian state), 'Umar would resort to another means to defeat Segu. In fact, the Bamana military prestige was still well-established, and the Bamana of Kaarta sought the aid of Segu to fight 'Umar. Even after the defeat of the Kaartanke army, the Segu Bamana decided to face 'Umar before he arrived in Segu. The occupation of Segu by 'Umar was achieved due to superior weapons used by the 'Umarian army.

Ahmadu, son of 'Umar and ruler at Segu.
Camille Pietri, *Les Français au Niger, voyages et combats*
(Paris: Hachette, 1885), p. 5.

CHAPTER 2

AL-HAJJ 'UMAR AND THE OCCUPATION OF SEGU

Thomas Hodgkin raised four significant questions in his 1963 article on the history of Islam in West Africa that are particularly important to understanding the trilogy of reform movements in nineteenth century West Africa. One, what were the objectives and dominant ideas of these reform movements? Two, to what sectors of the population of the Sudan did they primarily appeal? Three, how did their opponents and other sectors of the population react to their policies? And finally, how were the new states organized?[1] Although this is not a study of al-Hajj 'Umar's reform movement, these questions do help frame an analysis of the events in the Middle Niger with special reference to the Bamana. In this chapter my emphasis is upon the jihad launched by al-Hajj 'Umar and the wars between the Bamana and the Muslim populations during the period of 1860-1869.

Hodgkin and Ruth Schachter classify the 'Umarian movement, like others in the nineteenth century, as an attempt to achieve political unification, achieve social leveling, and resist European encroachment.[2] Mouhammed Hane makes a similar analysis, arguing that al-Hajj 'Umar had two objectives. First, he would make war and triumph the cause of God in the religious domain; and secondly, in the national domain he would fight to chase out the "immoral colonialism."[3] However, 'Umar had imperial goals of his own.

Al-Hajj 'Umar's Islamic Vision

Al-Hajj 'Umar b. Saidu Tal was born in 1211/1796 or 1209/1794 to

Seidu Usmaan Tal and Adama Ayse Caam.[4] His birthday was Aloar (Halwaar) in Futa Toro near Podor in present day Northern Sénégal. 'Umar's family were pious Muslims, and he learned Qur'anic principles from his father, a Muslim teacher, and various Moorish holy men.[5] Several hagiographers describe al-Hajj 'Umar as being a child prodigy, possessing extraordinary learning skills, and excelling under the scholars who taught him. Throughout his young adult life his erudition would continue to impress many with whom he had contact.[6]

'Umar left home around the age of 15, searching for a Muslim scholar who specialized in mysticism. In the course of his travels he met members of the Tijaniyya brotherhood, two years before his pilgrimage to Mecca. He made this pilgrimage in 1827, passing through Masina, Kong, Sokoto and Gwandu, Air, Bornu, Fezzan, Egypt and Jedda. He spent three years in Mecca, where, we are told, he studied the Tijaniyya under Muhammed ibn al-Ghali Abu Talib, local head of the Tijaniyya brotherhood who appointed 'Umar as Khalifa of the Sudan. 'Umar would argue in one of his works that "if Tijani is superior to all the saints as Muhammad to all the prophets, his brotherhood is superior to the others as the Muslim community to that of other prophets."[7]

On his return to West Africa, 'Umar created ties in Bornu and Sokoto by marrying into ruling families, which would prove significant both politically and socially. In Sokoto (1831-1838) he married Mairiam, Muhammed Bello's daughter. It has been argued that it was in Sokoto that he began to envision the possibility of leading a jihad.[8] In addition, he married Mariatu, a woman from a Bornu ruling family. His popularity continued to grow as he moved westward and he received gifts and slaves from various communities.

On his return to the Middle Niger from Mecca he was taken from the village of Anyemina and led to Segu where he was detained, or according to 'Umar's chroniclers, "thrown in a solid prison where he remained for sometime," perhaps at the instigation of family members reigning in Masina.[9] This sojourn in Segu would have important implications for the course of future events and in political decisions by the Segu Bamana, even before the major war with the Muslim leader twenty years later.

Tradition concerning this episode amply illustrates the tension in the mid-nineteenth century between the Bamana and their Muslim neighbors.

While al-Hajj 'Umar was praying one evening, Badyou, the Fama's sister, visited him, beseeching him to pray for her brother, Cèfòlò, because he was ill,[10] but 'Umar explained that he only prayed for Muslims. At this time, tradition has it that the Seguvians had arranged to arrest and execute al-Hajj 'Umar, but he escaped.

The Jihad

David Robinson argues that 'Umar had much experience in Islamic state-building before embarking on his jihad.[11] In Futa Toro he observed the weaknesses of the state founded by Sulayman Bal, and he analyzed other governmental structures during the pilgrimage. According to Tal family history, Allah ordained 'Umar seventy times to carry out a Holy War.[12] Upon arrival in Futa Jallon in 1840, the ruler Bubakar gave him permission to establish a religious center at Jaguker (Jegunko) where he taught the Tijaniyya order and attracted followers.

Shaykh Ahmad al-Tijani placed great emphasis on the essential role of the *awliya,* holy men, in guiding the believer to knowledge of God and salvation. 'Umar followed the tenet that true understanding was only to be attained through the mystical intercession of holy men with God. He supported the right to personal interpretation of the scriptures, and claimed the spiritual gift of *istihara*, ensuring him divine guidance in difficult times. These beliefs would be advantageous in his imperial designs. For example, by interpreting the scriptures as he saw fit, and claiming that the Tijaniyya were superior to all other sects, his jihad was easily justified, particularly when it came to attacking other Islamic states and polities.

Although al-Hajj 'Umar did not claim to be the Mahdi, he held Mahdist beliefs and his followers made the claim on his behalf. It appears that al-Hajj 'Umar made no great effort to reject these claims, and, of course, this made it easier to attract followers, particularly the down trodden in Sudanic societies. Vincent Monteil argues that he was not a prophet, but his life was compared to "the Apostle of Islam." His emigration to Dinguiray was his hegira.[13]

When al-Hajj 'Umar returned to the Futa from his pilgrimage, he preached that God had confided to him to lead the jihad. However, the young were not convinced of what they heard, and went to see 'Umar. When they arrived, he showed to them a mirror in which they saw their images in order to convince the young of Futa to join him.[14]

'Umar remained three years (1268/1849 to 1268/1851) in Dinguiray, teaching his disciples, ordaining the good, forbidding the bad, and dispersing the Tijaniya *wird*.[15] His success at instilling zeal in his talibes was attested by Faidherbe, a French governor of St. Louis at mid-century who remarked that the talibes marched against French weapons as if to martyrdom, as if they wished to die.[16]

During this period, al-Hajj 'Umar purchased military material, including canons, swords, and arrows, acquired from British merchants in Sierra Leone and the trading posts in Rio-Nunez, and Rio-Pongo[17] as well as French merchants in St. Louis.[18] In addition, he purchased horses for the talibes from the Saharan trader groups north of the River Sénégal. This trade would be instrumental in the jihad which was to come. 'Umar's followers also practiced cultivation, producing large quantities of grain.[19] The agricultural prosperity of Dinguiray was assured by the many slaves in the valleys of Bafing and Tinkisso.[20]

The fact that 'Umar was steadily buying firearms during the three years of his "preaching jihad," strongly suggests his design to advance to a "fighting jihad," or at least prepare himself for self-defense. By 1847 when he spent four days at the French post of Bakel on the Sénégal River, he had a considerable following of talibes from many areas.[21]

It was easy for 'Umar to recruit Futaka residents of Futa Toro to join his jihad. The Futaka who refused to live under French domination in the Sénégambia[22] emigrated; for them his movement offered an ideological home.[23] Others who had enthusiasm for the jihad dating to 'Abd al-Qadir's movement around 1190/1776, and resentment of the Qadiriyya and its ruling aristocracy were also 'Umar's supporters. Further east, others were dissatisfied with the results of the jihad by Shaykh Ahmad b. Muhammad in Masina, which had compromised the purist ideals of Islamic reform. More importantly, 'Umar's movement appealed to captives who wanted freedom, and those from the underclasses searching for military glory and/or quick material gain. For example, the slaves of Tuturubala profited from the invasion of 'Umar by escaping from their masters and finding refuge in Sonongho, a village of the Famas of Segu, where they founded a family line.[24] He was able to recruit people with multiple motives from many areas; together, these sub-groups formed what the French would call the *Tukulors*.[25]

'Umar had several factors in his favor which facilitated recruitment to his cause. First, he had a widely-known reputation as a man of religious scholarship, not only because of his pilgrimage to Mecca, but because he studied under several great Muslim teachers. Second, he had created ties with leading families through marriage, and made friends with leaders from communities across the Sudanic belt of West Africa. Third, he had created trade links with Europeans from whom he could acquire ample ammunition to outfit his army in the making. Finally, he had enough followers in the Futa Toro to create an agricultural base which would yield a surplus and produce a certain wealth.

Al-Hajj 'Umar began to articulate the objective of his jihad in the late 1840s. Early in the preparatory stage, his growing influence became a threat to established political leaders. The preaching of the Tijaniyya was not in itself strange; what was threatening was the socio-political implications of the *tariqa*.[26] Even in non-Muslim states, evangelicalism was known, and Muslim groups existed in these states, as the Moors did in Kaarta, and others in the commercial city of Sinzani in Segu. But, with al-Hajj 'Umar's movement, non-Muslims saw Islam as a force destroying existing socio-political institutions and replacing them with alien rule and institutions.[27] Perhaps the greatest threat posed by his campaign was his eagerness to "convert" if not to Islam, then to the Tijani way. It would appear that his jihad should have omitted other Islamic polities which by themselves, could spread the faith to non-Muslim communities. On the contrary, the paradox of 'Umar's proselytizing activities was that he would encounter and conquer more Muslim societies than non-Muslim states, the latter represented by the Bamana states of Segu and Kaarta. Even more feared was his policy of "wiping out" all who refused to convert.[28]

Two Muslim leaders, Ahmad b. Ahmad of Masina, and Shaykh al-Bakka'i, leader of the Kunta branch in Timbuktu of the Qadiriyya brotherhood at mid-century, recognized how dangerous 'Umar's campaign would be to existing polities. They saw that the "religious" movement

was not aimed at merely non-Muslims. In fact, the jihad would be conducted on two levels: to spread the Tijaniyya doctrine to other Muslim
societies, and Islam in general to non-Muslims.

At Dinguiray al-Hajj 'Umar prepared for the military jihad. The one-
time preaching or literary jihad (*jihad al-qawl*) quickly became the jihad
of the sword (*jihad al-sayf*), and from the moment he began to create a
perfect Islamic state. His enemies were delineated: imperfect Muslims,
African "polytheists," and those standing in the way of his expansion,
including the French. However, this stand against colonialism is unclear
in the early stage of the jihad itself and in the preaching to justify it. This
aspect seems to be highlighted in recent studies. The early chronicles do
not explicitly include the French as an object of the jihad. Kanya-Forstner
argues that the jihad was waged primarily against other Africans, and
'Umar could thus be expected to demonstrate a degree of flexibility in his
relations with the French.[29] It was only when the French refused to sell
him arms and began to arm his enemies that 'Umar's attitude changed. In
the 1840s 'Umar assured the French that his campaign would be conducted against "animists." Of course, we have to consider this as a strategy to keep the French out of the struggle and to continue using them as
a source of arms.

Eventually, al-Hajj 'Umar's army consisted of an elite cavalry, mostly
Futaka; "converted" sofas, mostly Bamana; and irregular Fula auxiliary
cavalry armed with lances, recruited from local populations of former
slave herders. Wane provides a detailed composition of the army which
consisted of four legs and an arm:

1. *Ngenaar*: soldiers from Boseya and Anyam
2. *YirlaaBe*: some people from Laao and the HebbyaaBe
3. *Toro*: those of Bundu
4. *Junfuntune*: a guard composed of Fula from Futa Toro,
   some Hausa, Tuubu or group of converts, and some Suufa
5. *Murgula*: the arm, formed contingents led by Alfa 'Usmaan[30]

The voluntary recruits from Kaarta were enrolled in the ngenaar. The
people of Kaso, Jafuna and Bakuna were incorporated in the yirlaaBe;
those of Gidimaka were with the *Toro;* the Fula of Futa Jallon were the
largest group in the yirlaaBe; however, others were placed in the murgu-

la. Each unit was divided into three arms: *Jungo soy-soy* (avant garde), *Jungo baafal* (arm of the door, charged with attacking the *tata*), and *Jungo boowal* (arm of the exterior, a reserved unit destined to guard the enterprises of the exterior).

Although booty was shared, the Amir al-Mu'minim, "Commander of the faithful," was entitled to a fifth of the booty. Weapons, firearms, and horses were normally appropriated directly. 'Umar's forces manufactured gunpowder locally, and taxes were sometimes collected in saltpeter. Moreover, gunsmiths would accompany the army to make bullets.[31]

An 'Umarian chronicle asserts that when the Bamana attacked the 'Umarians in 1852, 'Umar had not received the explicit order from Allah to launch a jihad. Then, the message of Allah and Shaykh Tijani ordained him to pursue the jihad, but he refused until the "pagans" attacked them because "the Holy War is permitted to Muslims who are oppressed." Allah revealed to 'Umar on Monday 21 *Dhu-al-Qaada* 1268 (September 6, 1852) after the prayer at dusk that 'Umar was authorized to launch the Holy War.[32] Finally, 'Umar decided in 1858-59 to have his people emigrate en masse to escape French domination.[33] The call to emigrate was a means to safeguard the Islamic forces, and preserve the chances of an ultimate victory over the French.[34]

The Bamana of Segu and al-Hajj 'Umar

One of the earliest encounters between the 'Umarians and the Bamana of Segu occurred when the Seguvians aided their sister kingdom, Kaarta, against the 'Umarians in 1855 at Sutucule where they were defeated. 'Umar continued to Koniakari where he built a *tata, or* wall. Afterwards, he assembled many troops and said, "I build this tata for the French."[35] After the Bamana clashed with 'Umar at Guidiume, Yelegmine and Médine, 'Umar continued to march to Nioro with many Futaka and Fulani.[36] The 'Umarians faced the Bamana again in the cause of Karunga where the 'Umarians repulsed the Bamana Massassi leader, Kanja Mamadi, and the soldiers of Segu abandoned the cause, and returned to Segu. In addition, many of the Kaarta Bamana left Nioro and migrated to Bèlèdugu.

When 'Umar attacked Jagunte (Gangunte) in August 1856, killing the leaders, he committed aggression against the Fama of Segu since Jangunte was a tributary of Segu. The Jawaras, an independent band from Kaarta, and the Massassi Bamana had gone to find refuge in Jagunte under the protection of Segu.[37] However, al-Hajj 'Umar was not prepared to attack Segu. Mahibou and Triaud argue that 'Umar had for a long time considered the eventuality of an attack against Segu. The distance from Futa Toro and the presence of Masina posed problems to his strategy.[38] Jangunte, although semi-independent, was, as mentioned, a tributary of Segu. 'Umar claimed to have attacked the area not to provoke the Fama of Segu, but to put down the Jawara Rebellion. As a result, he sent a talibe, Matmady Celare, to see Torokòrò Mari, Fama of Segu, to tell him that he had no animosity towards him, the Fama; he only wanted the Jawaras.

Torokòrò Mari's relationship with 'Umar looms large in the oral testimony. When 'Umar escaped from Segu, he left one of his followers in Barabugu who became an informer to Torokòrò Mari. The plan was devised that when Torokòrò took power from Cèfòlò, he would act like a Muslim and Shaykh 'Umar would come with an army and confirm him on the throne. In any event, Torokòrò converted to Islam. However, according to Bamana history, one of his wives betrayed him after she caught him praying in secret. She informed others, saying, "He is always in the water as a fish," meaning that he was Muslim.[39] Mage asserted that the Kuntigi accused him of wanting to deliver the Bamana to the Marabout ('Umar), and plotted the assassination after Torokòrò's collaboration with 'Umar.[40] In any event, Torokoro was killed, and his body was thrown into the river. For a week, the body failed to decompose, and neither a vulture nor fish touched it. He was later buried on the other side of the river by the head of a group of fishermen who found the body. Another oral source suggests that the 'Umarians pursued Torokòrò, and the Bamana decided not to save him.[41]

Koné argues that when Shaykh 'Umar was informed of Torokòrò's execution, he was furious. Not only did the death of Torokòrò needed to be revenged, the Bamana refused to elect one of Torokòrò's sons to be the new Fama.[42]

The Bamana did not wait for 'Umar to attack them because they refused to accept the expansion of the Futanke territory, particularly when

The court in Amadu's palace.
Abon E. Mage, *Voyage dans le Soudan Occidental*
(Paris: Hachette, 1868), p. 357.

it included the sister kingdom of Kaarta. However, the 'Umarians made the first act of aggression against Segu when they attacked Jangunte in 1856.[43] As a result, Ali sent an army to Danba. 'Umar assembled his military leaders at Markoya and told them that Segu had come to attack him, and Allah commanded him to make war against the *kaffirs*, or non-believers; the leaders accepted to make war against Segu.[44] 'Umar had assembled his troops at Markoya,[45] the capital of Bèlèdugu on November 20, 1859, beheaded all the men, and burned the city and the religious artifacts. The defeat of the Bamana had a profound effect since Markoya was a quasi-capital of Batair. After the defeat, Karuga, a Jawara leader, took refuge in Segu. 'Umar remained for several months, sustaining two attacks from the Bamana of Segu, the first in conjunction with soldiers from Bèlèdugu. "The Muslims killed even more enemies than in the preceding combat, and took 100 horses from them."[46]

In 1860 after spending 25 days at Damfa (Danfa), 'Umar learned that two Bamana armies arrived under the command of Baji, son of Ali, and Banta (Bonoto), reinforced by the Bamana of Fadugu and some Jawaras. The armies marched in two groups in order to put the 'Umarians between them. Nevertheless, 'Umar marched between them, and the Bamana followed and attacked the next morning at Ngani in Bèlèdugu. 'Umar, however, was prepared and won the battle on April 17, 1860,[47] but after winning the battle, the 'Umarians failed to chase the Bamana.

Before the next battle with the Bamana, 'Umar was able to get more followers from Nyamina, including the Maraka from Gulumba and

Médine-Sako, and Futaka recruits arrived from Nioro. The Seguvians placed a great army on the battlefield at Buntu, and again the 'Umarians defeated them. After the 'Umarians moved to Anyemina, the Bamana armies, led by Baji, later attacked them at Ghani. Baji was killed in this battle, and the 'Umarians took possession of many horses.[48] Then 'Umar sent armies to the villages of Tugunne and Jabal, killing the leader of Jabal and the men of Tugunne, but taking the women, children, and slaves as captives.

The Seguvians amassed a great army of 35,000 men at Watala lead by Tata, another son of Bina Ali, on 22 Safar 1277/September 9, 1860.[49] 'Umar marched to Watala with more than 15,000 men to face the main unit of the Bamana Seguvian army for the first time, in what became a four-day battle.[50] His army was shocked by the Bamana, who repelled them, forcing them to retreat with more than 300 dead. The cannons were left on the battlefield, and Samba Njaye (who later welcomed French emissaries and gave historical accounts to them) and thirty Wolofs tried to retrieve them; seven were killed and fifteen wounded.[51] 'Umar found a small abandoned village of blacksmiths, and for five days his people repaired gun carriages. The armies met again, and Tata, still esteemed as a hero for his bravery, along with his unit fought fiercely.[52] Although the Bamana fought with intensity, the 'Umarians had superior weapons and carried the day. In fact, the Bamana used guns manufactured locally.[53] In total, approximately 700 Bamana were killed, including Tata and a great many Bamana military leaders, and another 700 placed before a firing squad.[54] Muhammad ibn Ibrahim from Labe, a chronicler for al-Hajj 'Umar, who functioned in the court of Ahmadu, described the battle in these epic terms:

> . . . The contingents of Segu, their armies and soldiers advanced towards us; they were like mountains and dust, like pebbles or sand, so numerous were they. Then, the Shaykh, the saint, the pole, the mediator. . . went out and attacked them and scattered them. They did not even stand up to him for the time it takes to milk a ewe or bat an eye, before he inflicted upon them a terrible defeat and destroyed them and annihilated them with the sword, and ruined them. God, thereby, made Islam and its people victorious, and he humbled the forces of polytheism and its people.[55]

Muhammad ibn Ibrahim made no mention of the 'Umarian casualties, but the religious overtones are vivid. Of course, Ibrahim's dramatic and poetic version differs from Bamana versions which hail Tata and his soldiers as heroes. Tata was killed in the battle, and 'Umar took the village of Watala. According to one source, the defeat of the Bamana took three months and nine days, and the 'Umarians employed 776 guns.[56]

Although defeated, the Bamana did not submit to the yoke of the 'Umarians. On the other hand, the people of Sinzani did.[57] A Marabout of Sinzani, Konè Mama, wrote to 'Umar, asking him to come, for the people would surrender to him, taking the opportunity to free Sinzani from Seguvian control. The population of the village pledged allegiance to 'Umar when he arrived on October 15, 1860.

Two theories have been advanced to explain the submission. One, the Maraka of Sinzani continued cordial relations with the Bamana until they realized that the Bamana would lose, then decided to submit to the winner.[58] Since friction existed between Soninke families of Kuma and Sisse, it is unclear if both attempted to maintain a cordial relationship with 'Umar, particularly the Kuma family who wanted to regain control at the expense of the Sisse family and the Seguvian Famaw. The other explanation is that wealthy Muslim merchants in Sinzani welcomed 'Umar, believing that by submitting they could benefit from a decrease in taxes.[59] Only after the 'Umarians established rule did they realize that they had only changed masters, and the new one was constantly present while the Bamana Fama had been further away and required merely a tribute. French administrator Quinton argued that religion played no role in the decision-making processes of forming and/or breaking alliances although it is also argued that the Muslims leaders of Sinzani would have been happy to obey a ruler who professed the same religion.[60] Mahibou and Triaud add that the move averted the menace of Masina as well as removing them from the rule of Segu.[61]

'Umar exhorted that the peaceful cohabitation of Muslims and non-Muslims in Sinzani, which was habitual in the Middle Niger, was a travesty to Islam and accused the Maraka merchants of claiming Islam only in speech while submitting themselves to polytheism. 'Umar cited Uthman b. Fudi's *Sirai al-Ikhwan*, saying, "If it (Islam) is mixed with polytheism, it cannot be taken into consideration."[62] In general, the

Islamic communities in the Segu empire presented a major moral dilemma in the eyes of 'Umar, who resented the subordination of Muslims to a non-Islamic power.[63]

During his stay in Sinzani, 'Umar corresponded with Ahmadu (or Amadu III, Ahmad b. Ahmad b. al-Shaykh Ahmad Lubbu) of Masina (1853-1862),[64] debating the question of the conversion of Segu to Islam. Ahmadu Ahmadu returned a letter vehemently telling 'Umar that he had no right to attack Ali Witala because the latter was Ahmadu Ahmadu's vassal. 'Umar argued that Ali had not accepted in any fashion the authority of Masina, and Ali only sought aid from Masina to fight the 'Umarians. In addition, he replied that Ali preserved all of his gris-gris in Sikoro. Moreover, he considered this pretended vassal as an enemy who had sent troops to attack him ('Umar) in Kaarta. 'Umar said that Ahamdu Ahmadu's hostility toward him was clear in that Ahmadu Ahmadu had sent an army to Bakhunu against him.[65]

Alliance between Segu and Masina

Masina had been under Bamana political influence until the Fula Revolution in 1817, led by Seku Amadu (Shaykh Ahmadu Lobo), who dethroned Ahmadi Diko. Diko sought the aid of Segu to return to power during the reign of Fama Da.[66] Fama Da sent a large Bamana army to reinstall Ahmadi Diko, but Seku Amadu prevailed.[67] The war between Masina and Segu lasted until 1840, and "little by little" the Bamana "reconciled with their Muslim neighbors."[68]

The two states of Segu and Masina had been adversaries until the threat of al-Hajj 'Umar pushed them into an alliance, one which was both anti-'Umarian and anti-Tijani.This is an example of how political events shaped alliances in the Middle Niger during the nineteenth century. From the time of 'Umar's jihad to the coming of the French, alliances were created between leaders regardless of religious or other forms of identity. The reason that Bina Ali Jara accepted an alliance with Masina is clear: survival. Ahmadu Ahmadu, on the other hand, possibly had at least two motives for agreeing to the alliance. First, Masina had plans before the 'Umar's jihad to establish its own Islamic polity over Segu. Second, it was clear that al-Hajj 'Umar's jihad was aimed at both Muslim and non-Muslim states.

A leading advisor of Ahmadu Ahmadu, al-Hajj Seidou, suggested an alliance between Masina and Fama Ali, arguing that the people of Segu would prefer the rule of Ahmadu Ahmadu over that of al-Hajj 'Umar.[69] Ahmadu Ahmadu agreed to help Segu fight the 'Umarians in exchange for the latter's conversion to Islam. As a result, Segu was declared part of the Dar al-Islam under the tutelage of Masina. However, Ali was not obliged to attempt to convert the population. Ahmadu Ahmadu sent advisors and teachers under the direction of Ba Lobo, general of the army and governor of Fakala, to build mosques and to instruct the people in the fundamentals of the faith. One source argues that the soldiers were primarily sent to convert the people and build mosques rather than to prepare for battle.[70] In addition, Ahmadu Ahmadu sent a small column to Segu to assure the execution of the treaty with Fama Ali. As a result, many villages on the banks of the Niger burned their fetiches, and built mosques.[71]

In December 1860, 'Umar proposed to Ahmadu Ahmadu that the two work together to crush the Bamana and share the state and the spoils. Ahmadu Ahmadu, however, viewed the proposition as an insult, and ordered 'Umar to leave Sinzani. Ahmadu Ahmadu reportedly wrote,

> I give you the choice between submitting to me, as it is for you, the most restricted obligation, and return to the country from where you come. I accord you a delay of three days to make your submission or pack your bags, saddle your short-haired horses, and prepare your bestsoldiers, because I will send against your young people ages 20 to 25 years because it is individuals of your kind that the Prophet . . .said, "Kill them.[72]

'Umar responded that Ahmadu Ahmadu had become an infidel.

Ahmadu Ahmadu assembled an army of 8,000 cavaliers and 6,000 men as foot soldiers under the command of Ba Lobo in January 1861.[73] 'Umar responded by sending a letter to Ba Lobo, threatening him if that he took one more step on the territory of Segu, he would take Hamdallaye, the capital of Masina. Afterwards, Ba Lobo sent 500 cavaliers to warn Ali. With the messages, proposals and threats, it appeared as though the two sides were not eager to engage in battle unless forced to do so. The stand-off lasted two months before an incident brought the armies on the battlefield early in 1861.

Oral tradition relates that one day, fishermen from the two camps exchanged shots, and the talibes, thinking it was an attack, began to cross the river. Despite 'Umar calling them back, they continued, full of ardor, but the Masinanke killed all 500. The following day, 'Umar was unable to contain his army that wanted to avenge the deaths of the other soldiers. As a result, he divided the army in two columns, led by Alpha 'Umar Boila and Alpha Usman, surprising the Seguvians and the Masinankes; the latter returned to Masina while the Bamana escaped to Segukòrò. Another version is that al-Hajj instructed his men to attack the Bamana, and only attack the Masinanke if the latter attacked the 'Umarian first. This was done to preserve his prestige and his contention that he was waging a holy war. It was also argued that the army of Masina did not participate in the battle in the beginning. After seeing the 'Umarians with the advantage; however, they "swooped down" on the 'Umarian army, killing 400 men.[74]

Ahmadu Ahmadu sent an army of 2,000 to camp eighteen kilometers from Segu in order to join the Bamana army. Ali called 380 village leaders and their soldiers to Weita for a battle which was to begin on a Monday and last for three days. The Bamana won the battle on the first day. Ali is reported to have said to his warriors, "If we can kill the men of 'Umar, as we have killed them today, the Marabout is going to make peace with us."[75]

On the second day, the Bamana army and the army of Masina faced 'Umar in a battle which lasted until nightfall. On the third day, 'Umar was victorious, but Bina Ali and his principal leaders managed to elude the 'Umarians and found refuge in Masina.[76] Meanwhile, many of the Bamana abandoned most of the villages in the province of Segu before 'Umar marched into the capital, Segukòrò, on 26 Sa'ban 1277/March 9, 1861.[77] at same day 'Umar sent Alpha Ousman to attack a village in Segu; he massacred some of the inhabitants and captured others.

When Bina Ali arrived in Masina, he wanted to continue, but Ahmadu Ahmadu argued that he should stay in Masina, saying that he had 25,000 cavaliers to face 'Umar. Ali, however, insisted that some of his soldiers had followed him, and since they were stronger than the soldiers at

Hamdallaye, he should continue. He explained that he had assembled the military leaders and their men to fight 'Umar, but the latter had killed these soldiers and leaders except for those of Telingana and Gana. When Bina Ali described the chaplet which 'Umar carried, Ahmadu showed Ali one just like it, convincing Ali to stay in Hamdallaye, probably because he believed that Ahmadu possessed the same religious power as 'Umar. Later, 'Umar threatened to send an army if Ahmadu Ahmadu did not return Bina Ali to Segu.

Bamana soldiers had a reputation for being excellent fighters, and their fashioning an empire in the eighteenth century attests to their skills. Their defeat at the hands of the 'Umarians in itself did not discredit this repu-tation, for the 'Umarians had one great advantage over their enemies: more and newer European military weapons. In addition to the arms and ammunition 'Umar acquired from European merchants (the British in particular), he had captured two cannons from the French at Bakel, and two small mounted cannons had been taken from a French boat marooned on the Sénégal river. Merchants of Bakel and Médine competed with British agents from Bathurst and Sierra Leone to supply arms and muni-tions to the 'Umarians.[78]

Bina Ali wanted to make another stand at Banakoro, but loyal military leaders warned him that the army had disbanded. When 'Umar entered Segu, he took possession of the palace and treasures accumulated over the years by the Famaw Bamanaw. The gold alone in the treasure was report-edly worth 20 million francs.[79] The women and children of the royal fam-ily and the griots and captives were still at Segukòrò.

After the battle of Watala, 'Umar was called to meet Ahmadu Ahmadu who informed him of the conversion of the Bamana. But 'Umar suspect-ed a plot and refused to believe that the Bamana had converted by per-suasion or force. Furthermore, 'Umar had questioned Ahmadu Ahmadu's commitment to Islamic reform. Masina, in reality, had become a stum-bling block in 'Umar's goals to control the region, and needed to conquer Masina in order to connect Segu and Timbuktu. Discovering that Ahmadu Ahmadu had allied himself to the non-Muslim Bamana, 'Umar felt that he had the justification to attack Masina, finding a loophole in the Islamic law and custom defining who is legally subject to a declared jihad.

The debate over the "justification" of attacking Masina was conducted by Shaykh Ahmad al-Bakka'i of the Kunta in Timbuktu, leader of the Qadiriyya brotherhood (and 'Umar's next victim), and Yarki Talfi, scholar and ally of 'Umar and his surrogate in this dialogue. Ahmad al-Bakka'i gave moral and physical support to Masina and Segu, and proposed that Ahmadu Ahmadu proclaim himself ruler of Segu, depriving 'Umar of the one justification he had to attack Segu. This followed the principle that if the ruler of a state is a Muslim, then the people he rules are Muslim also.

Since the Muslims of Masina, as in Timbuktu, practiced the Qadiriyya, 'Umar could denounce the brotherhood as inferior to Tijaniyya doctrines. He also argued that Ahmadu Ahmadu's decision to ally himself with "pagans" pre-empted any right Ahmadu Ahmadu might have had to hide behind the shield of Islam.[80] Ahmadu Ahmadu, however, argued that the Seguvians had been converted; therefore, the basic principles of the jihad on which 'Umar had built his campaign no longer existed to attack Segu.

The Bamana regrouped in the provinces of Markabugu, Sanamadugu, Kaminiandugu and Bintugu.[81] The united armies of Bamana and Masinankes, led by Ba Lobo, attacked 'Umar in Segu in April 1861.[82] Ahmadu Ahmadu placed more than 50,000 men around the army of 'Umar, hoping to starve them.[83] One 'Umarian hagiographer reported:

> Ahmadu Ahmadu marched "hand in hand with the pagans with whom he entered very friendly and very solid relations to obtain goods from them the illicit character of which had been stigmatized by Allah."[84]

In other words, Ahmadu Ahmadu had compromised the Muslims after having been bribed by Ali Munzu with a thousand mithqals of gold.

After 'Umar defeated the armies and Ahmadu Ahmadu returned to Masina, Fama Ali took flight to Jebe. 'Umar's suspicions were well founded. The Bamana did not destroy their religious paraphernalia, but hid them from the Masinanke when they came to inspect Segu and to build mosques. The 'Umarians gathered Bamana religious paraphernalia and great statues from the palace without demolishing them in order to refute the claims by Ahmadu Ahmadu that the Bamana had converted and had destroyed their "idols."[85]

'Umar sent an army led by Muhammed Saidi Yanke to destroy Jebe. The soldiers killed many people, taking captives and large quantities of gold, silver and other booty. 'Umar then sent Alpha 'Umar and his men to find Ali in Baninko, but Ali had already gone to Tuna with those who had remained faithful. At Tuna, Ahmadu Yero Ba attacked and destroyed the village, taking many prisoners and booty.[86]

The Masinanke put an army of 30,000 men in the field, of which 10,000 were cavalry, in April 1861 at Koghe to retake Segu. After two weeks of maneuvering, the enemies clashed. The 'Umarians killed many of the Masinanke; however, Ali and his military leaders escaped with his best troops. Having succeeded in assembling an army, he went to install himself at Tuna where the Tangaraw, tied by a pact to the Ngolosiw, offered him residence. Meanwhile, 'Umar sent an army to capture Ali,[87] learning that Ali was in Daku. Nevertheless, Ali averted capture again, going to Fompona, and eventually rejoining Ahmadu Ahmadu. Like the other villages where Ali took refuge, this one was attacked in an attempt to capture him.[88] Meanwhile, Ahmadu Ahmadu sent representatives to 'Umar with a proposal to settle their differences, but the latter refused.[89]

'Umar called all the Bamana who had not revolted and remained in Segukòrò to tell them that Ahmadu, his eldest son, was appointed to command Segu, and they promised to obey. 'Umar then prepared for battle against Ahmadu Ahmadu. After a long battle, 'Umar marched into the capital, Hamdallaye, which the people had abandoned; many found refuge with al-Bakaa'i in the north, where they reorganized and found reinforcements.[90]

There is disagreement in sources about what happened to Ahmadu Ahmadu and Ali after the defeat. One is that Ahmadu Ahmadu was wounded in the battle, and was executed by the 'Umarians, but Ali was taken prisoner.[91] Others assert that both Ali and Ahmadu Ahmadu were wounded at the Battle of Theilwal, and that Ahmadu Ahmadu, seriously wounded, was executed. All of the Bamana noble princes captured with Ali were led to Hamdallaye. 'Umar publicly destroyed the Bamana religious instruments, the boliw, and eventually executed Ali because he obstinately refused to convert to Islam.[92]

Perspective on the 'Umarian Jihad

Trimingham has emphasized the violent nature of the 'Umarian jihad which developed into a military regime, "upsetting the balanced life" of many societies where "undiluted slave-raiding reduced many areas to unproductive steppes."[93] Al-Hajj 'Umar obtained firearms, it is reported, by trading prisoners of war, and boycotting European products. This view, however, differs from accounts which emphasize that 'Umar massacred the men and took the women and children as slaves to be distributed to his lieutenants and most faithful followers.[94] Of course, war captives were part of the booty, but, if he massacred all the men after a battle and distributed all the women and children, the number of captives available to trade for firearms would be limited. A balance clearly needs to be made between accounts that emphasize the "slaughter" of men, as some historians argue, and others that focus on the captives taken to be traded and/or distributed.

Violence in the jihad is sometimes highlighted by Arabic chronicles. For instance, the Chronicles of Oualata and of Nema state that at the battle of Mikouya (Markoya?), 'Umar killed a number of people, "which only God knows the number."[95] One should take great care in interpreting such passages because these chroniclers, especially hagiographers of 'Umar, were dramatic and often poetic in their descriptions of battles, attempting to highlight the grandeur of 'Umar, and often depicting the battles as being very one-sided.

The Bamana perspective of the jihad, and that of other groups for that matter, can be expected to stress the violence of events since they were the object of the jihad. The French accounts, which are sometimes more incriminating than the versions of local historians, are more complex. General attitudes and prejudices pertaining to the colonial world played a vital role in the French interpretations of these events. Mervyn Hiskett discusses the French attitude toward Islam, one which moved from being favorable and sympathetic to one of condemnation and prejudice based on French experience with the Algerian Muslims and on French imperialist designs.[96] The 'Umarians became "fanatic Muslims" in much of the French literature. However, Richard Roberts distinguishes the "fanatic Muslims" from "productive" Sudanese populations, arguing that the jihad was conducted by "an alien conquest army which had no ties to an agrarian base."[97]

The 'Umarians had developed an agrarian base during the "preaching" stage of the jihad, accruing surplus to trade for firearms and munitions as noted above. Subsequently, the 'Umarians developed an agricultural interest in Kaarta, and a grain market developed at Médine. According to John Hanson, the 'Umarians settlers, after reaping benefits of military conquests, protected their new positions by eliminating warfare in areas crucial to commercial activity.[98]

Raiding, according to economic historian Richard Roberts, was an outgrowth of the internal tensions in the 'Umarian army created by an unequal division of booty. Therefore, raids were a means of compensating for the differences between groups in the army, allowing them to operate independently, and directing discontent away from the regime. Lt. Sargolis, a French administrator, noted that when the soldiers displayed their displeasure when booty was limited, Ahmadu occasionally sent them to raid some villagers.

"During the 'Umarian period, the economy was based on predation and conquest," and 'Umarian rule failed to be "conducive to economic growth and commercial activity; incomplete conquest created geographical insecurity."[99] In fact, the "predation and conquest" owed much to the "incomplete conquest" and a lack of unity among the military personnel.

John Hargreaves raises an important quetion which underlies the ambivalence of modern African nationalists as well as French policymakers in the late nineteenth century and the military units following 'Umar. Did 'Umar and Ahmadu meld the people of their empire into a political state, or were they regarded by most of these subject peoples as alien oppressors?[100] This is also a question for modern historians.

While some historians have found the 'Umarians very inadequate in their ability to create a consolidated regime, one traveler witnessed some progress in that direction. Paul Soleillet, during his visit to Segu in 1878, remarked on the political and economic stability of the region. Traders moved freely in various regions of the state and in the Monday market could be found various African and European goods from Sénégal, Gambia and Sierra Leone.[101]

One difficulty in adequately assessing the 'Umarian period lies in the very brevity of the regime which lasted only thirty years. The military control of the 'Umarians never completely dominated the Middle Niger, as had their Bamana predecessors and the French who followed them.

The fact that the 'Umarians never gained control of the Middle Niger explains the militant nature of the regime after the conquest; in other words, neither 'Umar nor Ahmadu were able to graduate from the military stage of the jihad to establish a theocratic state based on Islam. This was largely due to the Bamana refusal to submit to a theocratic administration, other groups in open rebellion against 'Umarian policy, and the encroaching French efforts to gain control of the Middle Niger. Furthermore, the 'Umarian leaders failed to incorporate all of their newer recruits within a military organization, which may have dissolved many of the divisions within the military. Lastly, the death of 'Umar in 1864 opened a Pandora's box as his sons vied for power rather than submitting to Ahmadu, who could have possibly created the state based on Qu'ranic principles which his father had envisioned. This leads us to consider, then, these three aforementioned factors and their roles in the disintegration of the 'Umarian state.[102]

Control was secure in the immediate vicinity of Segu, particularly on the right bank of the Niger between Bamako and Sinzani. However, in distant provinces the situation varied. For instance, Ahmadu's brothers failed to truly acknowledge Ahmadu's authority. Tijani, a cousin, according to Méniaud, had thrown off the yoke of Segu until Ahmadu reclaimed it in 1891.[103] Moreover, Aguibu sought collaboration with the French. Lastly, Kaarta and outlying regions might have been "responsive" to Ahmadu, but communications were interrupted by the Bamana of Bèlèdugu.

Internal Division in the 'Umarian State

One of the major obstacles facing West African polities on the eve of colonialism was that of rivalry over succession. Too often ruling regimes were weakened by contenders vying for power, either motivated by their own ambitions or coaxed by others. The 'Umarian state faced this problem at the most inopportune time, that is, in 1863 when the state needed all of its manpower to fight external threats. It seems clear, as Hanson and Robinson argue, "'Umar's death, and the destruction of armies, sons, and disciples in the ashes of Masina threatened the very existence of the mission and the embryonic state which he ('Umar) had launched."[104]

It appears that 'Umar attempted to avert this situation by naming his successor, rather than waiting for other political factions to elect a ruler after his death. However, some of the learned 'Umarians preferred to elect the best candidate in the community as Caliph. After taking Segukòrò, 'Umar officially and publicly named Ahmadu, also called Lamdioulbe,[105] as his successor:

Everything which was given to me . . . esoteric and exotic knowledge, the secrets and revelations and and outpourings (of divine emanations) and the wirds, all of it, indeed, I give it entirely to you and give you full authority in it and authorize you to give it.[106]

Then he instructed the community, "This one is your Shaykh. Anyone for whom I am the Shaykh, this is his Shaykh. Seek from him all the good you wish in this life and the next, you will find it."[107] Another source claims that 'Umar called all the notables, and consulted the people of the Futa about who should succeed him as caliph. Realizing 'Umar's decision, they chose Ahmadu. The people, then, pledged allegiance, and ordered the subjects to follow Ahmadu. Yet another source reveals that 'Umar said to the people, "Be witnesses, turn toward him, I have given my powers to him, I reserve nothing." However, one historian argues that there is no conclusive evidence that 'Umar had named one of his sons successor, and these reports are suspect.[108]

If indeed 'Umar officially named Ahmadu as his successor, the public coronation failed to prevent problems between Ahmadu and his siblings. Ahmadu's brothers refused to accept his position as inheritor of the state, and plotted to create power niches for themselves. Perhaps 'Umar was thinking of this when he placed some of his sons over territories with the understanding that they would look to Ahmadu as their political and spiritual leader, and instructed them to obey and respect Ahmadu in all circumstances.[109] On the contrary, by placing Mustafa, an ex-slave, in Nioro, son Abibu in Dinguiray, and son Mukhtar in Koniakari, 'Umar established divisions within the state. When his nephew, Tijani, reestablished control over Masina with a new capital at Banjagara, the 'Umarian state became virtually three semi-independent polities: Segu, Kaarta and Masina. Each of the leaders had talibes faithful to them. However, revolts from without only postponed an inevitable confrontation, which occurred in 1870 when Abibu and Mukhtar conspired to take Nioro.

Writers seemed to agree that Ahmadu was young and inexperienced.[110] It has been argued that 'Umar gave his sons and followers little political and military training. However, 'Umar reportedly tested his sons, Ahmadu and Makki, in combat against the Bamana in Markoya in 1860, and made a clear choice of Ahmadu in a public gathering. Ahmadu was "cautious and reserved," and had a reputation for parsimony; Makki, on the other hand, was flamboyant and generous. He was a poet and patron of scholars.[111] However, following the course of events, it may be argued that age and experience would have done little to alter the outcome. There is no doubt that Ahmadu lacked the spiritual credentials of his father so important in maintaining the political status he inherited. In fact, the disciples and soldiers in Segu continued to look to 'Umar for leadership after the Ahmadu's selection at Segu.[112] Nevertheless, Ahmadu was no less qualified than any of his brothers, cousins, or other learned men who followed 'Umar.

Although Ahmadu was intelligent, he did not present himself to the people in the manner of his father, whose personality cemented the 'Umarians. At most, Ahmadu could claim legitimacy based on the legacy of his father. The fissure in the 'Umarian aristocracy demonstrates that even this claim was insufficient to garner Ahmadu the necessary loyalty to create a strong theocratic polity.[113] Although Ahmadu was calm and calculating, he was indecisive despite being able to call on learned men who had served his father, some of whom counseled Ahmadu in political affairs.[114]

Pietri suggests that much of the problem between Ahmadu and his brothers existed since childhood. Abibu and Mukhtar were the sons of Aissata, the Sokoto princess, and were of royal lineage. On the other hand, Ahmadu was the son of an ex-slave. Therefore, Abibu and Mukhtar were humiliated and insulted to serve Ahmadu, the son of a slave, and many of the talibes agreed that their royal lineage gave them leverage.

Ultimately, Ahmadu was forced to take arms against his brothers in 1870 in a costly civil war. Abibu and Mukhtar plotted with other brothers Muniru and Daye to revolt against Ahmadu. In addition, Abibu and Mukhtar refused to aid Ahmadu in his struggle against the Bamana resistance movement in Kaarta between 1871 and 1873, preferring attack Ahmadu at that very time. Daah, another brother, left Farabugu with 500 to 600 soldiers to go to Fuladugu Alarbala while the other brothers left Nioro to go to Kita.[115]

Abibu began to intercept and take tribute en route to Segu. In addition, Mukhtar and Abibu drove out or persecuted Ahmadu's supporters in their territories. Meanwhile, Muntaga attempted to preserve his position by offering support to whichever side had the advantage at a given point during the struggle. Abibu and Mukhtar began their campaign in 1873 during the rainy season when the river would be high, making transportation very difficult. Ahmadu crossed the river to attack in December, during the dry season, and Muntaga deserted his brothers, providing military support to Ahmadu. With this victory, Ahmadu was able to establish control over Kaarta. However, he faced greater problems with the talibes, Masina remained independent, and the Bamana continued their attacks.[116]

Abibu and Mukhtar decided to take Nioro from Mustafa in 1870, who informed Ahmadu of his brothers' intrigue.[117] Abibu claimed to have had a letter from 'Umar, who entrusted Nioro to him. Ahmadu defeated Abibu and Mukhtar and led them in chains to Segu, where they were still living when Soleillet traveled to Segu in 1878 but died soon after. However, other reports say that only Mukhtar was led to Segu. French reports state that Abibu and Mukhtar were taken to Segu where they were placed before a firing squad.[118] Gallieni, a French administrator, affirms that Mukhtar was a prisoner in Segu during his visit, and it was problematic to Abibu to have his brother in Ahmadu's hands. Abibu also had a stratagem, for he held Ahmadu's mother in Dinguiray. Ahmadu agreed to release Mukhtar in order to obtain his own mother's release.

Mage maintained that the 'Umarian defeat at Sinzani in December 1863 was due to malcontents in the cavalry, comprised of Futaka from Futa Central who were unhappy about a man from Futa Toro commanding the army. The old tensions between the people from different regions of the Futa were acted out within the army.[119] Samba Njaye asserted that some of the Talibe resented Ahmadu, supporting the claims of Abibu and Mukhtar to share in their father's inheritance.[120]

An additional problem in the military was its class structure. The military consisted of basically two groups. The first was the elite cavalry

troops which usually consisted of Futakaw of the same aristocratic class
as in the state structure. The remaining troops formed a secondary class
of new Muslim converts, irregular Fulbe cavalry armed with lances, and
Bamana sofas who had joined 'Umar. Although the term "sofa" represented the cavalry in the Bamana army, these Bamana soldiers were foot
soldiers in the 'Umarian army who maintained the name associated with
the Bamana military identity. The term came to represent all foot soldiers
in the 'Umarian army, distinguishing them from the talibe elites. In brief,
the military included both communal, geographic, and class divisions.
Moreover, a particular resentment toward the Bamana *sofas* deepened the
division.[121]

What distinguished the talibes as a class was that they were learned,
often regarded as religious leaders. They acquired additional recognition
since they had been with 'Umar during the establishment of the state, per-
forming civil and military functions. Moreover, the talibes were leaders
of the Futaka contingent of the army which formed the nucleus of the military.[122] Many of the talibes from the Futa lived in Nioro and Koniakari,
centers of resistance within the state. Furthermore, 'Umar basically relied
on recruits brought in from Futa Toro, but Ahmadu made greater use of
local recruits, creating more resentment, and thus motivating him to use
more local recruits.

Class divisions and resentment within the army were further exacer-
bated by the unequal distribution of booty. A distribution system based on
status in the military was introduced rather than individual merit, as had
been the custom in the Bamana army.[123] Booty was of the utmost importance, expressed in an 'Umarian text: "The booty kept up the spirit of the
army."[124] The 'Umarians followed a method of distribution based on
Islamic law whereby Ahmadu claimed one-half of the booty. The cavalry
would receive more than the foot soldiers although the new converts and
volunteers having military experience with different philosophies of
booty distribution might have been dissatisfied with the booty they
expected and received. The problems with booty raise questions about the
motives of many of the followers and their loyalty to the jihad itself. After
the death of 'Umar, it seems that the ideological basis of the jihad was
weakened, if not destroyed, and the possibility of material advantage for
soldiers was differently prioritized. Nevertheless, Ahmadu guarded the

treasures in Segu, refusing to distribute them to the talibes on the grounds that the jihad had not been completed, and the treasures were needed for fighting wars.[125] Ahmadu's intentions are unclear, but his argument was prophetic.

One explanation for the antagonism of Segu talibes from Ahmadu was discontent with their economic situation, particularly if they joined the campaign for material gains. Some of the former talibes who had fought with 'Umar, receiving much bounty from raids during the war, had fallen into misery when the conquest ended. Occasionally, Ahmadu would send them to raid villages in order to calm them, but the raids depopulated villages and created more hostility toward 'Umarian rule; it also destroyed tax bases.[126] Gallieni argued that they exhibited "fanaticism for their religion," but, in reality, they were "very dissolute in their acts and in their manners."[127] Perhaps he was making reference to the talibes appropriating goods from the people in the villages to compensate for booty they had not received, or out of greed.[128] The talibes in Segu also had less booty, and shared fewer political offices than those in Masina and Kaarta. The rulers in those latter areas needed dependable talibes in their opposition to Ahmadu. They did so by sharing the wealth, thereby providing an economic stake for the talibes to protect. By the 1880s a concentration of the talibes had moved to Kaarta, forcing Ahmadu to rely even more on sofa forces comprised of local recruits.

The major problem for Ahmadu in 1884 was his brother Muntaga who made his move to throw off the yoke of Ahmadu. Muntaga received aid from his brothers, Amidu, Muniru and Daah. In addition, Tijani, ruler of Masina, informed him of Ahmadu's moves. Ahmadu was aware of his brother's plot, or at least suspicious, especially after Muntaga refused to present himself before the Sultan in Segu. 'Umar had required that all his sons go to Segu to celebrate the Prophet's birthday, *Tabaski*, a law which Ahmadu finalized. Ahmadu, then, found new recruits, and organized his forces to attack Nioro. It was only at his camp at Nyamina that he told his followers that he planned, in fact, to attack Kaarta. They had assumed that he had been preparing to attack the Bamana of Bèlèdugu.[129] It is unclear why it was necessary for the secrecy. Perhaps the situation with the talibes during the previous campaign against Nioro had made him cautious about the attitudes of his soldiers. By the time he arrived at Bakun,

Muntaga and his men went to oppose him.[130] Ahmadu had defeated his brothers by the fall of 1885, and many of Muntaga's followers disbanded after Muntaga was killed.[131] Ahmadu, however, was pressed to remain in Kaarta in an attempt to consolidate his victory. In addition, the Bamana stepped up their resistance during the Kaarta campaign, blocking all communications between Segu and Kaarta, and Ahmadu's army was too weak to try and force its way through Bèlèdugu. Ahmadu had to also fight Muhammad Lamine who had encroached upon 'Umarian territory in 1886.[132]

The structure of the 'Umarian state was never on a solid foundation. David Robinson argues that part of the problem was the composition of the original jihad, which paid little attention to administration and the construction of an Islamic state after supplanting the non-Islamic regimes. "The mission which 'Umar claimed to have received from God was the destruction of 'paganism,' not the construction of Islamic societies."[133] However, as Robinson himself realizes, 'Umar's energies were consistently applied to constant mobilization and constant warfare instead of recruitment efforts, military training, and state-building on the basis of Islamic law.[134] Evidence suggests that recruitment continued as new major trade routes, protected by Ahmadu's soldiers, permitted new recruits to enter Segu. However, it is unclear who exactly recruited these new followers, and it has already been noted that the talibes resented Ahmadu's reliance on local recruits.

'Umar did have a stable structure in the early stages of the jihad from 1840 to 1859, however, where he did in fact address all the elements that Robinson argues were lacking in the state. Its development was virtually impossible because 'Umar never ceased pushing the frontiers of his state, and he died before being able to consolidate it or to apply Islamic law in any systematic fashion. In this respect, Robinson's analysis seems appropriate. But, it is specious logic to assume that 'Umar had no intentions of constructing an Islamic theocracy.

Early colonial writers emphasized the lack of effectiveness of Ahmadu's leadership. For example, Ahmadu was characterized as being young and not having the spiritual or political qualities of his father, nor having proven his worth to be awarded leadership upon the basic principle that each head of state prove him/herself beforehand.[135] Ahmadu also faced the problem of following a founder of a state, and having to compete with a revered personality. Moreover, it seems clear that Ahmadu inherited many of the problems of the state when he inherited the Caliphate, and these were problems that seemed to confound 'Umar himself. After all, 'Umar was killed during a revolt in a supposedly conquered territory.

The inherited state was defined by boundaries created by military campaigns, rather than a political, religious or economic design. The wars of succession took their toll on security in the 'Umarian state. In addition, new recruits seemed to lack the ties to Islam or the ideology of the original jihad that characterized the original recruits from the Futa. The jihad had shifted from that of a "preaching jihad," and the preoccupation with wars prevented 'Umar's objective to catechize new recruits. This became clear when scant booty for the troops created resentment and discontent.

The paramount problem that 'Umar failed to resolve was the tension between his sons. One of the major causes for civil wars in African polities was the rivalries for the throne. The Bamana and the French took advantages of the cleavages within the state to advance their own agendas.

Entrance to Amadu's palace at Segu-Sekòrò.
Abon E. Mage, *Voyage dans le Soudan Occidental*
(Paris: Hachette, 1868), p. 211.

A soldier of Mari Jari led to execution.
Abon E. Mage, *Voyage dans le Soudan Occidental*
(Paris: Hachette, 1868), p. 429.

CHAPTER 3

THE BAMANA:
A POLITY IN TRANSITION

Arguably the most difficult problem for Ahmadu was the war efforts of the Bamana. Indeed, from the Bamana perspective, the 'Umarian conquest can be viewed as a temporary setback from which they soon recovered.[1] By no means was the 'Umarian conquest an accepted fate. The Bamana war against the 'Umarians can be divided into two phases. The first was the battle against the 'Umarians at the time the 'Umarians were creating the empire, and the second was the campaigns after the Battle of Thiewal in 1861, staged from new headquarters where they employed new strategies.

Bamana reaction to the 'Umarian occupation was varied. Obviously, different Bamana groups had different approaches to the 'Umarian administrators. Not only were there different reactions between the various castes and groups, but there were also differences between subgroups within a larger group, i.e. the Tònjòn. The most cohesive reactive force appears to have been the Bamana nobles, who had the most to lose, not only wealth and power, but social and political status as well.

In some respects, the Bamana war against the 'Umarians was forced to operate underground, employing guerilla tactics. Although the Bamana had a reputation of being great soldiers, this legacy of military supremacy did little in the face of superior weaponry of the 'Umarians. The

Bamana had few French arms, rather guns made or refurbished by them-selves[2] or acquired from other sources. For some time the French had been supplying arms to the 'Umarians because they were attempting to court them. It was later in the Bamana campaign against the 'Umarians, in the late 1880s, that the French would promote trade in arms to the Bamana.

The Bamana and Islam

One of the hagiographers of 'Umar praised the seizure of Segu as marking "the end of paganism, and from that moment on, the light of Islam shined a brilliant flame."[3] This was far from reality. Generally, the Bamana society of Segu was not Islamized by the 'Umarians. The *Kòmò* and other secret societies provided for the spiritual life of Segu.[4] After the 'Umarians' conquest, the Bamana "continued to drink their beer, *dolo*, as before the conquest, and to worship their *Kòmòw*." When it was time for harvesting they drank to their *Kòmòw*, and continued their religious cer-emonies. "Everyone knew that they remained always Bamana because they ate mixed animal meats which are forbidden by Islam. To the Bamana meat was meat."[5]

After subduing Segukòrò, 'Umar imposed tenets of Islam, at least in theory. After defeating the combined armies, he imposed the *Risala* of Ibn Abi Zaid al-Qairawani as the Islamic code, replacing the Bamana judicial institutions, and he demanded that the non-Muslims go to the mosques. 'Umar also ordered the shaving of heads, abstinence from alcohol, and the prohibition of consuming the meat of dogs, horses, or sick animals.[6] The tension between occupation forces and the local Bamana population was heightened since often the Muslim communities were of foreign ori-gin and resisted assimilation into the non-Muslim Bamana society on reli-gious grounds as well as due to differences of language and tradition.[7]

Little of the forceful proselytizing techniques in Segu and Kaarta was carried over from the practice of the preaching jihad in the Futa, where time was taken to actually teach converts. Instead, 'Umar ordered many of the Bamana who refused to convert to be executed.[8] Even when some Bamana leaders professed to be converted, 'Umar denied their claims and executed them.[9] By using force, 'Umar further alienated a society which viewed his conquest in social and cultural terms, not just political change. The loss of freedom and coerced conversion created deep resentment. Islamic practices were adopted and followed mostly in the riparian villages of the Niger River where the 'Umarian talibes could oversee the new institutions. However, 'Umar's power base did not include a general conversion of the Bamana, who completely refused to adhere to Islam. Religiously and politically, he failed to cross "the two rivers, neither the Bani nor the Niger, and failed to conquer the Bamana."[10]

After the death of 'Umar, the Islamization process, like other aspects of the regime, began to falter. Ahmadu created two Muslim cantons, Tuba and Nyamina, and decided to make the head of Nyamina the head of the province, with authority over the non-Muslims of Fadugu, Tukuruba, Messekele, Gana and Doeribugu. This authority was more nominal than real because the Bamana victoriously resisted the Pan-Islamism of Ahmadu.[11] In 1864 Mage discovered that the Bamana refused to recognize Salam.[12] Non-Muslims continued to fight to regain religious and political freedom, and little by little the 'Umarians lost their authority and prestige (which was precarious at best) among the conquered. One explanation for this is provided by Jules Brévié who argues that Islam was never adopted by the Bamana to the 'Umarians' full liking, but rather it was imposed by force (as had been done to groups of the Sahara), and the Naturists had always actively rebelled against religious oppression. Islam could only develop in the Sudan, thanks to secular support, but as soon as that secular power was removed, the religion "died, suffocated under the rich vegetation of Naturism which, rustic and indestructible, pushed vigorous rejection when the moral condition of its life re-established itself."[13]

The practice of Islam under the 'Umarians was heavily infused with Tijani ideas which created problems, especially among the Muslim population who followed the Qadiriyya. In fact, 'Umar reportedly burned the books of the Qadiriyya in Segukòrò.[14] During the time of 'Umar the Muslim *Qadis* (judges) settled problems of divorce, and land and other disputes. The Qadis were named by the *Qadi* of Segu.[15] The 'Umarians, however, had partial claim to be judges in that "they were not right because they only judge by their intentions and not by the laws" except in some cases when they judged the people with a book called the

Samurudang d'Arrissala.[16] The Bamana, however, very rarely surren-
dered to the judgements of the Muslims. Instead, the Bamana resolved
their own problems.[17] They did so on the various levels of the Bamana
judicial system, meeting in a designated place in order to discuss the
cases. The unconverted Bamana refused to consult the Umarians unless
the problem concerned or implicated a 'Umarian.[18] However, some of
those who converted came to pose their problems before the Muslims.[19]

The Bamana attitude toward Islam was also due to 'Umarian political
activities. 'Umarian occupation was not viewed as spiritual, nor philan-
thropic. "Everyone spoke of the wickedness of the Futaka because they
raided each village after they conquered it. The 'Umarian conquest was
not spiritual because even where the Quadiriyya existed, it failed to stop
the 'Umarian from attacking."[20] Not only did they monopolize all the riches, the tax was heavy and at any time could be doubled in the same year.[21]
The 'Umarians left a legacy of cruelty and wickedness because the talibes
became "an oppressive and self-seeking aristocracy."[22]

The 'Umarian occupation was severe from the Bamana perspective.
Those who accepted Islam remained in Segukòrò, but they were not
numerous. Those who converted were considered to have feared the
'Umarians, for those who did not fear them never accepted their domination.[23] The few Bamana who remained were quasi-Muslims. For instance,
some converted Bamana kept dozens of wives, and some disregarded the
rituals of ablution. Other ceremonies such as child naming, *denkundi*;
marriage, *furu*; and, funerals, *sudon,* for example, remained Bamana.
Even if a Marabout came to give a benediction, the Bamana performed
their own religious ceremonies after he left. The majority of the Bamana,
particularly those in the villages of the hinterland, continued to worship
their Boli and Kòmò, and no mosques existed in these villages.

The Bamana equated acceptance of Islam with the acceptance of
'Umarian power, which thus limited the scope of possible conversion, in
that the 'Umarians "came with news to Islamize the countries, but in reality they came to command the country by force. They liked power too
much, and had little time to Islamize the countries."[24] This jurisdiction
was very severe for the Bamana since the 'Umarians attempted to force
Islamic principles on the communities. Of the major restrictions on the
Bamana, one was the limitation on the number of wives allowed. "If you

had ten wives, they left you with four. The six they took and made them slaves."[25] Another issue was wealth. The 'Umarians raided the wealthy, seizing whatever riches were available. In addition, they had a reputation of taking beautiful girls by force to marry. (This was also a complaint of the Sòmònòs.) In short, "the Bamanaw were nothing for them ('Umarians) because they killed the Bamanaw and buried them."[26] It is this kind of treatment that led the Bamana to repudiate Islam.

Those who had embraced Islam before the arrival of 'Umar, like the villages of Togu, Dugubal, and others, did not resist 'Umar since he was more powerful than they. Nevertheless, they preserved themselves and continued their former practice of Islam, but not the Tijaniyya 'Umar preached. Robinson points out that 'Umar built mosques in the capital and countryside.[27] However, a local historian, Tiam, asserts that the 'Umarians built only two mosques in the country, one at Segu and one in Barueli.[28] Some mosques had been constructed by the soldiers and teachers of Ahmadu Ahmadu before the 'Umarian invasion.

The biggest stumbling block to Islamization in the Middle Niger seemed to be the 'Umarians themselves.[29] Their behavior made it difficult to entice the Bamana to Islam. Of course, other problems existed. For instance, the Bamana had religious practices of their own, and to displace one set of beliefs with another is no easy task. Those who had already been Islamized before the coming of 'Umar had not embraced the religion by force and "cruel" coercion. Many of the other Bamana families kept their Bamana religious rituals and paraphernalia, and many fled from Segu to install themselves "behind" the Bani River.

Bamana Soldiers

The Bamana soldiers had greater bargaining power than the other groups in their society. Being professional soldiers, they could sell their skills to whomever would bid for them. For example, some joined the ranks of 'Umar and later fought with Ahmadu. Some of the Bamana Kuntigi fought with 'Umar when he marched against Masina after the Bamana loss in the Segu campaign. Nevertheless, their loyalty was not trusted. When the soldiers returned to Segu, they gave great gifts to

Ahmadu. Ahmadu, however, informed them that he had been warned of their desire to betray him. As a result, he called them to a convocation on March 23, 1863, and had the talibes surround the Bamana soldiers, telling them "You wanted to betray me; I am going to punish you." However, he realized that most of the soldiers had weapons under their clothing; therefore, he sent them to 'Umar, who had them executed on the bank of the river. Mage, in recounting this episode, explained that the Kintigiw, like the other Bamana, wanted vengeance and liberty in the form of the autonomy, culture, and religion they practiced under the old regime.[30]

Loyalty was important to the militaristic philosophy of the Tònjòn, a philosophy which tied the soldier to his military commander. It is true that the temporary dismantling of Bamana political power in Segu motivated individual interests to carve an economic niche in the political vacuum. Oloruntimehin argues that the Bamana created new socio-political institutions: not only banditry, but the creation of a professional soldier class who fought for personal interest as well as the Bamana cause against the 'Umarians.[31] The concept of professional soldiery already existed. During the 'Umarian period it is important to make a distinction between the professional soldier who fought for the state and loyal to the ruling aristocracy, and the soldier who was by definition a mercenary and thus gaining employment, and who owed no allegiance to any particular person or ideology. Essentially, some Bamana soldiers fought as a means of livelihood, and the causes of the regime or person(s) to whom they offered their skills mattered little. Mabèrè Kanu, a former captive and a general in the Segu Bamana army, is an example. When Kanu was sent to help the Cisse revolt in Sinzani in 1868, the governor of the state offered him the command of his armies and other rewards to retain him. As a result, Kanu left the Jaras to head the Sinzani forces, and convinced other military leaders like Ntò and Boliebugu to join him, creating problems between the two allies. Disagreements erupted between Ntò, Boliebugu, Kanu, and the governor over the issue of booty distribution. Consequently, Ntò and Boliebugu withdrew their men from the service of Sinzani and attracted some of Kanu's men, occupying several villages within the sphere of Sinzani, including Sibla, Sanamadugu, Markala, Gomako, Boliebugu and Mikha. The Cisse ruler then made Ntò the new commander of the Sinzani forces and head of Markadugu, causing Kanu to leave Sinzani and again collaborate with the Bamana of Segu.[32]

Because of the political instability, small autonomous groups could operate for their personal gain, and leaders could exert control over small or medium-sized bands of soldiers. Even in this sense the Tònjòn structure survived because an individual soldier had to exert influence over a band of men even if he could not establish control over larger groups.

Loyalty, however, was retained by the Jara family from many soldiers who continued to serve the Bamana state throughout the thirty-year period of 'Umarian occupation. Many the cream of the crop of the military continued to support the Ngolosiw. In fact, the major disunity in the Bamana military did not come from "warlord" competition because no one leader could garner enough influence. The major problem for the Bamana war efforts was Ntò. From 1861 to the French conquest, Ntò and the Ngolosiw, particularly Karamòkò Jara, vied for the position of Fama; Ntò, however, had no valid claim to the position. This competition in itself demonstrates that the Bamana people considered the Bamana state at this time far from dissolution from the 'Umarian invasion. In addition, both Ntò and Karamòkò Jara fought the 'Umarians. Indeed, many of the population never officially submitted to 'Umarian rule. In anticipation of the future return of the Bamana to Segu, the question of succession, as we shall see below, had already begun to surface.

The Bamana-'Umarian Thirty-Year War

After the 'Umarian invasion, most of the Bamana evacuated the villages closest to the capital.[33] Even the leaders who remained in Segu had planned to revolt in March 1863. However, Ahmadu learned of the plot from spies.[34] Kènyè Mari Jara, brother of the Fama Ali Jara, called on Kaminiandugu to fight, closing the route which the 'Umarian troops took to enter the country. This route would remained closed to the 'Umarians for the next thirty years as Kaminiandugu became the principal theater of war during these years.[35] From 1861 to 1870 Kènyè Mari led a military campaign, recapturing some of the villages from the 'Umarians. Many of them were located near Segukòrò, now the capital of the 'Umarian state. The battlegrounds on the two banks at Sama and Segukòrò caused the people to leave "rich country" and move toward territories of the interior or to large fortified villages. The roads became dangerous, and commerce was completely closed down since the caravans were forced to choose other routes.[36]

Kènyè (or Kègnè) Jara, better known as Manjè but also known as Masala Mari, was one of the first to react after the Ngolosiw were chased from Segu. He was strong-willed even to the point of stubbornness. He and his followers were able to chase the 'Umarians to Dugukuna in one battle, forcing the latter to cross the river. Manjè proclaimed that he would fight because "strangers came in my country."[37]

Manjè was the governor of Masala, from which he acquired the name of Masala Mari. He assassinated Torokòrò Mari (also known as Bale Jara), but left the title of Fama to his younger brother Ali Jara, governor of Weita so that he could avoid creating the impression that his action against Torokòrò was a thirst for power.[38] Manjè fought at the side of Bina Ali against 'Umar, and most notable for his roles in the battles at Tio, Kaku and Tuna.

When Ali went in exile after the rout at Kaku and the fall of Tuna, Manjè refused to follow. He decided to stay and continue the struggle. He lived at Tuna and with the Ngolosiw and an alliance with Tangara he created a unified base for his actions.[39] Kènyè Mari made Tuna the headquarters of the Bamana state, waging war in the direction of Sinzani and Segu, and causing Ahmadu and the 'Umarians to be "seized with panic," even in the capital city.In Ali's absence he assume the leadership of the Bamana armies. However, it was only after the execution of Ali that he became the new Fama; he was crowned at Tuna. From that moment, he put forth all his energy and courage to liberate his country. Although a man of character, he was considered obstinate in his decisions. "He did not retreat from any excess when the interest of his cause demanded it."[40]

Manjè mobilized all who were discontented with 'Umarian administration. He went first to Shuala near his cousins who aided him to recruit some contingents in Kola and Kuruma who promised their alliance.[41] After crossing the Joliba, he returned to Bèndugu to cross Kaminiandugu where he apprised the population aware of the situation and acquired some allies among the local leaders. He reinforced his troops with recruits from these regions, and returned to Tuna, his capital, and prepared to face the 'Umarians.[42]

In August 1863 Kaminiandugu entered the war. When the 'Umarians under Ahmadu completely evacuated the right bank, the Segu Bamana established themselves in front of their former capital and continued the struggle. The talibes charged with collecting taxes in Kaminiandugu returned to Segu, complaining of the dissent in the region, and requested the support of the army, which Ahmadu refused. Meanwhile, some Bamana soldiers of Kaminiandugu went to Bamabugu, captured and executed forty talibes. Eventually, the population of Kaminiandugu was reduced considerably by the war between the Bamana and the 'Umarians.

The military maneuvers in Kaminiandugu in 1863 were encouraged by partisans of Manjè. Bubu Sise of Sinzani sent his nephew, Brehima Ncini, to make contact with Manjè. Manjè assured the Maraka city of his support and promised aid at an opportune moment.[43] The success of the Bamana military in 1863 encouraged Manjè to engage the 'Umarians. The actions of Kaminiandugu permitted him to enlarge his territories by rallying some leaders of that region.[44]

During the Kaminiandugu and Sarraudugu offensives, there was no revenue for Ahmadu. As a result, the millet price increased fivefold in 1864 and 1865.[45] In 1864 matters worsened for Ahmadu as the Maraka of Nyamina revolted, led by an ally of Kènyè Mari, Bethen Suko. Moreover, the Bamana of Kala, who also never recognized 'Umarian authority, joined the provinces on the offensive. Meanwhile, Masina under Ba Lobo regrouped. By 1864 Ahmadu was, in effect, surrounded by Bamana forces on the offensive and other groups in revolt.

Also in 1863 Ahmadu enraged the people of Sinzani by raising the taxes because he needed more resources. When representatives from Sinzani came to explain that the tax was too high (500 measures of cloth valued at 800,000 cowries [local currency] at least), Ahmadu raised the tax to 1,000 pieces of cloth. Although this increased tax was extracted, the people subsequently rebelled, a revolt which lasted for two years.[46]

The Bamana of Sinzani created additional problems in December 1863. Ahmadu sent an army under Alfa Abdul to Sinzani to face the Bamana troops at the site where the Bamana troops had defeated the 'Umarian force, and Abdul was killed in the battle. Then Ahmadu united the armies of Nioro and of Tierno Alassane (or El Assane Ba) to attack the inhabitants of Sinzani, aided by the Bamana who succeeded in also defeating the 'Umarian forces. According to Mage, the 'Umarian armies entered with little resistance because the Bamana had already left the village. The talibes, entering from the west entrance, began to pillage the village, taking salt, cowries, cloth, cotton and captives. The Bamana left by the other entrance and doubled back by another route to surprise the talibes from the rear. At the first shot from the Bamana, the 'Umarian soldiers who were on lookout fled the scene, and the reserve 'Umarian unit followed. The talibes who were still inside the village mounted the walls, and seeing the army in flight, fled themselves, taking the booty they had gathered. The Bamana attacked them, forcing the army to return to Segu in disorder. The talibes abandoned the captives en route, and threw their guns in the river in order to cross more expeditiously. Ahmadu decided to attack Sinzani again in February 1864 when the Bamana again put up great resistance, killing and wounding the 'Umarians, who failed to take any booty. After Alassane failed to defeat the Bamana, another source related that Ahmadu himself besieged the city for three months. Unable to defeat the troops of Sinzani, the 'Umarians retreated never to establish full control over the area again.[47]

While Kènyè Mari was waging war on one front, Mari Jara who would later become the last Bamana Fama, led other Bamana in battle. In March 1864 Ahmadu was alerted from Masina when two sofas taken prisoner in the previous campaign escaped and told him about Bamana military actions. In April 1864 Mari Jara and his army attacked Dugassu and Ahmadu had to dispatch a contingent to defend the village. Also in April, the Bamana attacked two small Bamana villages to the south of Segu, Minianka and Nagassola, which had submitted to 'Umarian authority. The Bamana threat was so feared that when Ahmadu demanded that village leaders to supply men for an army to lead Mage to Hamdallaye, they refused, explaining that if the army left for Masina, the Bamana in Segu would revolt and take the city and kill everyone. Ahmadu, therefore, was forced to wait on contingents from Nioro.[48]

In September 1864 with the aid of his cousin Dugaba Kulubali of Shuala, Manjè launched operations in the zone of Farakò on the left bank of the Joliba where he raided the harvest.[49] Manjè escaped to Tuna after a stay in Moninpèbugu and Kaminiandugu. In spite of the defeat at Togu,

he enhanced his image among the Bamana and continued to receive reinforcements. His authority was now exercised over Kaminiandugu, Saro,
Moninpèbugu, and Bèndugu which recognized him as Fama.[50]

In January 1865 the Bamana forces occupied Toghu, a village of
Sinzani, and the 'Umarian forces failed to uproot them, losing arms and
ammunition, including 120 barrels of gun-powder and many war drums.[51]
Ahmadu returned to Segu to assemble another army, but lost in the next
attack.

By the end of 1865, Bamana victories had permitted Kaminiandugu,
Sinzani, Sanamadugu, Marakadugu, all on the left bank of the Joliba to
be free from 'Umarian domination. The 'Umarian province of Segu was
reduced to a portion of territory between the Joliba and Bani from Dna to
Koké. Only Nyamina on the left bank was under 'Umarian control.
Bèndugu, Saro, Kaminiandugu, Moninpèbugu, Marakadugu, Sanamadugu and Kala recognized the Ngolosiw as the Fama.[52]

By 1867 Manjè was receiving the support of many Bamana villages,
including some on the left bank of the Bani. Then, he formulated a new
plan of action, and temporarily established himself at Kènyè, a village to
the southwest of Segu, which had his name. He fortified the village and
began to systematically and regularly attack and raid the area around
Segu that had submitted to Ahmadu. He wanted to make his residence the
core that united all the Bamana even if that should lead to shortages (such
that millet was valued at 100,000 cowries [80,000 in Bamana numera-
tion]).[53]

Ahmadu won his most decisive battle against the Bamana in 1868 at
Kènyè. At this time Ahmadu was forced to recall most of the 'Umarian
garrison to Segu. Famine was everywhere because Manjè's soldiers had
burned the harvests in a scorched-earth policy. In this manner the Fama
also rallied those who came to seek protection, peace, and food at Kènyè.
Ahmadu attempted a decisive action to put an end to this situation, and
laid siege to Kènyè. For almost a year Manjè and his army withheld the
assault, enduring enormous deprivations. Hunger obliged the besieged,
who had exhausted all their reserve, to feed themselves, using radical
means.[54] Yet they continued the defense. An 'Umarian agent charged
toward the village in an attempt to jump the thick wall with his horse, and
was hit by the defenders. They committed an act of imprudence by open-

ing the gate to identify the body. Instantly, the 'Umarians surged and massacred the garrison and residents at Kènyè. The town was destroyed,[55] and Manjè lost twelve children in the battle.

Ahmadu's struggle against the Bamana was viewed as a continuation of the jihad, providing him credibility in the eyes of many Muslims. The incident was epically depicted by Muhammad ibn Ibrahim.

> We captured them as booty as soon as they came in sight, the booty kept up the spirit of the army.
> We instantly killed any of those dogs who followed us, and captured the women and children.
> That bright night was illuminated by the moonlight in a celebration which made the children happy.
> We slept opposite our enemies, because of our joy and abundance of booty, thinking of the place we had made.
> We slaughtered many fat infidels.
> Whoever spent a night with us expected violence.
> For there, the Banu Mari were put to the sword, their women and children became slaves.
> They have no sultan or king, for they are devils as well as infidels.[56]

However, a Bamana source credits the Bamana loss simply to hunger. When Manjè reformed an army at Tuna, the soldiers wanted to wait until the millet was cut before going to battle, but Manjè refused. Subsequently, the village fell due to famine, not Ahmadu's strength.[57]

After the defeat, the Bamana who had escaped Kènyè faced Ahmadu in 1872 (now with the support of many Futaka from Nioro) at Gemukura where they had established a new base. Ahmadu attacked Gemukura at dawn, setting fire to the village while the people were sleeping.[58] The people escaped to Kagoro, a village beside Gemukura which the Bamana had built.[59] The recorder of this event, Sa'id b. Ahmad or Seidu Jeliya, prime minister of Ahmadu in the 1880s and 1890s, described events in a religious tenor.

> And when the Commander of the Faithful, Ahmad al-Kabir al-Madani al-Mansur, heard about that (the revolt of the Bamana), the fervor of the people of Allah welled up in him along with the fury against the enemies of Allah. There upon he began to prepare the

armies and to dispatch them to make jihad against them and to gain victory for Allah Most High and His Messenger and the believers by fighting them.[60]

The Bamana rebounded with a major victory over the 'Umarians at Guigne, and disrupted communications and trade along the major commercial artery between Segu and the West. The Bamana threat to Segu increased during Ahmadu's absence in the early 1870s. Mustafa Jeliya Turè, an advisor of Ahmadu stationed in Segu, expressed concern over the Bamana forces and the fate of Ahmadu.[61]

Manjè committed suicide at Kaana, and his body was buried in the *Masa Blon* (great vestibule of leaders) with the honors of a leader. The people of Kaana hoped that the special burial would bear witness to Manjè's bravery. The oral historian, Cèkòrò Tangara, sees the suicide of Manje as an act of pride, brought on by his disappointment at seeing the 'Umarian conquest of his patrimony. His disappointment was pronounced because he had a highly evolved sense of Bamana identity; he wanted to defend and conserve his people at any cost.[62]

Manjè succeeded in leading the Bamana in successful campaigns. These successes not only explain his qualities as a born leader, but also the courage, and the tenacity which Manjè proved.

> His conviction for the defense of the Bamana cause in the eyes of his people was a symbol of all that the ethnic group venerated as ideal. He knew how to synthesize the sentiments of originality and the aspirations of all those (of his people) who the Futaka had frustrated and desecrated, in their conviction as with their goods humiliated and held up to ridicule.[63]

Despite his stubbornness and his refusal to listen to the advice of the counselors and other members of the royal family, he succeeded in gaining the support of certain princes like Karamòkò Jara and certain military leaders like Mabèrè Kanu, Kaana Dugu, Ncè Jara and others, who were driven by the same ideal as he.[64]

Despite his success, he was unable to reconquer Segu. The reason rested more in the military domain than because of political strategy. In short, the Bamana army had inferior armaments. The 'Umarians used guns which were newer models and better constructed than those of the

Bamana, and they had a greater number of weapons. The cannons which were left from the days of 'Umar were a decisive factor at Tuna. Of course, the great error made at Kènyè was the final downfall for Manjè.[65]

With the ability to acquire necessary reinforcements from other areas of the state, particularly Nioro, Ahmadu was able to keep the guerrilla attacks outside the nucleus of Segu. Although the movement of Kènyè Mari failed to topple the 'Umarian state, it did circumvent Ahmadu's political and economic goals.

Several villages continued to obey and be devoted to the Jaras throughout the 'Umarian period and beyond, including Sele, Koro, Say, Saro and Niga.[66] Four other major areas remained submitted to the Bamana Famaw: Kaminiandugu, Markadugu, Bintugu and Sanamadugu. Each village furnished contingents, requested by Mabèrè Kanu, and these men assembled at Sama-Fulala. Kanu took counsel with the head sofas and the leaders who were his assistants for particular maneuvers.[67]

Information compiled by the French suggests that the force which could be convened by the Bamana military leader consisted of 2,000 fantassins (infantries) armed with guns or lances, and 600 cavaliers. In addition, a partial column of approximately 1,800 men, cavalry and infantry, assembled at Fanienema. These columns of Kaminiandugu and Bintugu, the stronger being Bintugu, were almost always mobilized, operating south of 'Umarian territory on the Bakay. The columns had constant communications with each other to facilitate movements and/or to join each other if necessary. Since Kaminiandugu was a strategic war base for the Bamana between 1861 to 1875, and situated between Segu and Hamdallaye, Bamana from other areas came to Kaminiandugu to continue to fight the 'Umarians. Even upon the arrival of the French, a large number of head sofas were still in Kaminiandugu and Bintugu; on one side, Kogue Ba, brother of the Fama; and on the other, Kissima, captain of the Bintugu column. Additionally, there were secondary leaders; the superiors, however, lived at Sama near the general of the army.[68]

The provinces of Markadugu, Kaminiandugu and Bintugu formed a stronghold for the Bamana nobles, forming a large crescent, overhanging and partly surrounding the 'Umarian capital of Segu in the north, south and east directions.[69] The Bamana of Bèlèdugu closed the routes west to Kaarta, and the Malinkes who followed Samori Turè controlled the south-

west corridor between the Niger and Bani Rivers toward Dinguiray and
Futa Djallon, leaving only two routes open leading to the states of Cèba
in Kènèdugu, one by the ford of Sorokòrò in Segu, and the other by the
ford of Cenda. The 'Umarian capital had, in short, "become their
prison."[70]

Karamòkò Jara and the other inhabitants of the left bank of the Joliba
and of the north crossed the river after the defeat at Kènyè and occupied
Marakadugu, the zone of Farakò, Sama, Kamala and other areas. The
presence of the princes (Karamòkò at Farakò, Sannye Baa, son of
Nyènèma Kòròba at Kamale; Weita Baa, son of Kirango Bèn at Bayo)
confirmed the submission of the left bank and of the North to the Ngolosi
power. Karamòkò maintained that entire zone under the influence of the
Jara dynasty until the problems between himself and Marakadugu Ntò
erupted.[71]

At the death of Kènyè Mari in 1870 the Bamana on the left bank of the
Niger and those of the Baninko were determined to fight desperately
against the 'Umarian occupying forces. However, the situation of the
Bamana located between the two rivers was delicate because of their
proximity to the 'Umarians who regularly attacked them. Therefore,
"they needed a moment of respite."[72]

The first successors of Manjè had neither the conviction nor the com-
bative ardor of their predecessor. They were content to administer the territory which had submitted to them although the polarization of the
Bamana state and people was still a major issue. These rulers launched no
direct military action against the 'Umarians, and only certain military
leaders and some princes living on the left bank of the Joliba or in
Baninko raided the 'Umarian garrisons and territory.

The designated successor of Kènyè Mari (Manjè) was Nyènèma II who
was crowned according to Bamana custom in 1873, and his authority was
recognized by Bèndugu, Kaminiandugu and Saro. Karamòkò and the others of the left bank (Marakadugu, Sanamadugu, and Monimpèbugu) submitted to the new Fama although they did not support his attitude toward
the 'Umarians.[73] Nyènèma II was not disposed to armed struggle. He
wanted to give his subjects time to renew their forces and lead a normal
life. He left Tuna and Bèndugu, which had become the "model" for the
struggle, and installed himself at Sanbala in Kaminiandugu, near Tuna in

a village retaken from the 'Umarians. It might have been symbolic that some Bamana Famaw made villages recaptured from the 'Umarians as their as their power base. He died in 1878 "after a reign without brightness."[74]

Mamura became Fama at Nyènèma II's death, but ruled for only seven days and was replaced by his cousin Nyènèma III, called Nyènèma Ncini, but better known as Masatoma. He was also crowned at Tuna as were the others, but preferred to make Moribugu his capital around 1879. His reaction to the 'Umarians was much like Nyènèma II. However, the subjects of Marakadugu and of the left bank of the Joliba, more engaged in the armed struggle against the 'Umarians, decided to revive their militant opposition. Ntò, the military general of Marakadugu, was sent to the Fama to request that he reconsider his attitude toward the struggle. Masatoma then prepared to take arms. He committed suicide in 1883.[75]

The Reign of Karamòkò Jara 1883-1889

Karamòkò Jara, son of Mònzòn, returned to Tuna to receive the investiture, an "act which seemed destined to rally the Bamanaw of Baninko." Then he returned to Moribugu and Sana for a year, motivating his subjects to resume combat against the enemy. Most of the Bamana recognized him as Fama of Segu.[76] Karamòkò's army was divided in 35 bolow of 1500, 2000 or 3000 men. The strategy of attack was that the bolow fired on the enemy one after the other, permitting constant firing. The soldiers' uniforms consisted of a shirt and a specialized trouser. They were armed with a gun, sword, pin, penknife, and a hatchet, called a *sèmè*. Each had a sack of *cous-cous* and another of water. The ammunition (powder and balls) was carried by the Sòmònò who divided it in 35 piles immediately before combat.[77] Bacekòrò Kulubali argues that Ahmadu took notice of the force the Ngolosiw had acquired and the danger it represented for him.[78] Mabèrè Kanu was made the general of the army, serving as the head Tònjòn. He was an unrelenting fighter, faithful to the Ngolosiw and devoted to the Bamana cause. After the death of Manjè, he had fought in the service of his successors. Under Karamòkò he accepted the supreme leadership of the army.[79] Karamòkò's first martial acts were to attack the

military convoys and the caravans entering 'Umarian territory, severely
testing the 'Umarian army. Karamòkò, however, failed to fully exploit his
victories. In fact, he had serious difficulties due to the dissension among
some of his military leaders, particularly Marakadugu Ntò. With the latter, the problem was rooted in the power struggle between Ngolo Jara and
Ntò's great grandfather, Zanketegela.[80] Ntò, at this time, formed an
autonomous "fiefdom" at Markadugu and Sana. Nevertheless, Ntò continued to fight the 'Umarians.[81]

Karamòkò established an army at Farakò on the Niger, and raided the
right bank. As did his predecessor, he made Farakò, a former village for
'Umarian sofaw, his headquarters. He failed to execute his plan by 1887,
however, since Madani divided his army in three parts, placing one section each at Nango, Massolah and Kogne, attempting to hamper
Karamòkò's movements.[82] Karamòkò was able to defeat Madani in three
battles: two at Weita, and the third west of Marakadugu.[83]

Although Karamòkò lived in Farakò, his sofas lived in Sama, a
Bamana village. The defection of the villages on the left bank of the Niger
which had broken from Segu to establish their independence had much to
do with Karamòkò establishing his post on the left bank as the center for
his partisans, many from Kaminiandugu. Although he had strong intentions to attack Segu, Karamòkò felt that he lacked the force to do so.
Delanneau suggests that he wanted to avoid compromising his influence
and chance a setback; he preferred to wait for a more favorable occasion.
In addition, Delanneau was convinced that Karamòkò was waiting for the
French to assist him, and he informed Karamòkò that the French would
not make war on Ahmadu.[84] However, it is unclear in the French records
when or if Karamòkò sought the aid of the French. In fact, the Bamana of
the right bank killed a Futaka after learning that he was a friend of the
French.[85]

Sarraudugu followed the success of Kaminiadugu, and assembled an
army which attacked Koghe. Ahmadu, who wanted to revenge his defeat
at Banbugu, sent an army to Markaduguba, and when the army of
Sarraudugu invaded Koghe, the 'Umarians attacked them. Afterwards,
Ahmadu sent an army to attack Sukuru, and executed the village leader,
Sukorokan, and his brother, Bilama.

The Bamana who made war against the 'Umarians continued to punish those Bamana who submitted to Ahmadu, seeing them as traitors. For example, Dugaba, a Bamana head of Sokolo, left Sinzani to attack the Bamana still submitted to Ahmadu. Ahmadu was forced to send approximately 500 men to face the attacking Bamana unit.

General Mabèrè Kanu continued to attack the 'Umarians from the right bank, and he led raids on caravans destined for Nyamina. The Bamana made all commerce impossible in the region under his occupation, as well as near Nyamina. The Bamana indiscriminately raided all the caravans which fell in their hands, creating problems for Ahmadu and for the French.[86]

Ahmadu had placed Yoro, who had been a sofa of 'Umar, in command over Bèndugu and the villages of Baninko and Sarro in payment for his services. But the Bamana revolted against his authority in 1886. Yoro attempted to quell the resistance by force, leading a column against them, but to no avail because the villages of the Baninko were tied to the Jaras at Farakò.[87]

Tautain wrote that Karamòkò decided to return to the other bank in July because of the need to attend farms. This was good news for Nyamina. However, the two months of tranquility were due to "raiders" going elsewhere, not to any French influence or presence.[88]

The majority of the skirmishes between the Bamana and the 'Umarians for some months had been to the advantage of the Bamana. For instance, in September 1886 the Bamana of Npere attacked a caravan.[89] Again, around the middle of October 1887 a band of Bamana composed of the people from Segala, Damfa and some from Karamòkò attacked villages faithful to the 'Umarians. Moreover, the route from Wolossebugu to Segu was cut.[90]

Karamòkò Jara led the Bamana in a campaign against Madani in Segu in late 1888 and inflicted several defeats in May and June. The French accused Karamòkò of being "so intoxicated with his successes" that he refused to take into account that not only had his sofaw attacked the caravan routes from Tuba, but also those from Nyamina and Konina which were within French territory. The people of Konina did, however, join Karamòkò. Meanwhile, about 400 cavaliers from Bèlèdugu quickly formed an army and invaded Nyamina. Consequently, the French mission reported that from Sinzani to Kurussi was in ruins.[91]

Karamòkò's relationship with the French was ambiguous. Although he had openly declared the French his enemies, he was also ready "to extend his hand" to them when they arrived at Farakò.[92] The French, as will be discussed later, were dishonest, cunning, and deceptive in their relations with Africans, but took offense when the same practices were used against them. Karamòkò did not approach the French, but the French sent missions to Farakò to meet him. Mamadou Racine,[93] after his arrival to Nyamina, attempted to bring Karamòkò Jara to the French and make him sign a treaty with them.[94] Also, the French used other schemes to win over Karamòkò, including getting other influential people to talk to him. Despite all the gifts the French sent, Karamòkò's response was, "When the owner of a camel has his camel fall in a well, and someone manages to get him out, he (the latter) will go with the camel."[95] Simultaneously, Underberg was planning to talk to Ntò, Karamòkò's adversary, despite Underberg having received instructions to not enter talks with Ntò in the event proposals with Karamòkò failed. It seems that the French realized that the Bamana were needed to remove the 'Umarians from power in Segu and the Middle Niger as a whole.

The French assessed the political situation in the late 1880s as one ripe for the destruction of the 'Umarian empire. Joce, representing a group of Bamana, had met with the French, informing them that the Bamana were prepared to keep Ahmadu contained in Kaarta. In addition, Farakò seemed to be a convenient base for French operations and an army of aux-iliaries.[96] However, Karamòkò had no plans for his power base to become a pawn to the French, nor to jeopardize his offense against the 'Umarians. Karamòkò reportedly instructed the French that he could not send the entire army, but would furnish two batallions, and explained, "Here, I sit next to powder. The Futa and me, we fight each other day and night."[97]

The French attempted to show their force by occasionally seeking to intimidate Africans. In 1888 the Almamy of Tuba, a protegé of the French, sent three messengers to Bamako to tell the French that the peo-ple of Konina raided the caravans from Tuba. The French Resident ordered the citizens of Konina to restitute Tuba for the men and stolen animals. The Koninans, who had already divided the booty with Karamòkò, refused to make restitution. Karamòkò told them that if the Commandant marched against them, he would come to their aid.

On June 25 Sidi Konè, head of Nyamina, also complained of the violence from Karamòkò. The French administrator sent a letter to Karamòkò, instructing him that he should not permit his sofas to raid the caravans coming to the French, and more seriously, he accused Karamòkò of permitting his forces "to commit these depredations on French territory." Karamòkò replied that he did not know how to read, and returned the letter. His sofaw continued to frequent Nyamina, menacing the area until the end of September. The French assumed that "the change of heart" in September 1888 was due to a French convoy on the Niger en route to Kulikòrò.[98]

From the moment Ahmadu left Madani in control of Segu, Madani was at war with Karamòkò Jara. On May 12, 1887 Ahmadu's ambassadors, including Samba Njaye, were in Kayes to meet the French Commandant Superior with the treaty of Guri in which, according to the French, Ahmadu placed his present and future states under the French protectorate. He thus opened his territory to French trade, authorizing navigation of the Niger and its tributaries. The Bamana were aware that the French had been courting Ahmadu, and they were suspicious of "the good relations established between the French and their eternal enemy, Ahmadu."[99]

When Ahmadu's brother decided to opt for complete independence, Muktar wanted to bring the Bamana under his authority in Jombokhu in 1873, but failed since the Bamana were disinterested in the civil wars of the 'Umarian state, preferring to focus on regaining their own independence.[100]

Other Bamana attacks followed. In 1874 the Bamana of Segala, northwest of Sinzani, joined the war effort. On November 16, 1879 some Bamana came to Jeigui and took property, killing several people and taking some captives. Led by Falike, some Bamana also took arms against Ahmadu in 1880. They swore to kill Ahmadu, but discord within their ranks prevented a unified front. Gallieni reported that in December 1880 the Bamana army had become emboldened with success against the 'Umarians at Banamba, and planned to march on Nyamina. Ahmadu attempted to organize forces, but the talibes refused to march against the Bamana. It was thus necessary for Ahmadu to form a new army. This was averted, however, thanks to his mother, Fatma, who interceded on his behalf and convinced the talibes to join him in Dukuna.[101]

Mansa Togoma, son of Cèfòlò and nephew of Karamòkò, rescued many villages from 'Umarian authority, operating from the left bank of the Niger. Many of the Bamana from these villages dispersed, finding refuge in the villages of the former Fama. Most of the Bamana and Marka villages of the interior, on the other hand, remained intact and waited for the opportunity to revolt.[102]

Since Ntò was an ally of the French, Karamòkò sent an emissary, his brother Cèfòlò, to the Resident in Bamako to complain about Ntò creating a state within the Bamana empire. The French told Karamòkò that he should abstain from any hostility toward Ntò.

The French moved carefully, and stepped up their machinations to protect themselves, pledging allegiance to many sides. A French mission was sent to the northern Bamana cantons under Ntò to re-affirm French readiness to fight Ahmadu, their common enemy. Simultaneously, the French signed a treaty with Ahmadu at Bamako. The French clearly doubted that Ntò was capable of fighting Ahmadu.[103]

The Bamana of Bèlèdugu

The Massassi dynasty of Kaarta and some Bamana Seguvians found refuge in Bèlèdugu after defeat at the hands of al-Hajj 'Umar. The Bamana of Bèlèdugu conducted the same type of warfare as those of Sambala and other areas. Digna, in Bèlèdugu, was in some respects a holy city for the Bèlèdugu Bamana because it was the principal bulwark for the defense against the 'Umarians. Digna and Wessebugu barred 'Umarian entrance into the country.[104] Diringua Mari, the Bamana leader, used Bèlèdugu as a base until 1869 when he died. His brother, Bussefi, assumed leadership of the struggle until 1871, recapturing towns like Farabugu and Lakmane, but failing in a skirmish to recapture Jala. He died in battle trying to recapture Gemukura, a campaign which ended in 1872 when the 'Umarians finally expelled the Massassi from Gemukura. Dama, a Massassi and other Bamana moved to Gore after losing to Ahmadu in an 1874 expedition.[105] Falike took the leadership role in 1880 and waged war until the coming of the French and the arrival of Bojan in

1890.

The Bamana leaders of Bèlèdugu sent representatives to the French post at Médine in 1875. The French wanted a treaty with the military leaders, but the Bamana were in need of arms, including double-barrel guns and revolvers, swords, and ammunition.[106] During this period the French decided to supply arms to both sides, hoping the 'Umarians and the Bamana would continue the war. Valière, the governor of Sénégal, wrote:

> In the interest of our colony, it is not bad that the King of Segu meet some difficulties and be obliged to fight in order to be master of the population of the Western Sudan. It could be dangerous the day when he would have reunited under his authority the countries lying between the Senegal and the Niger.[107]

After the Bamana attacked the Gallieni party at Jo, the French governor Brière de l'Isle instructed his military commander in the field, Desbordes, to use available forces to attack the Bamana of Bèlèdugu for pillaging Gallieni's party, and informed Ahmadu about French determination to avenge the Bamana action. Desbordes eagerly anticipated military action against the Bamana, ordering them to dismantle their fortification at Gubanko, Jo and Bamako, or be attacked. However, the Minister for the colonies, Admiral Cloue, disapproved of the plan.

When Gallieni left Bamako, the head of Turella alerted him that some Bamana had arrived at Bamako one day after Gallieni's party had departed. After learning that the French wanted to follow the route of Nafaje, the Bamana pursued them, dividing in two columns in order to sever the route. The stronger unit followed the Joliba (Niger) River to the ford of Turella in order to attack the French while the other marched to Nafaje. Gallieni's party was able to escape because the ford was not crossable.[108]

During Gallieni's sojourn at Nango, he heard about other activities of the Bamana. He learned that the Bamana military in Kaarta was expanding, thus blocking all communications between Segu and Nioro. Later, Ahmadu sent a detachment of talibes and sofaw to occupy Nyamina to protect it against Bamana attempts to regain their autonomy.

Eventually, the Bamana military movements began to be co-ordinated in larger campaigns. Karamòkò Wale, son of the founder of the Bamako

Saharan community, joined the Niare, Bamako village heads who were his hosts, and the Bamana of Bèlèdugu to fight the 'Umarians.[109] In 1884 the Bamana of Segu and Kaarta joined the Bamana and Mandingo of Bèlèdugu. Bèlèdugu sent reinforcements to help Segu Bamana fight 'Umarian forces in Nyamina, Tubakura and Konina, forcing the 'Umarians to withdraw.[110]

The Bamana wanted to exploit the internal strife within the 'Umarian state just as those factions had earlier attempted to take advantage of Bamana disunity. Bamana attacks intensified during the times of the 'Umarian Civil Wars in 1871 and 1884. In 1884 Ahmadu left Madani, his son, in control of Segu, and installed himself in Nyamina with loyal troops. When en route to Nioro, he took the greatest precaution crossing Bèlèdugu where Bamana opponents lived.[111] After defeating his brothers, Ahmadu was blocked by the Bèlèdugu Bamana from returning to Segu, and his talibes were reluctant to leave Nioro. As a result, Ahmadu need-ed a larger arsenal which he attempted to get from the French by con-vincing them to lift the ban on the sale of arms; he did this by removing his trade ban on French commodities. The French initially refused, but later, Gallieni lifted the ban on arm sales when the French needed help to control Mahmadu Lamine.[112]

By 1885 the Bamana of Bèlèdugu had assembled troops and repaired their tatas, and Ahmadu was operating from Nioro to create an army with his brother Muntaga to fight the Bamana of Bèlèdugu, and to return to Segu. Ahmadu began to be menaced by Kumi of Grand Bèlèdugu. In addition, the Bamana and Marka of Segala, Murja, and Damfa united, waiting on a signal to march against Ahmadu if Ahmadu made an offen-sive move. Karamòkò Jara's army occupied Kolimana, then Nyamina. A head sofa, Sidi Konè, waited to evacuate the villages on the right bank. In addition, Mabèrè Kanu and Boliba, principal military generals of Karamòkò, assembled troops to oppose Ahmadu. In summary, all the Bamana provinces of the left bank decided to annihilate Ahmadu's forces. By early fall (October) 1885 the Bamana of Bèlèdugu and the Markas of Markadugu closed the route of Segu. An army left Segala to aid Daba, who wanted to continue the struggle against Ahmadu.[113]

When Ahmadu established a quasi-capital at Nioro, he attempted to pit some Bamana of Bèlèdugu against other Bamana, in an effort to maintain communications with Segu. He attempted to attract certain canton heads of Bèlèdugu, hoping to exploit the jealousy of some who were disputing who should command the troops. The leaders of Thieorebugu and Kumi were the more ardent. When Joce, nephew of the head of Kumi, was named to command the column, the canton of Theiorebugu allied with the 'Umarians. This was the background engendering the animosity between the two regions.

When in 1886 the people from Seibabugu in the canton of Massantola demanded to found a village within the boundaries of Dumi, Kerejo Traore, uncle of Joce, persuaded them to make common cause with the people of Kumi. In short, to share the land meant to share the problems of the people. Subsequently, Kumi had the largest numbers of soldiers to oppose the passage of the 'Umarians. The people of Bamabugu also accepted an alliance with Kumi, but it was short-lived, for in less than two years, they abandoned Joce to join Theiorebugu.[114]

The French Resident was confident of the commitment of a great majority of Bamana leaders to their cause. But it was unlikely that the Bamana of Bèlèdugu supported "their cause," not knowing the real intention of the French. They were, however, true to their own cause: to be free of the yoke of the 'Umarians. Hoping for French support in the Bamana enterprise, the Bèlèdugu Bamana put their good will, their herds and their crops at the service of the French. However, some French observers feared that this loyalty could end at any time if the Bamana of Bèlèdugu realized the true intentions of the French. One Resident expected that one day, the Bamana would ask, "Are you, yes or no, on our side or the side of Ahmadu?" No longer counting on the French, the military leaders assembled men to fight for their cause.[115]

The Commandant at Bamako believed that Siniki Sako provoked the Bamana of Bèlèdugu against the French saying that the campaign of Mahmadou Lamine carried a severe blow to the power of the whites. Although the French were unafraid of a military movement by Sako, they considered him to be influential enough to cause many problems with his speeches.[116]

By 1887 a great many villages of Bèlèdugu had detached themselves little by little from the French and some were even hostile to the French. When the head of Doerebugu sent his son to greet Commandant Loyer to tell Loyer of his satisfaction with being under the French protectorate, the Commandant believed that the leader was insincere.[117]

The Bèlèdugu Bamana formed a column in March 1887 to attack the 'Umarians in Kaarta. The French commandant insisted that the Bamana never attack the 'Umarians because they had nothing to gain, instead counting on the French to remove the 'Umarians. But this advice was based heavily on a false overconfidence by the French military. The Bamana in general did not wait on the French, and eventually the Bèlèdugu Bamana began to doubt the French and distanced themselves from them. The commandant acknowledged this fact in the same report, which argued that this resulted from half-promises made to aid the Bamana against the 'Umarians. This shows from the outset that the Bamana did not put all their hopes on French commitments and actions.[118] When Ahmadu threatened to attack some villages in Bèlèdugu, especially Kumi, and the people demanded the help of the French, the French had no intention of aiding them. Tautain stated that the African still did not believe the treachery of the French.[119] The treaty signed between the French and Ahmadu on April 24, 1887 produced, according to the French observer, "the most deplorable effect on the Bamana of Bèlèdugu, who asked with just cause what confidence could they have in a power whose acts contradicts their promises."[120] The already weak relationship between the Bamana of Bèlèdugu and the French deteriorated further. Consequently, the French held a meeting with Bamana leaders in Bamako, and relations improved between May and October 1889 except for the Bamana from Massantola and Sirakoroba. Representatives from Damfa and Murja went on their own to renew relations which had been weak for some years. They promised their support to make sure that the caravan routes would be open. Nevertheless, the Bamana of Bèlèdugu, according to the French administrators, continued to disrupt the territory.

The Bamana believed that Ahmadu would attack them, and feared that the cavalry would destroy their harvests. Meanwhile, Ntò had become an ally of the French, and he attempted twice to attack Nyamina, which resulted in further Bèlèdugu Bamana suspicion toward them. The Bèlèdugu Bamana accused the French of having tricked them, and they refused to accept further advice from the French. During this period, Tukoroba, Konina and Markabugu united to attack Ahmadu, who repulsed them.

During 1888 and 1889 a mission composing of Captains Ruault, Septans and Underberg attempted to rally the Bamana. Some villages closed their doors, refusing to enter relations with the French. With pressure from neighboring villages, they sent representatives to Bamako to meet the Commandant Superior. Yet Damfa and Massantola, and the states of Karamòkò Jara failed to send ministers. Some emissaries did go later to either Bamako or Nyamina to explain their actions. During these summits, the French were able with gifts and speeches to convince the Bamana to see the 'Umarians as a common enemy to all. Afterwards, the French were assured that they could count on all the Bamana of Bèlèdugu against Ahmadu or Madani.[121]

The major factor in the 'Umarians' failure to consolidate their control in the Middle Niger was the Bamana who refused to accept or even nominally acknowledge 'Umarian overrule. The literature (i.e. Oloruntimehin, Kanya-Forstner, Roberts, Robinson, Hanson, etc) near-universally accepts the 'Umarian or French perspective of Bamana activities as simply a "resistance movement" to the 'Umarian regime. However, the Bamana saw their activities as a war waged to maintain their own regime and regain their autonomy over their lands after having been forced in exile. Several points support this assessment. The Bamana ruling classes continued to exist throughout the thirty-year 'Umarian domination, only operating from new headquarters; leaders continued to hold their titles, and the institution of the Tònjòn remained intact while other functionaries continued their duties.[122] Even the French referred to the Bamana rulers as "kings." Although the Bamana Empire did not survive in the sense of the mobile empire of Samori Turè (actually, it was unnecessary for the Bamana), it is evident that its administrative infrastructure remained untouched despite 'Umarian efforts to crush it.

Some of the Tònjòn fought on the behalf of the Ngolosiw, and others operated as independent bands. Often, the independent bands carried out raids, reflecting the organizational capability of the Tònjòn leaders.[123] The isolated attacks were not all banditry, however. The Bamana had lost in direct battle against the 'Umarians; therefore, guerilla warfare tactics provided a much more successful method of preventing the 'Umarians from achieving complete control of the Middle Niger and outlying regions. The

Bamana guerilla warfare disrupted peaceful trading on major raiding corridors upon which the rich economy of the Middle Niger depended.
Nyamina, a major trading town, was for a time around 1865 almost
deserted. The caravan routes which ran through Bèlèdugu were virtually
closed, causing Ahmadu to provide armed escorts for some caravans.
Since fewer caravans moved in and out of the state, revenues from taxes
were reduced.

The ʻUmarian army was spread throughout the region, attempting to
limit the Bamana attacks, protect caravans and enforce tribute payment.
Not only were the commercial routes valuable to the state treasury, they
were requisite for mobilization of ʻUmarian troops, particularly permitting new recruits from the Futa to arrive at Nioro or Segu.

Despite the dedication of manpower Ahmadu was obliged to use for
escorting the caravans, many traders avoided the major routes, taking
safer routes to avoid Bamana soldiers. Not all the pillaging might have
been connected to a conscious war effort, but the cumulative effect of
these acts still helped the cause.

Bamana soldiers also sporadically attacked villages, taking and/or
destroying livestock and other property, which sometimes resulted in
famine.[124] For outlying villages, this did little to promote confidence in the
ʻUmarian regime.

The Bamana who refused to acknowledge the ʻUmarian regime were
not sources of tax revenue, thus making it necessary for Ahmadu to seek
other means to collect revenues much needed to support the war against
the Bamana. When he increased tribute and taxes from the people firmly
under his control, he created additional malcontents, encouraging other
populations to seek their independence from ʻUmarian rule, as happened
in Sinzani in 1863.

"The reality between the Bamana and the ʻUmarians was war, night
and day because the ʻUmarians only had power between the two rivers.
All the rest was Bamana (territory), and was against al-Hajj ʻUmar."[125]
Many of the Bamana migrated behind the Bani and Niger Rivers, and the
state of Segu was never entirely conquered by the ʻUmarians. There were
always centers of Bamana military activity; therefore, "social peace was
never maintained because the Bamana completely refused Futaka occupation." The Bamana maintained their efforts for thirty years against the

'Umarians, employing any available method to disrupt the 'Umarian state, from raiding caravans to guerilla warfare. They even appealed to Samori Turè to unite with them against the 'Umarians.[126]

That which so many call the "Bamana resistance" to 'Umarian occupation was essentially a continuing struggle of a state against a foreign aggression. Seydou Thiero poses the question of the definition of a state: Is it a "machinery of domination by a class," or a "form of government?" By any of these definitions, he argues, it is "undeniable that Kènyè Mari and his successors exercised a state power." He asserts that often the definition of a state is shaped by the European development following the bourgeois revolutions. However, the state has multiple roles, including guaranteeing the existence, and life, interests of a people of assuring their development and realizing their aspirations. The Bamana state was an expression of the exercise of the power of the authority (*fanga*).[127]

CHAPTER 4

THE INTRIGUES OF THE FRENCH

It has been emphasized that the 'Umarians wanted to avoid confrontation with the French because neither al-Hajj 'Umar nor Ahmadu was confident enough to openly face the French in combat. But, the French, too, were avoiding combat with the 'Umarians for various reasons ranging from their military inadequacy to inadequate financial and political support from Paris.[1] For thirty years the French would use diplomacy, not war, in an attempt to gain their objectives. Both sides negotiated treaties while each concentrated on other difficulties: the Bamana war and internal schisms for the 'Umarians; the movements of Samori Turè and Mahmadu Lamine, and disagreements in policy-making within the colonial office for the French.

It is portrayed in our literature that only the state of 'Umar blocked the progress of French expansion into the Middle Niger, as if no other state might have hindered French movements.[2] In forming this assumption is the "respect" given by historians to the 'Umarian state (as to other Islamic regimes) at the expense of non-Islamic polities. In fact, the Bamana state of Segu was a major hurdle to both the 'Umarian and French designs to control the Middle Niger.

From 1880 onward the French became an ever-increasing nuisance to Ahmadu. The French interest in negotiating a treaty with the 'Umarians was to enhance political stability, promote commercial development and consolidation, and above all, protect the region from European rivals, particularly the British.[3]

It has been argued that 'Umar had no intention of fighting the French, but it might be more accurate to say that he had strong reservations about fighting the French, for he did entertain the idea, and he did attack the French at Médine and other posts. Perhaps the outcome of that skirmish motivated him to reassess the situation. Yet al-Hajj 'Umar attempted to collaborate with them in an effort to keep them outside of his sphere of operation. 'Umar's communications with the French suggest that his jihad was primarily directed against "Black kaffirs" rather than French Christians.[4] However, the operative word is *primarily* which suggest that secondary foes existed.

The French saw themselves as the great saviors of the downtrodden under 'Umarian rule, or at least this was one of the justifications which has been put forth for their actions.[5] The power base of the 'Umarian state was recognized by the French: "The military demonstrations of the Toucouleurs crossed the conquered country and 25 years of domination without rival gave them a great prestige."[6] Even before the final French move to gain control of the Middle Niger, they were contemplating the dissolution of the 'Umarian state.

Regarding the French simply as traders, not as future overlords, 'Umar offered to permit them to trade in the state as long as they paid customary tribute. He was reported as saying:

> The whites are only traders. Let them bring merchandise in their ships; let them pay me a good tribute when I'm master of the Blacks, and I will live in peace with them. But, I don't wish them to erect permanent establishments or send warships into the river."[7]

The French rejected this overture because they were unable to see themselves as tribute-payers to an African regime, a position beneath their national dignity and an outgrowth of "Catholic triumphalism"[8] and racism. Ye the French consented to negotiate with the 'Umarian state in order to promote their commercial and political agendas.

Louis Faidherbe sought to co-operate with 'Umar, signing a treaty with him in August 1860. The French considered this treaty a great victory, but Faidherbe distorted 'Umar's intentions and exaggerated his own influence. One of the important measures in the treaty was the agreement of a delimitation between areas controlled by each power. The text also recognized 'Umar as a "religious chief, a political power, and a territorial strength." For the French, on the other hand, free commerce was the most significant provision of the text.[9] The French attempted to convince 'Umar that they had no intention of challenging his power, nor that of his son if he died.[10]

Faidherbe's successor, Pinet-Laprade, had a different attitude. Viewing Islam itself as an enemy, he attempted half-hearted negotiations with Ahmadu after the death of 'Umar. The prevailing view was that the militant Islam of the 'Umarians was a serious challenge to French civilization, Christian religion, and social order. Although some Frenchmen might have looked favorably on Islam in West Africa during the early nineteenth century, this soon changed. The French explorer René Caillie commented on Muslim fanaticism and made other negative statements about Muslim powers in the territory in which he traveled. Likewise, Paul Holle and Frédéric Carrère were typically hostile to Islam.[11] Furthermore, the war against Algerian Muslims heightened suspicions of an Islamic threat to French rule. Moreover, "ethnographer" Henri Duveyrier, like many Western Europeans and French policy makers in West Africa, assumed that Western European, Christian values were superior to other cultures and religions.[12]

The next attempt to sign a treaty was in the hands of Abon Eugene Mage after the reported death of 'Umar in 1864. In Saint-Martin's analysis, Mage and Ahmadu developed reciprocal esteem for each other. The rapport thus established between the 'Umarians and the French lacked the inequality and sense of superiority of the French which characterized subsequent relations. More importantly, these negotiations also reflected the subordinate position held by Mage and French interests in 1863.

The Mage Mission arrived in Segu in 1863 with hopes of negotiating with 'Umar. Ahmadu was suspicious of the French emissary, and detained the group in Segu for more than two years, informing them that it was too dangerous to leave. Mage explained that he was on a peace mission because the governor wanted to send someone to see 'Umar, explaining, "If we make war against those who offend us, we desire peace with all the good people." The French government, added Mage, recognized Ahmadu as King of Segu, and 'Umar as master of Masina.[13]

Ahmadu delayed informing the French of 'Umar's death in Masina, perhaps in an attempt to maintain political stability and to keep the French in the dark in order to keep surveillance of their movements, or to make sure the news was true that his father was dead. In any event, the instability of the routes this time worked to the Ahmadu's advantage. After the death of 'Umar, the emissary decided to negotiate with Ahmadu, who signed a treaty which permitted French trade, subject to a ten percent tax on caravans entering the state, just as 'Umar had earlier stipulated.[14]

Ahmadu never trusted the French, but negotiated with them to keep routes open so that recruits could come from the Futa when needed. Nevertheless, he was adamant that the French recognize his authority and pay the import duty. In addition, he rejected Mage's appeal to build a trading post, aimed at establishing a commercial monopoly and political control for the French. Ahamdu, not sure of his father's death, claimed that he lacked the authority to cede land. In this and subsequent negotiations, the main objective of Ahmadu was to acquire cannons and other munitions. Subsequently, Pinet-LaPrade refused the tax measure, and the French governor failed to ratify the treaty or to send the mountain guns and cannons which Mage had promised to Ahmadu.[15]

In 1871 after Ahmadu had gone to Nioro to re-establish control, he sent Samba Njaye and Bubakar Saada to Colonel Valière in order to buy cannons, but Valière refused to sell any to Ahmadu. Again in 1874 Ali 'Umar, a former companion of al-Hajj 'Umar, traveled to Saint Louis with Tambo Bakhiri, one of Ahmadu's ministers, to negotiate a treaty with the French. This time, Valière considered sending a small military mission to help Ahmadu modernize his army. Valière wanted to build permanent trading posts in 'Umarian territory, but building stone structures required special authorization. He sent his proposal to Segu, but the 'Umarian emissary, Tambo, was believed to have been killed during the uprising in Jafunu en route to Segu, and the governor thought that Ahmadu had ended the negotiations. Although Governor Valière was willing to negotiate with Ahmadu, his successor, Brière de l'Isle, was opposed, preferring to provide military support to Ahmadu's enemies.[16]

Paul Soleillet went to Segu under the pretext of a peace mission, but also wanted to gather information for a tentative railroad project passing Segu. He attempted to make a treaty in 1878 following the 1876 French attack on Logo, a dependency of Ahmadu. The French justified their action as protecting French commercial interests, and the territory of the French protégé, Sambala of Médine. During these talks, Seydu Jeyla, Ahmadu's minister, informed Soleillet of Ahmadu's intentions of possibly establishing relations with the British, and he carried letters from the British official in Bathurst to establish regular transactions between Segu and the Gambian trading posts. A Dr. Gouldsburg in Bathurst wrote a letter to propose commercial relations and offer an alliance.[17]

The British commercial links with the interior were strong in the 1870s. In 1879 over 1000 Seguvian traders are reported to have visited Sierra Leone. Also, a British merchant and member of the Gambia Committee, T.T.F. Quinn, maintained a subcontractor on the Upper River named Abibu Diub whom Soleillet met in Segu in 1878. In 1880 most of the European goods found in the Upper Sénégal area among the Bamana of Bèlèdugu and the 'Umarians on the Niger were of British origin.[18] Realizing the threatfrom the British, the French negotiated with Ahmadu. In fact, the French had been attempting to curb British trade to Segu since 1848. Raffenel wrote a letter to the Fama of Segu in 1848 to convince the Fama that merchandise from French agents in Sénégal was "more beautiful and less expensive" than that from "the whites of Gambia and Sierra Leone."[19] The French realized that their protectorate treaties failed to hamper former commercial connections. Even though the Julas of Galam knew that the French possessed Bakel "for years and years," it did not stop them from buying gold in Bambuk and selling it in Gambia and Sierra Leone, knowing that the French treaties were null for the most part.[20]

The subsequent French emissary was Joseph Gallieni who traveled to Segu to try his hand at signing a treaty with Ahmadu in 1879. Instead of going directly to Segu, Gallieni attempted to create alliances with anti-'Umarian groups, signing treaties with the leaders of Kita to build a fort in their territory in exchange for the French promise to assist them in an effort against the 'Umarians. He also approached the Bamana of Fula-dugu and Bèlèdugu. However, the Bamana had no confidence in the French, knowing that Gallieni was heading to Segu to see Ahmadu, and sensing that his party had only come to survey Bamana territory in order to help the 'Umarians against them. Gallieni reported that in many places the Bamana believed it was necessary to exterminate "the whites who came to Bèlèdugu to deceive the inhabitants and aid the Tukulors to sub-jugate them."[21] The leader of Guinina challenged Gallieni, citing as an example when 'Umar came with words and gifts much like Gallieni, say-ing that he wanted to protect them, but subsequently enslaving them. Gallieni's party was attacked at Jo by the Bamana; their supplies were taken, fourteen were killed, and eleven were wounded.[22]

After arriving near Segu, Ahmadu forced Gallieni to stay at Nango. According to one local version, an old woman saved his life because he had so supplies.[23] Njaye and Marico informed him that the route from Bakhoy was closed to Europeans, and he should have passed through Nioro, taking the route which Mage had taken. Ahmadu's displeasure was evident, and Gallieni sent two interpreters, Alpha Sega and Alassane, to give an exact explanation as to why he took the Bèlèdugu route, arguing that he knew the Bamana had intercepted the Kaarta route. The explana-tion, however, failed to sway Ahmadu, for the interpreters reported that they received a poor response, and the inhabitants, especially the talibes, wanted to "make the four whites who came disappear."[24]

Gallieni's attempt to negotiate with both sides failed. After failing to attract Bamana to his intrigue, he found that these attempts jeopardized relations with Ahmadu. Ahmadu's suspicions were further intensified by a letter he received at the time from Abdul Bubakar, head of Bossea, informing Ahmadu that Gallieni was mapping the stronger regions of the empire to facilitate a later expedition. In addition, one of Gallieni's past digressions came to haunt him. Khamo, a former Malinke leader whom Gallieni had refused to see, went to Segu, further agitating the situation. As a result, Ahmadu delayed sending a minister to Gallieni. He also remained "deaf" to Gallieni's complaints about their destitution in Nango. Gallieni's interpreter, Alpha Sega, always found "a closed door" when he presented himself to the sultan.

Finally, on October 31, 1880 Gallieni gained an audience with Seydu Jeyla, Ahmadu's minister, which led to a series of negotiations. Seyda Jeyla outlined the major problems Ahmadu had with the French:

1. Ahmadu had not received the cannons which Mage had promised.
2. Ahmadu's representatives were badly received in Saint Louis in 1874.

3. Mage had specified in the treaty that the people of the Futa could come to the empire with their wares, but this had not been permitted.
4. The French had sustained the Bamana rebels and gave asylum to their leaders.
5. The French seized Logo by force and killed Niamody without warning Ahmadu.
6. The French had built a fort at Bafulabe.
7. They had passed through enemy territory to reachNango.
8. The 'Umarians wanted any treaty they signed to bemeticulously observed.

During the second conference, Jeyla presented Ahmadu's propositions which included that the French recognize Ahmadu's authority in all the countries conquered by 'Umar.[25] French merchants could establish themselves in the empire; Ahmadu would protect the merchants, but they could not meddle with the commercial routes which had met the needs of the Julas; Ahmadu could give navigation rights in the territory from the Niger to Timbuktu to the French, but they had to use canoes; the French could have a Resident at Segu, but he had to be a Black Representative who would follow Islamic laws; and the post at Bafulabe had to be destroyed. The minister agreed to drop the final request after considering Gallieni's rejoinder. Ahmadu's minister emphasized that the treaty be recognized in all parts, aware that French governors had changed treaties in the past.

Although the exact time is difficult to determine, oral history includes a chapter on Franco-Seguvian relation that features an incident with a missing shoe. Perhaps it occurred with Gallieni since the event happened in Nango. According to the account, the French Representative spoke of an agreement with al-Hajj 'Umar, one with his signature, asking if such had been shown to Ahmadu. The Representative asked if 'Umar had delivered a shoe to his son, one which was "guarded like a man's life." Ahmadu, however, did not want to answer the question. Then, the Representative opened his bag and removed a shoe, and Ahmadu believed that the man had stolen the shoe from him. Therefore, he searched for the shoe which was in his possession. After he found it, he showed it to the Representative. The Representative then said that Ahmadu was the chosen one since he had the match to the shoe. The French Representative then opened the heel of the shoe and removed a paper written in French and Arabic, supposedly with a signature of 'Umar. When Ahmadu opened the heel of the other shoe, he also found a piece of paper in Arabic and French. The French pointed out that Ahmadu must accept the agreement, seeing the signature of his father, but Ahmadu refused.[26]

Meanwhile, Gallieni's stay in Nango began to erode his confidence. When he heard that the Bamana had cut all communications between Segu and Nioro, Gallieni feared that Ahmadu would retain him at Nango until the road was opened. Gallieni was uncertain because it was becoming evident that Ahmadu was less naive than Gallieni had believed.[27]

During the third conference, it appeared that arms were the main concern for Ahmadu, for Jeyla conceded some points to Gallieni in exchange for cannons and gunflint. In fact, arms were the motivating factor for Ahmadu's relationship with the French. He needed a steady supply of them to subdue the Bamana and to extinguish internal insurrections.

Jeyla adamantly refused to accept a white resident. Furthermore, he demanded 50,000 francs, 2,000 guns, 4,000 barrels of powder, 10,000 bullets, 4,000 swords, 1,000 pieces of cloth, and 1,000 sacks of salt. Gallieni insisted that the demands were "out of proportion with the situation." Nevertheless, a treaty was signed at the fourth meeting, on November 3, 1880.

While awaiting Ahmadu's signature, a fever epidemic took its toll on the party; their provisions had been exhausted, and Gallieni complained that they suffered due to the slowness and lassitude of the 'Umarians. By December Gallieni was convinced that Ahmadu was holding him prisoner at Nango. This episode demonstrates the extent to which a foreign party could be at the mercy of the ruler of the country, especially when the aliens were defiant of local authority.

Ahmadu exhibited his skills of playing cat and mouse equal to those of the French. He argued that he left the French at Nango for their safety, but explained to Gallieni:

> When one is in a country, it is necessary to submit oneself to the custom of that country. It is a bad envoy if it does not understand that it is necessary to wait on the treaty. The blacks are not like the whites; they do not like to hurry themselves, and at the moment I am busy with my army.

Ahmadu would not be intimidated by Gallieni; the more the latter complained, the more the former made him wait. Gallieni's negative and condescending attitude only intensified Ahmadu's resentment.

Ahmadu was also enraged with the hypocrisy of the French authorities who sent Gallieni to arrange a commercial treaty while other French parties aggressively encroached upon 'Umarian territory and continued to try to organize anti-'Umarian forces. Perhaps this too was a factor in Ahmadu's treatment of the French party.

According to an oral account, Ahmadu's refusal to see Gallieni was because he was adhering to 'Umar's prophecy which warned that several French missions would come to Segu, but only the first (Mage) would be peaceful and should be received. The others, he warned, would have hostile intentions and should be refused entry into Segu.[28]

Finally, on March 10 1881 Gallieni received the signed treaty. He later explained that the criticisms of the treaty from his superior were unmerited, and that two elements in the document were unacceptable. One, articles that called for the deliverance of cannons and guns were not possible. Two, the Arabic text failed to conform to the French version, and this undermined in part the political and commercial concessions that Ahmadu made. Desbordes later wrote that the treaty was rejected because of the contradiction between the two texts.[29] Both failed to explicitly say who was to blame for the discrepancies.

One part of Gallieni's problem in negotiations with the 'Umarians was his racist perspective. The negative attitude toward Islam at mid-century among the French authorities in Sénégal and the Middle Niger has been noted previously. Yet racism was a glaring factor which receives little if any attention. The problem was more than a clash of cultures, and the role of Hiskett's "Catholic triumphalism" might not have been the determining factor in the racist view.

Gallieni repeatedly made racist comment about Africans in general, and Ahmadu as an individual. For example, while waiting to negotiate with Ahmadu, he wrote,

It was useless and even dangerous to insist and, before the stubbornness of that ignorant and superstitious nigger; the best was to wait until all the suspicions dissipated. . . ."[30]

It would have been difficult for Ahmadu to not recognize Gallieni's racist attitude and stereotyping of black Africans. In his letters to Ahmadu, he combined both an Islamic phobia and racism. He described Ahmadu as a black and Muslim sovereign, "professing the most profound fanaticism for his religion, using the imagery and pompous style peculiar to the Orientals." Gallieni continued to insult him by use of general stereotypes, characterizing him as "cruel and shrewd as all of his kind."

Gallieni claimed that the Bamana recognized the superiority of the whites while the Muslim Futaka, especially those of Segu, felt that they were equal to whites.[31] Gallieni believed the 'Umarian view of the French was that of an avid people of conquests and enemies of their religion. This might have been an accurate assessment, and it is obvious that Ahmadu's astuteness in perceiving the deceitfulness of the French irritated Gallieni. Considering his attitude of superiority, perhaps Gallieni expected to easily deceive Ahmadu.

The French attempted to place themselves atop the 'Umarian state, taking advantage of the political, social, and commercial organization in existence, without waging war and being responsible for its ramifications. Consequently, for almost ten years between 1880 and 1890 they attempted to gradually bring the 'Umarian state under their control by making treaties from the hierarchy as well as at lower levels. When this strategy failed to produce any real results, they looked at other options, mainly to exploit tensions between 'Umarians and the enemies of the 'Umarian state. In 1885 the governor in Sénégal questioned whether to continue actively seeking an alliance with Ahmadu or to build "a close alliance with the countries that want to live under French protection."[32] The governor disagreed with the minister, and counted on Ahmadu's brothers to dissolve the state. He wrote, "The presence of the brothers of Ahmadu could become an advantage. It seriously complicates the situation if one strictly follows the ministerial instructions which order the alliance with him (Ahmadu)."[33] He believed that an alliance with Ahmadu damaged the image of the French in the eyes of those opposing to the 'Umarian state.

The French were delighted to see the problems which Ahmadu's brothers created. Minister Armand Rousseau thought that the best means for the destruction of the 'Umarian state was to "divide and conquer." He hoped for war between the brothers as long as it did not close the markets or prevent the French from obtaining supplies.[34] The French were willing to use a wait and see approach. Lt. Col. Frey wrote that he told Ahmadu's brothers while they were in Kita meeting with him that the French would remain neutral in the internal dispute. Frey wanted to develop a rapport with Ahmadu in order to assure him that the French had no intentions of being hostile. He advised the brothers to submit to Ahmadu so that the state could be peaceful.[35] But many of the actions of the administrators were dubious, which did indeed damage the image of the French in everyone's eyes, since neither side could trust them, knowing the French were wooing both Ahmadu and his enemies.

By 1884 the French had been examining their alternatives. The minister of Marine wrote to the governor in the Sudan that the latter's predecessor had authorized aid to the Bamana of Bèlèdugu to the degree that he could spare his forces without compromising the essential operations. Then the minister warned that to engage in a struggle with local adversaries without being absolutely forced into conflict would be impolitic. He preferred to permit Ahmadu to clearly define his intentions, at that moment, to would attack Bamako or Nioro. If he attacked Bamako, the French would stir the people of Bèlèdugu to revolt and march to stop Ahmadu from ravaging the area which furnished necessary supplies to the French. However, if Ahmadu marched on Nioro, the French could still incite Bèlèdugu to attack the 'Umarians, but not until Ahmadu's attacks on frontier villages would provide a pretext for actively intervening.[36] It was indicative of French policy and attitudes that they saw themselves in such an influential position that they could have groups of people make military moves by their command at this juncture. However, the Bamana needed no incitement to attack, only arms.

Ahmadu wrote a letter to the French administration in the fall of 1884, complaining about the trickery and the hypocrisy of the French policymakers. He wrote that the 'Umarians had been deceived because the French had refused to fulfill the conditions of their treaties. In addition, he accused the French of attempting to usurp more power than the treaties permitted. Moreover, he informed them that he knew that the texts of these treaties had been altered. Ahmadu also pointed out that he had no need of boats, nor the gifts the French promised him until he could be sure of the purpose of the French mission, and the exact goals of their policy.

Apparently, the French had made some reference to the rivers being natural routes (for commerce and transportation), for Ahmadu responded that each country has a leader, and God had placed the territory in the leaders hands. Finally, he stressed that God did not like "doers of wrong."[37]

Another problem with treaties was that the French insisted on treating the territories with which treaties were signed as protectorates, despite the African signatories having a very different understanding of the function of the treaties. Even twentieth century historians of colonialism still refer to these treaties as creating protectorates.[38] The 'Umarians, on the other hand, saw the French as equals, at best. 'Umar made it clear that the French were traders, not overlords, adopting his father's position. He signed treaties to attain political goals, not to obtain protection from the French. Most of the French individuals sent on "peace treaty" mission had a major problem seeing 'Umar or Ahmadu as equals, which was often a major obstacle in negotiations. Ahmadu reacted against French aggression between 1881 and 1882 by closing caravan routes linking Kaarta to French posts in the Upper Sénégal, making French commercial activities difficult and sometimes impossible. In 1882 the new governor, Rene Senatius supported Desbordes' mission, authorizing the use of force to break resistance to those opposing the French program.

Desbordes' activities intensified in the early 1880s. In 1882 he attacked the 'Umarian empire by forcing 'Umarian leaders to leave Murgula, an area hostile to the French regime. These provincial leaders were posted there to prevent the French from reaching the Niger River, indicating that Ahmadu anticipated the French conducting military maneuvers. Desbordes did not attack the leaders, but invited them for a "peaceful" discussion; when they arrived, unarmed, they were forced to go to Kaarta.[39] Desbordes installed a puppet ruler at Murgula. He reported to his superiors that 'Umarian military strength prevented people from allying with the French.

At Bamako' Desbordes negotiated with Karamoko Jara and his brother, Titi, in 1883. They consented to the construction of a fort, and promised to co-operate with the French against 'Umarians. Oloruntimehin argues that the various groups in Bamako, non-Muslim Bamana and Muslim Saharan populations, were split over issues other than those of the 'Umarian state. The Saharans only accepted the French presence from a French show of force; they preferred to negotiate with Samori Turè.[40]

By 1883 one French official believed that the principal objective of their policy towards Ahmadu and Samori Turè should have been to prevent a struggle between the two because the result of a single winner would unite nearly all the Upper Niger populations under his leadership, and the consequence would be fatal for the French. Furthermore, the potential ruin of the country by such a war was a major concern, prior campaigns of Turè being cited as proof of that.[41]

The French saw their occupation of Bamako as a direct counter to Ahmadu's authority. André B"me argues that it was the French presence at Bamako which prevented Ahmadu's return to Segu after the defeat of his brothers.[42] However, it seems clear from various contemporary French accounts and reports that it was the Bamana who prevented Ahmadu's return to Segu, severing all communications between Nioro and Segu. In fact, Bamako was located south of Segu, not between Nioro and Segu.

Between 1883 and 1890 the French at Bamako intervened in the Middle Niger as much as possible without engaging in open conflict. If there had been any doubt about French imperial motives, Ahmadu could be sure of them by the end of this period.[43] After 1883 the French advance stopped, for in 1884 ministerial instructions tied the hands of local administrators, stipulating that all decisions come from the French parliament. However in 1885, some administrators continued to question whether an alliance with Ahmadu was expedient. The governor in Sénégal argued that it was necessary to inquire of the commandant superior of the Upper Sénégal if he believed it was possible and useful to create an offensive and defensive alliance with Segu, noting that Ahmadu was the principal obstacle to the expansion of French influence in the Middle Niger.[44]

For his 1885-86 campaign, Colonel Frey was given instructions to begin negotiations with Ahmadu at Nioro. Frey assumed that Ahmadu would be successful with his planned attack against Bèlèdugu in 1885, and he was concerned that Ahmadu would turn against the French after that campaign. Ahmadu had assembled approximately 15,000 men around Nioro, planning the invasion. Some informants claimed that he would march on Bèlèdugu, and others asserted that he wanted to attack

Guidimakha. In any event, 500 cavaliers and 400 fantassins left Nioro for Guidimakha.

Frey wrote a letter to Ahmadu, reminding Ahmadu of a previous invitation Ahmadu had given him to visit Segu, and informing Ahmadu that he wanted to talk with him, assuring Ahmadu of his sincerity in all he would say and promise. He added,

> I abhor untruthfulness and you will find nothing in my acts which would be contrary to my declarations. Of your side, I have hoped that you will act the same in my regard. My first speech is a speech of peace and of friendship. The French want peace because peace is favorable to the development of commerce. Our desire is to maintain good relations with the natives who are around us in respecting scrupulously their customs and their religion.[45]

Meanwhile, the Bamana had been blocking Nyamina, ransoming all the caravans which left the area. When Sidi Konè, head of Nyamina, complained to the French, Delanneau explained that he could do nothing since Nyamina was a dependant of Ahmadu and his sofas should protect it.[46] This was done to draw Nyamina into an agreement in order to get French protection. One French administrator reported that Nyamina wanted to enter relations with the French, but warned that it should be handled with prudence because Ahmadu's soldiers constantly monitored them.[47] Ahmadu, according to French records, corresponded with Delanneau over the control of Nyamina, warning, "Do what you want because you are stronger, but if I can harm you, I will not miss the chance."[48]

The French received information that Karamòkò Jara had planned to occupy Kolimana and Nyamina. Karamòkò Jara continued to menace Nyamina with his sofas. The latter also were powerless over the his sofas pillaging the caravans attempting to enter Nyamina.[49] This caused Sidi Konè to move most of the inhabitants to the right bank while waiting to evacuate the rest. He complained of the plunders and rampaging by Karamòkò's followers.

Although Delanneau continued to think that an alliance with Nyamina was very important, Sidi Kone and the leader of the captives, Mocabile, opposed an agreement with the French in the name of Ahmadu, even though the brother of Konè, Sabidiane, desired their arrival.[50] Meanwhile, all the Markas of Nyamina and Tuba acted in secret collaboration with the French, but Kone insisted that he never demanded French protection nor support; instead, the French ultimately installed themselves without his consultation.[51]

The French signed a treaty, placing Nyamina and dependant villages under their protection on September 14, 1885, an outcome from an instruction in January 1884 which saw the alliance of Nyamina as "one of the most important political achievements" obtained on the voyage of 1885 because only Nyamina had a cannon on the right bank which remained under the sway of Ahmadu and considerably obstructed French political action. The French were careful to maintain the appearance to Ahmadu and the Bamana that Nyamina freely came to them.[52]

Frey noted that the commandant of Kita later asked not to approve the treaty with Nyamina, arguing that it would create difficulties with Ahmadu. Frey placed Europeans in the posts occupying points on the supply lines, and he instructed the commandant at Bamako to take great care in relations with Nyamina since the treaty had not been approved by the governor.[53] At this point in 1885, the French were still hesitant in severing all ties with Ahmadu. Frey warned the governor that it was imperative to not approve the treaty with Nyamina before knowing the results of the negotiations he had started with Ahmadu, and argued that Delanneau demonstrated more zeal than prudence in his haste to conclude a treaty.[54]

Meanwhile, the French were attempting to come to agreement with Bèlèdugu. The French strategy was that if Ahmadu attacked and defeated the Bamana, he would be too weak to oppose further French penetration, and the French would attack under the guise of an alliance with the Bamana. However, if the Bamana had success against Ahmadu, his would still be a weakened state. After Ahmadu defeated his brothers, the French could no longer rely on division within the 'Umarian regime. The Bamana opposition to the 'Umarian state began to be more attractive to the French.

Fortunately for Ahmadu, the French were obliged to direct their attention toward Samori Turè in 1886 due to the growing influence of Mahmadu Lamine, who was preaching and recruiting in Khasso. Ahmadu probably erred when he expelled Lamine's son, Soybu, from his territory. Nevertheless, this action caused the French to rethink their approach to

Ahmadu. Consequently, Gallieni signed another treaty with him in May 1887.[55]

Yves Saint-Martin argues that the period from 1860 to 1878 was one in which the 'Umarians desired to conserve peaceful relations with the French. Saint-Martin based this assessment on the fact that Ahmadu continued to negotiate with the French despite their encroachment upon 'Umarian boundaries, and their broken and/or invalidated treaties. Also, each of the French missions had to ultimately depend on Ahmadu's hospitality although the degree of hospitality differed from mission to mission.[56] Although Gallieni constantly complained, he survived his first mission because of Ahmadu, leading Kanya-Forstner to maintain that "despite the gravity of the aggression (of the French), Ahmadu reacted with extraordinary moderation."[57]

The "peaceful" period, however, was marked with some violence especially on the commercial routes. The attacks on the routes by the talibes were a major concern for the French. For example, although some messengers (Julas for the most part) came two or three times in the name of Madani to assure the French that the 'Umarians were and would always be their faithful allies, Underberg stressed that the talibe leaders of Segu raided and ransomed the caravans along the route of Wolossebugu. Delanneau informed Frey that Ahmadu's soldiers raided a caravan coming from Tobokura, claiming that Ahmadu had intentions of stopping all caravans coming from territories under French occupation. Earlier, a 'Umarian band had attacked a caravan of Masina, killing about twenty people in December 1878.[58] As for the French, they made military forages from Murgula and Bamako. In short, the period of "peaceful diplomacy" was also one marked with sporadic military maneuvers.

Kanya-Forstner argues convincingly that internal problems, not the overwhelming superiority of the French, provide the best explanation for Ahmadu's failure to act after 1883. The French were not as formidable as they have been presented by colonial and post-colonial writers. The overextended, rapid military movement of the French created communications and supply problems. In this respect, the French had repeated the same logistical error that al-Hajj 'Umar had made. In addition, other Muslim leaders and disease weakened the French during the 1885-1886 period, but Ahmadu's internal problems prevented him from taking advantage of this. Both sides were, thus, forced to rely on diplomacy although it seems evident that they had other objectives in mind. Open conflict was untimely, but this period of "will for peace" would abruptly end as new French administrators in the field became impatient.

Page one of a treaty between Archinard and the people of Sinzani. Archives National du Mali IE-4 Traité entre le Colonel Archinard et les Gens de Sansanding, 10 avril, 1890.

Amadu's army crossing the Niger.
Abon E. Mage, *Voyage dans le Soudan Occidental*
(Paris: Hachette, 1868), p. 503.

CHAPTER 5

THE DEFEAT OF THE 'UMARIANS

One of the major issues in the historiography of the European conquest of Africa is the role of the Africans in this "conquest." Our literature generally focuses on the activities of the Europeans, thereby, de-emphasizing the role of the African soldier. The Bamana serve as a good example in that the occupation of the Middle Niger in 1890 was largely due to their thirty-year war against the 'Umarians and their active role in the actual military campaign against the Segu-'Umarian state.

Raymond Betts argues that by the end of the nineteenth century a growing literature concerning the importance of brute force as an essential factor in human activity was being accepted in Europe. French colonial theorists had acknowledged the role of force in imperialist conquest, but this had not been woven within any colonial doctrine. The philosophy of the "survival of the fittest" and the struggle it implied became one of the major reasons for concern over the seemingly limited economic resources of the world. "Overseas expansion," Betts explains, "was considered obligatory for any nation wishing to assure its share of these resources." The French perceived the indigenous peoples as lacking the skills to utilize the wealth in their territories, and this prevented more capable people from enjoying it. "Rousseau's noble savage uncorrupted by civilization should not be allowed to prevail where such conditions exist."[1]

The early 1880's in the Western Sudan witnessed diplomatic and military movements of the French which culminated in the conquest of Segu in 1890, and much of the remainder of the Niger Valley by 1893. We have reviewed previously the conditions which favored the early phase of diplomatic activity. The period of diplomacy gave way to a more aggressive phase at the end of the 1880s when the French would use diplomacy to merely legitimate their military campaigns. This military phase can be understood by the low cost of military recruitment, the growing insecurity of commercial routes, and shifting French imperial structure affecting the Middle Niger.

Richard Roberts suggests that the 1881 army of French Colonel Borgnes-Desbordes resembled the 1859 'Umarian army under al-Hajj 'Umar. Both marched across the region in the same direction; and although both recruited a variety of local populations, the officers were mainly from a single racial group. Both armies offered social mobility, material benefits, and spiritual rewards for the troops, and the leaders of each maintained the loyalty of their troops by distributing booty.[2]

The economy of the Middle Niger did little to benefit French posts, located on the periphery of the major trading corridors and centers. For example, the caravans from Burè (one of the two major gold-producing areas) to Nioro, had no interest in traveling to French posts where they could not sell their principal merchandise, slaves, and where they would have received less profit than at Nioro.[3] Also, disruption (caused by the guerilla warfare and "normal" attacks on caravans) forced the caravans to take longer routes in the early 1880s. For instance, in 1881 a caravan from Burè was attacked by the people of Kalé, 25 kilometers from the French post of Bafulabe, prompting the merchants to complain to the French. According to one report, the caravans had been highly susceptible to being raided and having the merchandise stolen over a four year period.[4]

The increased costs of insecurity because of the Bamana war virtually destroyed the Bamako markets. The French were unable to influence the trade in their favor because merchants could avoid zones under French influence. Ruault overestimated his power to influence the regional economy and the producers' readiness to respond to the demand for products not usually found in markets near Bamako. It was not until 1889 that Bamako could meet its own requirements.[5] As a result, the French could stop trade, such as of horses, to Samori, for example, only by paying higher prices or bringing a larger area under their control. Although the market improved by 1889, the prohibition of the trade with Samori (which comprised the bulk of the transit through Bamako) hurt Bamako since merchants avoided the area, instead crossing to Nyamina, Segu and Sinzani.[6] Even the Frenchman Colin had trouble arranging a caravan in 1883. He explained that one could not find 'Umarians to cross the Malinke and Bamana country beyond Bafing. When the commandant of Médine hired a group of 'Umarians to take some provisions to Kita, they insisted that it would be necessary to replace the carriers at Bafulabe. In addition, the doctor's caravan had to avoid Segu because it was doubtful that Ahmadu would permit a caravan sponsored by a French doctor to cross the Niger.[7] It became increasingly important for the French to intervene in the Niger market, in order to secure the region for other colonial projects, especially the plan to construct a railroad. French intervention into the economy provided a solution to two problems. One, it was reasoned that the Niger Valley would be a marketplace for food supplies; two, the French could use control over the economy as a tool against their enemies.[8]

During the early 1880s Colin published an article explaining these commercial problems. According to him, the commerce of the Haut-Sénégal was far from prosperous when compared to what it could be. Even at Bakel and Médine, the commerce had diminished notably. He blamed it on several causes, particularly the political situation.[9] The French post at Bamako was situated on the fringe of the commercial zone. Trade in the Middle Niger was flexible and resourceful, its methodology created over time when political and economic conditions often changed, making adaptation key to survival. Since paying higher prices was an unrealistic option, the alternative was to control a larger area. Controlling enough territory to intervene in the economy meant the destruction of the 'Umarian empire. In 1878 the seizure of Sabusire by the French was due to the position of the village which controlled access to the 'Umarian state from Médine.

Gallieni's advice to Louis Archinard was that the French policy in the Sudan "must be neither pro-Tokolor nor pro-Samori, but exclusively French, and we must look on all these chiefs as people to be ruined and made to disappear before very long."[10] However, de la Porte instructed Archinard to avoid complications with the Muslims, and Archinard had been given further instructions to abstain from taking any important measures without authorization from the governor of Sénégal. His instructions included this statement:

> It is important that you refrain from taking anymeasure as important, so great of consequence as could be that attack on Kunjan without consulting the department and the governor of Sénégal under the authority of which you were placed. The easiness of telegraphic communications between the Sudan, Saint Louis and Paris should permit you in all circumstances to ask for my formal instructions before taking any action of war . . . [11]

Archinard insisted to the governor that he sought peace, but that Ahmadu and Samori had plans of war, and that Ahmadu was eager to come to blows, being stubborn and obstinate. He warned that if the French failed to respond to the aggression, the enemy would succeed. He did not want Ahmadu to assemble enough support throughout Kaarta to become strong enough to cross Bèlèdugu to return to Segu. Therefore, the best means to stop Ahmadu would be to attack Segu. Archinard suggested that the French should create a new post in the midst of a Futaka population in Kaarta, and return Segu to Mari Jara, the Bamana ruler, so that Ahmadu would lose prestige and power. Also, a representative should be left in Segu so that Mari Jara could not "abuse the victory which we will give him." He further claimed that Ahmadu, in alliance with Samori, believed that as soon as he would attack the French, Samori would follow. He reported that the Ahmadu-Samori alliance was cemented by their exchange of daughters for marriage. Samori's strategy was to force the French to divide their forces.[12]

Despite the argument in his communications to the governor, Archinard was confident that the Bamana would soon be strong enough to overthrow the Futaka without any real aid by the French. Gallieni had believed that the 'Umarian state would fall at the death of Ahmadu, which might have been the overriding factor in his attempts to maintain diplomatic relations with Ahmadu and buying time until Ahmadu's death, when a succession issue might erupt. It had become clear that Ahmadu

would refuse to be a puppet ruler as the French had hoped since none of
the negotiations over the previous thirty years or more had gained the territory of Ahmadu.

Until the late 1880s the problem Ahmadu faced was to find the best
defense against French encroachment on the 'Umarian state. Not only
were the French involved in other expensive military expeditions against
Samori Turè and Mahmadu Lamine, there were problems with railway
construction in Sénégal. The French were unable to openly attack the
Sudanese states because of an under funded colonial budget, and, hesitant
to finance such a war, they preferred to wait until the empire would crum-
ble from within and/or be destroyed by anti-'Umarian groups.

By the time Archinard was appointed the political climate had
changed. First, Mahmadu Lamine had been defeated, ironically enough,
with the help of Ahmadu. Also, the French signed a new treaty with
Samori Turè in 1888. Forts had been provisioned, roads had been
repaired, and the railway had reached Bafulabe. More importantly, the
Bamana had intensified their campaign against the 'Umarians. Yet the
French Ministry was still satisfied to continue its "wait and see" policy.
Archinard, however, would alter this policy.

Much has been written about Archinard's eagerness and aggressive-
ness, and it is well established that he had problems with the colonial
Ministry. Archinard wanted to push ahead with the conquest of the Sudan,
perhaps, as had been suggested by Kanya-Forstner, motivated by his
denial of a promotion to lieutenant colonel, and for the personal glory of
conquering the Sudan, something his predecessors had failed to accom-
plish.

When Gallieni instructed Ahmadu to evacuate Kunjan, Ahmadu
replied that a French attack on Kunjan would violate the treaty of Guri.
The French had a history of destroying 'Umarian military posts (Sabusire
(1879), Gubanko (1881) and Daba (1883)). Gallieni, in this instance, told
Ahmadu that the campaign on Kunjan was not directed at his state, but to
promote peace and stability. However, the seizure of the post would put
the French in a stronger military position; it would also force Ahmadu to
the brink of war. The French recruited troops from neighboring posts for
the attack that was launched in 1889. In addition, the French had been led
to believe that only 300 soldiers were in the Kunjan post as was the case

when Gallieni had left it. But the people had prepared for an attack, sending reinforcements led by Bukari Fofana, and by removing all the thatching from the roofs in order to prevent the spread of fire. The double walls of Kunjan stood up well to the 80mm mountain guns, withstanding the attack for eight hours.

Archinard wrote, "The people of Kunjan resisted well and the bombardment (was) prolonged." One tirailleur was killed, and three were seriously wounded. A number of the auxiliaries were killed during the pursuit and the raid which followed, and some tirailleurs were lightly wounded.[13] Archinard timed the attack on Kunjan to coincide with the drafting of the promotion lists. However, the news reached the Ministry after appointments had already been made.[14] As justification for his strategy, Archinard argued that Ahmadu had a hostile attitude after ceasing all relations in April 1888, following the evacuation of Kunjan.[15] In odd contradistinction, in October 1889 Archinard wrote to the commandant in Kayes that relations with Ahmadu had been good during the winter, and that all his letters were courteous.[16]

Ahmadu ordered cavaliers to parade along the right bank of the river, and he increased the thickness of the walls of Koniakari. He also raided caravans which crossed the 'Umarian state to trade at Médine. At the end of May 1889 Ahmadu's troops attacked the railroad at Talaari, and on June 3 fought a heavy engagement with the French at Kalè.[17]

Archinard wanted to take advantage of Ahmadu's attack on the Bamana of Murja, claiming that the Bamana had signed a treaty of protectorate with the French and had demanded French assistance. Archinard also cited some acts by Madani to justify his attack. For example, he claimed that Madani stopped couriers that Cèba, King of Kènèdugu, (and at that time a pawn for the French), sent to the French at Bamako, and that he raided the people and caravans which came to trade with the gunboats at Kulikoro. Moreover, Madani fined those who furnished wood to the gunboats. He even stopped the Fula of the right bank from selling livestock to the French. When the commandant of Bamako wrote to Madani, the commandant asserted that Madani responded insolently to the letter.[18]

The occupation of Lontu "produced a great agitation and a salutary effect" in that it contributed to the difficulty of Ahmadu in finding supporters to avenge Kunjan. The French had several operational goals aimed at the Seguvian state, including military demonstrations against Kaarta where Ahmadu was stationed. They also pressed for political action with the Bamana of Bèlèdugu and demonstrations against Madani and the occupation of Nyamina. The other goals would solidify French encroachment in the Niger region.

Captain Ruault headed a mission to travel in Bèlèdugu to convince the Bamana to make an important diversion near Murja, east of Kaarta. When the mission of Ruault, Septans and Underberg travelled to Bèlèdugu to entice the Bamana to enter relations with the French, some villages closed their doors, not wanting to talk to them.[19] But the meetings, gifts and news of French military activity at Kunjan provided the French with a confidence that they could depend on the Bamana of Bèlèdugu as allies.

The major problem, however, was not, as the French believed, to unite the Bamana of Segu and Bèlèdugu, but to win Bamana collaboration with the French. The Bamana of Bèlèdugu were prepared to treat the French as a possible ally, but the past French relationships with Ahmadu continued to raise suspicions among the Segu Bamana. The Segu Bamana knew that the French had given a chair, symbolic of friendship, to Ahmadu during one of their visits.[20] In addition, Karamòkò Jara, then the Fama, maintained distrust of the French even though several African leaders in Bamako attempted to persuade Karamòkò to accept the French offer.

Archinard also wanted to make the territory of Aguibu, brother of Ahmadu, a French tributary. Archinard carried gifts, including six Europeans chairs to Aguibu. Archinard wrote Aguibu a letter (22 February 1889) arguing that the destruction of Kunjan had nothing to do with his plans to seize Aguibu's state. In this letter, Archinard's language was similar to the 'Umarian correspondence with a religious overtone, saying, "God gave me the force, I use it for that which is just." Aguibu failed to reply, but responded by raiding territories between Tinkisso and Niger. A small French column was sent to Siguiri to face Aguibu's soldiers, but the French force dispersed without fighting.[21]

At this juncture Aguibu shifted his strategy and became a "docile instrument in the hands of the French." St. Martin and Oloruntimehin have proposed hypothetical explanations for Aguibu's sudden change, ranging from his desire to receive gifts from the French, to the possibility of French assistance in replacing Ahmadu atop the 'Umarian state.[22] In addition, self-preservation is another motive to consider since Aguibu's territory was virtually surrounded by the French and effective communications with Ahmadu were near impossible. His intentions can only be the source of speculation, but the fact that he became a French pawn removed one more threat to French policy.

Archinard's next move was to attempt to set 'Umarian leaders at each other's throats by using Muniru and Ahmidu, who had been given asylum by the French when they revolted against Ahmadu in 1885, and sending them to Banjagara where the French hoped they would strengthen their anti-Ahmadu forces.

Unlike Aguibu, who finally yielded, Murtada of Kulu refused an invitation to St. Louis extended by the French, affirming his loyalty to Ahmadu. Consequently, Archinard threatened to arrest him if he attempted to travel to Futa Toro where Archinard suspected him of seeking allies for Ahmadu. Although Archinard felt confident that neither Aguibu or Ahmadu would attack the French after the seizure of Kunjan, he placed an arms sale embargo on the region as another means to weaken his foes.

If Ahmadu wanted to attack French posts in 1889, as the French maintained, the fear of a Bamana attack on Nioro was a constant worry for the 'Umarians since a 'Umarian attack away from Nioro would leave the town vulnerable to the ever-present Bamana threat. Ahmadu ordered districts of Fansane and Tomora to store grain and not sell any part of this harvest. He sent emissaries to seek allies with Samori Turè; Ali Buri Njayi, the ruler of Buurba Jolof; Abdul Bubakar, the Almamy of Bosseia in Futa Toro; Bojan, Chief of Logo in Khasso; and Alfa Yaya, Almamy of Futa Jalon. Archinard responded by building a fortified post at Nyamina in 1889, knowing that Ahmadu was forming alliances on a vast scale.

Ahmadu had left his son Madani to rule Segu while he stabilized politics in Nioro. Just as when Ahmadu's father left him in Segu, this act signaled a major turn in 'Umarian politics. Although Madani was in a much better position than Ahmadu to attack the French at Nyamina, he failed to act or react, seeing the French installation as a threat against the Bamana; the Bamana, ironically, thought that the French at Nyamina represented a move against Madani. In Archinard's estimation, Nyamina was indispensable to Ahmadu if he had hopes of returning to Segu, realizing that Ahmadu could not safely cross Bèlèdugu. The only way for Ahmadu to avoid Bèlèdugu was to travel during the rainy season when the water was to the north of the country. But without refuge while passing through the high waters, he would likely encounter his enemy, Karamòkò Jara. Although the Niger, when the waters were low, had many fords, Ahmadu had been harassed by the Bamana in these areas.

The occupation of Nyamina gave Archinard two advantages. He could keep Ahmadu from returning to Segu without first negotiating with the French, and the French could be in a strategic location to attack Segu without fearing a rear attack since Archinard felt he "operated in friendly country among the Bamana, natural allies of the French."[23] The treaty with Nyamina in 1883 gave the French "rights," but the Sarrakole inhabitants, facing raids by the 'Umarians on the right bank, and by the Bamana on the left bank, demanded more than French occupation.

By August of 1889 the Jara nobles had still refused cooperation with the French, convinced that the French were not to be trusted. However, Archinard, determined to gain their trust, sent a mission under Lt. Marchand to Farakò with a promise to reinstate the Jara family as rulers of Segu, a position which the Jara family considered to still be theirs. He also sent forty pieces of Vosgien cloth, and forty liters of tafia as gifts. But the mission failed. The family reportedly said, "The French make alliances with everyone, and friends with everyone, even their enemies; they make promises that they don't keep."[24] In effect, the mission created the fear that the French would march against Farakò.[25]

The Bamana were not interested in replacing one group of interlocutors with another. By December 1889 Archinard had succeeded in gaining an alliance with the Bamana, perhaps due to the fact that the Bèlèdugu Bamana had accepted an alliance. The French concluded an agreement with Karamòkò to gain "free trade," but this was the extent of the agreement as far as the Bamana were concerned. Only Ntò was placed under French protection.[26] Saint Martin asserts that a secret alliance was made with Mari Jara in exchange for the support of his soldiers, stationed at Samafula and Farakò. The soldiers were to be ready by the end of 1890, furnishing several thousand backup troops and porters for the French.[27] According to Bacèkòrò Kulubali, Marchand was sent to woo Mari Jara who received Marchand and talked with him. Marchand promised the Fama aid, military aid, it being understood.[28] With the help of the governor of Sénégal, Clement Thomas, Archinard convinced the Ministry in Paris that it was necessary to attack Segu in order to attain French goals.

Archinard had been organizing his final assault on Segu in 1890 for more than a year, storing food and ammunition, including two 95mm field guns with 1000 Melinite shells. He built bridges to create a route to Farakò and permit ninety-five pieces hitched to six mules to follow the column from Bamako to Segu; and, he recruited Africans as auxiliaries.[29] Bamana recruits who were waiting to enlist also were trained.[30]

The Seizure of Segu

Archinard attacked Segu with 3,600 men at 5:30 a.m. on April 6, 1890, bombarding Segu with a cannon after having placed his army "behind the river."[31] After the French shot cannons from behind the river, the Sacred Baobab on the edge of the river was hit, and the Bamana sent two slaves to speak to the French.

The so-called "attack and seizure" of Segu was, in fact, more of a "march and occupation" of Segu because Madani and his army fled Segu, leaving it defenseless. The French occupation lacked any glorious elements of military maneuvers or bloody battles.

The Sòmònò families of Cèro, Jirè and Dembele provided river transportation for the French force. The Sòmònò aided the French to expel the 'Umarians so that the Bamana could re-establish their authority and because the 'Umarians had proven themselves inhumane.

> If they wore a beautiful bubu, the Futaka took it from them. If they had a newborn among the Futaka, the Futakaw collected the cowries of the Sòmònòw for the baptism. When the Sòmònòw returned with fish, the Futakaw met them and collected it. One day in September, the Sòmònòs had left to fish behind the river. When they had some fish, they gave the fish to their wives, who put the fish in some baskets and closed them with stalks of peanuts plants. The fishermen told the women to say to the Futakawwhen they asked that they had returned from the peanut field. But, unfortunately the young Futakaw chased the women, forcing them to drop their baskets. They took allthe fish in spite of what the women had said. The

Sòmònòw were fined a large sum of money.[32]

The Sòmònòs claim that the 'Umarians took all their property; there-fore, for them the French were the source of total liberation from 'Umarian control over Segu. They had wanted to chase the 'Umarians from Segu, but they lacked the means to do so.[33]

Traitors were reportedly among the 'Umarians who assisted in the defeat of the 'Umarians at Segu. One episode in oral literature supports this claim. Archinard sent two black and two white men to ask Cèrno Abdul if he could aid him in removing Ahmadu from power. One of the black men was named Kanja. The men wore grand *bubu* and turbans like the Saharans. When night came, they walked in the village to determine which side should be attacked. The daughter of Ahmadu and wife of Abdul, entered her husband's house[34] and said, "I smell an odor in your house. That odor is not the odor of a Muslim because the odor resembles the odor of a being who is not cleansed." Then Abdul responded to his wife, menacing her, "Who could be in my house without your seeing him?" After threatening her, she left to go to her father to say, "Papa, I smelt an odor in our house. It is not the odor of a Muslim to me. My hus-band must be in keeping with some other people." When Abdul began to suspect his wife, he demanded of the four men that which the French promised him upon their arrival to destroy Ahmadu. They responded, "The French told us that when you ordered them to depose of Ahmadu, they will give you the power." Then, Abdul told them,

> No army could combat Segu between the two rivers because the power of the Futaka is only between the two rivers. All the Bamana of the other banks of the rivers are against Ahmadu and are prepared to combat him. So, it is necessary to go behind the Niger in order to bombard Segu, for there is no other means except that."[35]

After that the four men left to rejoin Archinard in order to inform him of the plan of attack. A few days later, the French arrived behind the river and bombarded Segu, causing its downfall. When the French entered, they arrested many 'Umarian supporters, and those who refused to sub-mit were killed by the French. Abdul had planned to take Madani and deliver him to the French.[36]

The wrestling of Segu from 'Umarian control was easy because

Madani had placed the talibes on the river banks to prevent the French from crossing the river, and the army was caught in the open when the French bombarded the city. The bombardment prevented the defenders from returning within its walls; therefore, they fled north.[37] A Sòmònò, Koda Cèro, informed the French that Madani had abandoned the city, and had given orders to others to evacuate it.[38] Many 'Umarians dispersed in the small villages; some went to Duguninkòrò or returned to the Futa, and others took refuge in the Sòmònò quarters.[39]

The 'Umarians who remained in Segu made their submission, and a palaver was held on April 11, 1890 when Archinard proclaimed Mari Jara as Fama of Segu, but under the control of a French Resident and a company of tirailleurs. Nango and Sinzani were placed under the direct administration of France, and following the expulsion of the 'Umarians, the goods of the former occupiers were confiscated. Seven thousand Futaka were escorted to Kaarta or Futa Toro, but none arrived; some escaped and others died en route.[40] Ahmadu's family and nobles were led to Kita, then to Kayes. Meanwhile, Archinard was preoccupied with finding and taking the famous treasure of Ahmadu which Archinard reported as being worth $500,000 (but was valued at $250,000 at Kayes).[41] The Bamana, on the other hand, wanted the French to kill the 'Umarians who had taken refuge among the Sòmònò, according to one historian. However, the French complained that they were unable to tell the difference between the Futakaw and the Sòmònòw. When night fell, the Bamana put nets in front of the doors of the Sòmònò' houses, instructing the French to kill those families which had no nets in front of their doors. When the Sòmònò learned of the plot, they put nets in front of everyone's door so that the French could do nothing.[42]

The seizure of Segu alone did little for the French agenda. If, as Roberts argues, Ahmadu never integrated Segu into the larger 'Umarian state, and Segu remained the weak link in the empire, the occupation of Segu only removed 'Umarian control from a marginal outpost, albeit the capital. It is clear that by 1890 the stronghold of the 'Umarian state was Nioro. It is counterintuitive that Segu had been designated the capital of the 'Umarian empire, considering its precarious location in respect to the larger state. Perhaps to take the seat of previous Bamana power was intended to symbolically mark the 'Umarian conquest. Whatever the case, the Bamana army surrounding Segu had isolated the capital from the strong 'Umarian outposts. Therefore, it became essential for the French to control Kaarta in order to effectively remove 'Umarian influence in the Middle Niger.

After Segu, Archinard attacked Wolossebugu, winning only after a street-by-street battle. He took only 300 regular troops (because the water supply was scarce), but he depended on several thousand Bamana auxiliaries. The Wolossebugu army consisted of Muslim Bamana loyal to Ahmadu under the orders of Banjugu Jara (who later shot himself rather than be captured). In the two-day battle, two Europeans were killed and eight wounded (of the 27 in battle). In addition, thirteen *tirailleurs* were killed and 26 wounded. No numbers were given for the casualties for the Bamana auxiliaries "who bore the brunt of the final assault." Six hundred bodies, however, were found when Archinard entered the fortress.[43]

When Madani fled from Segu, Mari Jara's cavaliers pursued him, but failed to overtake him, and Madani was able to re-join his father in Nioro. Later, Ahmadu's army then suffered a defeat at the hands of the French-African army on June 6, 1890 at the village of Bugura.[44] However, Ahmadu continued the struggle, attacking the railway at Talaari, and skirmishing along the Kayes-Bafulabe line. Forty-three in the French-African army were killed in one battle. Early in June, the 'Umarians attacked a train leaving from Bafulabe (en route to Kayes), and several in the French-African army were killed and wounded. A few days later some Saharan fighters joined Ahmadu.[45] From June 12 through 15, Archinard led an attack on Koniakari, sending raiding expeditions into neighboring districts. Captain Ruault arrived at Koniakari with a flotilla on the morning of June 16 after having fought en route since the previous evening. The French reported that the loss for Ahmadu was great, and after the battle, all of his people took flight, but that losses for the French-African troops were minor.[46] Fighting continued in Koniakari and surrounding areas until September when the French-African column was disbanded and the annual floods isolated Koniakari. Ahmadu later tried to retake the town, but failed. The loss of Koniakari can be attributed to poor communications during the rainy season, many non-Futaka soldiers deserting the 'Umarian army, and the superior weaponry of the French.

Ahmadu divided the his forces at Kaarta, placing the Bosseia group under Cèrno Bokar; the Toro group were under Cirè Eliman, which included about 5000 troops stationed to block French advance from the south. The *Irlabe* (YirlaaBe) under Cèrno Ibrahim Sibe were based in Jala, guarding the southern flank; and the *Lao* group under Abdulaye Ali were stationed at Jelia. In addition, Ahmadu had remnants of the Seguvian army under Seikolo, a chief sofa, guarding the east against any Bamana attack from Bèlèdugu. The main concentration, led by sofa General Bafi and Ali Burè, remained at Nioro.

The significant battle occurred on January 1, 1891 at the pond of Mael, near Korriga where 10,000 'Umarian soldiers were under the command of Al Buri Njaye. Following this battle, Njaye regrouped the army between Kolomina and Yuri, south of Nioro, in what has become known as the "Battle of Kolomina." Two days latter, the struggle ended in a loss for Ahmadu who had participated in a ten hour battle on the second day. Ahmadu was ultimately defeated by the Bamana soldiers, for only 120 white soldiers marched with Lt. Marchand in that battle.

Ahmadu's army made a last stand at Yuri in January 3, and more than 3,000 of his soldiers were killed or captured.[47] However, Ahmadu escaped, going north to negotiate with the Saharan Mechdouf and Ould Nacer the right of passage within their territory. Another source asserts that Ahmadu went to Nema with an army on January 26, 1891, and faced adversaries in another battle, but the groups with him betrayed him. As a result, he left Nema with people from the Futa and went to Wowarbe.[48]

When a column from Koniakari marched on Nioro and a Bamana column marched on Bakhunow, the Futaka population evacuated Dianghirte to go to Tuna. When Ahmadu reached Hammake with forty cavaliers and some fantassins, Ali Buri and many runaways joined him, enabling Ahmadu to leave Hammake with 1300 to 1400 soldiers.[49] Moreover, Al-Hajj Buguni, who attempted to rally populations, joined Ahmadu in Nampala. Ironically, when the army passed by Jura, a large Bamana village, it was welcomed. At Jenné, Alpha Musa and Jon Kunda joined Ahmadu, and the *sofas* of Musa followed him to Banjagara. Ahmadu Tijani, nephew of Tijani, sent 100 horses to Ahmadu. Even the Chief of Sokolo, who had signed a treaty with Tautain in 1887, entered relations with Ahmadu after becoming discontent with the French.[50] It was clear that Ahmadu still had a certain degree of influence despite French reports to the contrary.

Ahmadu reached Masina and supporters proclaimed him ruler. Ahmadu's younger brother, Muniru, had served as king after the death of Tijani's son, Seydou Tamsir (Tapsiru), in 1888. For two years, Ahmadu organized the state of Masina and prepared to face the enemy.[51] Although reports of Ahmadu's great problems circulated, the French governor worried that after some months, Ahmadu could again become a dangerous adversary.

The Conquest of Segu: A Re-examination

The "French" conquest of Segu was a simple occupation of a city abandoned by the 'Umarian military which had operated away from the city before taking flight. In reality, the major battles followed the march on Segu. The notion of a "French" conquest is more complex because such conquests as that of Segu in 1890 (and many other European occupations of African states in a similar light) are generally described in the European literature as European conquests. However, two very important elements in this characterization should be emphasized.

First, the military and political glory with which the French administrators adorned themselves was largely an imaginary construction. The 'Umarian empire was already weak and fragmented by 1890, a state of affairs which owed little to French intervention.[52] Not only had the internal rivalry weakened Ahmadu's forces, but the Bamana disrupted virtually every aspect of the 'Umarian empire. The Bamana of Bèlèdugu disrupted 'Umarian communications along the periphery of the state as well as in main centers like Nioro and Masina. His incapacity to subdue the Bamana of Bèlèdugu prevented Ahmadu from integrating Segu into the larger state. In addition, the Segu Bamana disrupted trade by raiding caravans, and made it impossible for Ahmadu to establish security so that trade could flourish at a level comparable to the years before 'Umar's invasion. Both Bamana groups and periodic guerilla attacks by smaller Bamana columns diminished the tax base of the state considerably. After Ahmadu left Segu, the 'Umarians completely evacuated the left bank, and the Segu Bamana returned to occupy the area in front of their former capital, continuing the struggle.[53] In addition, when Ahmadu left Madani in Segu, it signaled the strategic importance of Nioro.

Due to the ever-present Bamana threat, Ahmadu was unable to consolidate his empire, leaving Masina virtually independent. By 1890 it was clear that the Bamana had achieved what Archinard's predecessors had wanted: the 'Umarian state had practically disintegrated. One of Ahmadu's political weaknesses was that he failed to attempt to negotiate with Bamana leaders in any way to prevent this. Negotiation with the French was an ongoing process for over thirty years, yielding little if any positive results for the 'Umarians.[54] The tactics of the Bamana had been very successful to the point that they were close to taking Segu. They had already made it impossible for Ahmadu to return to there. Morevoer, the defeat of Madani was easy.

The second pertinent element in analyzing the conquest is the virtual absence of the role of Africans. This reflects the broader historical literature on the European conquest of Africa which largely ignores African participation in the "scramble for Africa." Yet, it was the Africans who conquered Africa for the Europeans.[55] The case of the Middle Niger serves as a good example. African participation in the theater of operation goes beyond the "divide and conquer" philosophy whereby Europeans exploited cleavages within the African regimes, or sought allies in those who opposed the ruling regime. The French attempted to do both, operating on the internal schisms within the 'Umarian Empire in addition to attempting to rally 'Umarian opposition groups.

Who actually conquered Segu? At most, the French supplied a handful of officers and ammunition for the war in the Middle Niger. In virtually every other respect, from providing food to providing transportation, Africans were the major actors in the struggle against the 'Umarians. Archinard's African army consisted of 720 regular soldiers, 32 French officers, and 1,500 auxiliaries.[56] The army, consisting of African recruits, which the French marshalled, often relied on friendly villages to supply food.[57] In addition, the French employed Africans as porters to transport foodstuffs and equipment. As has been discussed, the Sòmònò were indispensable in their provision of riverain transportation for the army, an instrumental service in the campaigns against Ahmadu and Madani.[58] Even after those campaigns, the Africans in particular made consolidation possible. For instance, in 1891 it was a column of Africans that arrived in Sinzani from Segu in response to news of hostility in the region.[59]

Bamana soldiers played significant roles in two capacities. Some Bamana had already joined the French army before the attack on Segu. These soldiers were already skilled in military techniques and were familiar with much European weaponry since the French and British had traded arms widely in the region. In addition, Bamana were skilled in building and repairing weaponry, a necessary asset, since at times, they could not acquire arms from the French. Moreover, these soldiers were familiar with the terrain. Their military skills created opportunities in the French-African army just as it had done earlier in African armies. Eventually, some even infiltrated the officer corps.

The Bamana army, in short, separate and distinct from the French-African army, made the "French conquest" of Segu possible. For example, Mari Jara prepared for the final battle against the 'Umarians with the general of the Bamana army. He mobilized the available contingent of Marabugu, the bolow of Bèndugu and Kaminiandugu.[60] Lieutenent Gatelet estimated that the Europeans had 742 soldiers, of which only 103 were Europeans, and 570 non-soldiers. Mari Jara, however, had a thousand soldiers, 338 cavaliers and 818 porters.[61] It was the Bamana cavalry who chased Madani to Nioro. Moreover, it was the Bamana auxiliaries that made the seizure of Wossebugu possible, for the French had only 300 regular troops, mostly Africans (only 27 Europeans were in that campaign). And, it was the Segu Bamana army which defeated the 'Umarians at Mael, when only 120 soldiers marched with Marchand. More importantly, the Segu Bamana army often fought independent of the French recruited army during the struggle against the 'Umarians.[62] Although French records show that the participation of the Bamana and other African soldiers and civilians was the most important component in winning the war, published French accounts have created a colonial legend. It is also clear that the French needed the Bamana more than the Bamana needed the French in attaining their respective goals. The French lacked the money and the manpower to attempt any conquest on their own. In fact, their financial problems had as much to do with French policy during the pre-conquest period as the fashion in which they would attempt the conquest. Not only did the participation of Africans assure the removal of the 'Umarian power from the Middle Niger, but it would be instrumental in the administration which followed.

San Farba, influential griot of Segu.
Abon E. Mage, *Voyage dans le Soudan Occidental*
(Paris: Hachette, 1868), p. 223.

CHAPTER 6

THE BAMANA WAR
AGAINST THE FRENCH

After the defeat of the 'Umarians at Segu, the French attempted to re-establish the political structure which had existed under the Bamana prior to 1860 although with minor changes. The French wanted to take advantage of the rich commerce which flourished in the Middle Niger, and it was important to stabilize the region so that the trade routes could again be secure. The French attempted to rule the region through the Bamana, but the Ngolosi refused this arrangement.

Archinard was responsible for having changed the political balance of power in Segu. He refused to place all the areas of Segu under Bamana control for the fear that they would victimize those who supported the 'Umarian regime. Bojan was installed at the Nango where many Bamana slaves from Kaarta lived, and Mademba Sy, a Sénégalese Futaka agent, was installed at Sinzani.[1] By putting enemy rulers or potential enemies in contiguous areas, the French created a check and balance mechanism and pursued their "divide and control" strategy in order to contain Bamana power. Bojan, a Massassi Bamana from Kaarta, and a puppet for the French, aggravated the situation by attempting to lure those Segu Bamana to join him who did not want to live under Jara rule. Moreover, the French gave Bojan the arms, ammunition, and the horses captured in Segu, strongly substantiating the Bamana belief that Bojan was brought from Kaarta to be used against them.

Archinard credited himself for the "crowning" of Mari Jara as King of Segu in April 1890. However, from the Bamana perspective this was a matter of little consequence since the succession had already been determined by the Bamana while the 'Umarians were still in Segu. As discussed above, the Bamana nobles maintained the succession of the Fama while in exile, and the Jara family in the diaspora remained the dynasty which ruled the Bamana state. Therefore, Archinard did not reinstate the Jara family as rulers and nobles, but ceremoniously reaffirmed their established positions.

Archinard attempted to use pre-colonial African institutions in a system of indirect rule, placing the French atop the Bamana organization. If successful, such a strategy would have greatly reduced administrative expenditures for the French ministry while reaping the benefits from the political economy previously based on Bamana rule. The most significant change was that the French administration was placed atop the economic and political systems while the judicial and social institutions were largely left to African rulers.

The major problem with this model of indirect rule was that Mari Jara's political power was limited by the new political order. During the palaver between himself and Mari Jara, Archinard said, "The French came to take the country of Segu, not in order to govern it themselves, but to return it to the Bamana, the former owners."[2] This account is similar to an oral account which reports that Archinard said to the Bamana, "Our mission was to chase the 'Umarians, and we have chased them. We will say nothing to you. After having said that, they would do nothing to the Bamana."[3] However, this was not the case. Archinard established rules which would limit the authority of the Bamana Fama. Of course, these limitations were made to insure "the prosperity of the country" and the "development of commerce."[4] The Fama would have political authority over other Bamana of Segu, but that was the extent of his new authority because the Bamana could wage war only after consultation with the commandant. Even if war was waged, the French would not aid the Bamana. On the other hand, the French insisted that the Fama provide soldiers to the French when necessary. Two other provisions in the arrangement with the French occupying force severely reduced Bamana influence. First, the Sòmòno and Bozo who were, admittedly, of special interest to the French because of their importance for commerce and navigation, were placed directly under French authority with no obligation to the Bamana Fama of Segu. When the French arrived, "They made new laws in saying to the Sòmònò that they were not like the Bamana. They were to give fish to the French when the latter needed it."[5] The French employed the same revenue system which the 'Umarians had inherited from the Bamana rule. The Sòmònò were to pay an annual tax in rice, millet, salt, butter, etc. and a daily tax in fish, milk and eggs. Moreover, half of the receipts from river passage went to the French Resident.[6] The role of the Sòmònò was also to transport the whites when the latter needed to go on military maneuvers, and to transport arms.[7] As a result, the French could exclusively benefit from the taxation of these groups. Nevertheless, the Fama was expected to give half of all revenues from the Segu market, allow the passage of caravans, and permit free navigation on the Niger. Moreover, the commandant would have complete authority in issuing permits to caravans and barges in order "to avoid raids." Another matter of controversy was that all properties of Madani and the 'Umarians belonged to the French, "who chased them" from Segu.[8]

Archinard's administration was very much an adhoc construction which repeated some of the same errors that 'Umar had made. For instance, several attempted administrative changes were implemented prematurely. Archinard's proposal put all matters relating to revenue directly under French authority. Mari Jara and the four military leaders "understood and agreed to this arrangement," according to the French, because the Fama declared that "he would never have been able to take Segu" and the agreement was in "exchange for what the French had done for him."[9] Many of the measures, in short, did not follow the pre-existing political arrangement in the Middle Niger under Bamana rule.

In essence, the Bamana no longer headed their "re-established" empire since the French Resident had the right to know everything. Theirs was merely one of several states reconstructed and carved out by the French, leaving the others (formerly under Bamana control) beyond the authority of the Fama. To add further insult to the re-established Bamana authorities, individuals like Bojan and Mademba Sy, who were puppets, were allowed to provide a check on Bamana power.

The Massacre of Mari Jara

Mari Jara was around 58 to 60 years old at the time Archinard marched on Segu, yet he was still vigorous. He spent most of his time alone. It was said that he had a passive character and was a quiet man, but one who seriously reflected on issues before making a decision. However, the French saw him as useless in that it was almost impossible to judge the length or the character of his reign.

At the death of Karamòkò Jara on August 13, 1889, Mari Jara became Fama as the legitimate heir, being the eldest brother. He was not immediately proclaimed as Fama although he was the Fama by right of birth and was recognized by the military sofa leaders. Instead, the proclamation occurred on the fortieth day after the death of Karamòkò when the new Fama was installed in the *jomfutu,* the royal house, as was customary. During this period the change of reign was customarily kept a secret and the new Fama reigned under the name of the former Fama.[10]

Mari Jara had lived at Kamale before the death of Karamòkò. Then, he moved to Farakò. He, his counselors, and his guard lived in the jomfutu. The general of the army and the sofa leader who commanded the columns lived at Sama Fulaba, a military town.

Mabèrè Kanu was the general of the army. Other military column leaders, in order of command were: Songoba, Madon, Cèkòròbabugondje, Babugu Baje, Masseme Mame, Bambugu Songo Boi, Nerekoro Bugu, Banan Koro Tenema, and Mpieba Bingue. In addition, the Bamana army had four section leaders: Bolo Tigui Songoba, head of the permanently garrisoned guard; Mpe Bèrè, second in command to Songoba; Digui Seme, leader of the young sofa enlistees; and, Bantago, who had just arrived from Kamaniadugu. The counselors included Kirango Ba, the nephew of Mari, and Garanke Karamòkò, who was very influential.[11]

The Bamana were encouraged by their successes against Madani's army, in particular the battle at Mindanga. Nevertheless, the ultimate goal of the Ngolosi Fanga was to regain total control of Segu. If in 1880 the Bamana had inferior weaponry, that situation began to change from the time that Ahmadu rejected the protectorate of the French proposed by Gallieni.[12]

Ntò, ally of the French, vowed to never obey Karamòkò as long as his reign lasted.[13] Ntò was depicted as a brave, energetic leader who knew how to make sure his decisions were executed even when he could not do so himself. He was very confident, and his enemies recognized these qualities and feared him as a rival power. Moreover, Ntò was a leader of a large Bamana army, and had great success against the 'Umarians. However, he gradually isolated himself from the larger Bamana war effort, and began to fight to create a polity for himself. After becoming very powerful, he refused to recognize Karamòkò.[14]

Mari Jara sought reconciliation with Ntò, wanting to bring him into the regular Bamana ranks. Mari Jara emphasized that Ntò had a falling out with Karamòkò, following the poisoning of Togoma and Mònzòn, but he should not have had a problem with the Jara dynasty as a whole. Ntò had refused to submit to Karamòkò, but he vowed to assent to the legitimacy of the Ngolosi Fanga, and therefore, he could submit to another Fama.

The French believed that Mari Jara was disposed to accept the submission of Ntò, who had no hatred of the new Fama and no reason to persist in a revolt. However, Mabèrè and the other sofa leaders would never permit Mari Jara to accept the submission of Ntò. The French doubted that he would enter the royal fold, and the two sides had some contentious encounters.[15]

Ntò had many devoted partisans, and his successes were uncontestable. The villages were divided in their loyalties between Ntò and Mari Jara, but Mari Jara had thirty under his control, including the military villages of Farakò and Sama Fula. Ntò, on the other hand, had only thirteen, with Sinzani remaining undecided. The villages which supported Ntò were located to the north and in the interior while those which followed Mari Jara were found in the south and on the river. They were divided as follows:

VILLAGES LOYAL TO MARI JARA

Farakò Sama	Fula	Boyau	Suba	Kalabugu
Ceribugu	Mamurula	Memana	Dibugu	Tenu
Doguiba	Niugu	Sanamadugu	Dosseguela	Makarela
Tonguelo	Jonteguela	Kuna	Kokri	Donguebugu
Tiambugu	Toimana	Sirabele	Kamale	Jadu
Kolodugu	Niebebugu	Seroicala	Werla	Duro

VILLAGES LOYAL TO NTÒ

Markabugu	Suma Marka	Songani	Delaba	Sonogo
Negnebugu	Misserebugu	Ntòsama	Kemedale	Molado
Niempene	Ngolobabugu	Ntòfafano	Sinzani (undecided)[16]	

As one historian argues, Mari Jara was naive, as were many African rulers of the period, in that he failed to clearly understand the effects of regional geo-politics, and above all, the presence of the French.[17] Despite Mari Jara's craftiness, which seemed to characterize the Ngolosiw, he was a victim of the "respect for words given to another," summarized in the Bamana saying, *ke ko de ye fo ko ye,* "a thing done is a thing said."[18] But the French words were far from truth and held little integrity. Mari Jara thought that the arrangement was meant to promote commerce, and the French had no other preoccupation than the prosperity of their business, like all the Arab businessmen in the region. For him, then, the Resident Underberg was, in accordance with agreements concluded with the French, a representative charged with commercial interests of the French community. Added to this agreement, however, was the stipulation that the Fama could call the Resident to aid him to defend his power.[19]

Little has been written on the murder of Mari Jara and his nobles. This is interesting in light of the fact that the French took great pains to describe virtually every situation and incident in great detail. Nonetheless, the French records and subsequent accounts based on these reports, mention only in brief the suspected plot of Mari Jara to attack the French and to kill Bojan and the French Resident Underberg. As a result, specific incidents remain clouded in mystery.

After the Bamana returned to Segu, it was soon clear that Mari Jara would not be a pawn for the French, and Archinard wanted him removed. Archinard had not been satisfied with the reception given to him by Mari Jara and the villages under his control.[20] The justification for ousting Mari Jara was that the Fama allowed his partisans to raid villages newly submitted to the French. However, the real reason was that Mari Jara wanted to rule alone, and Underberg refused to permit another authority to overshadow his own. Mari Jara considered himself the legitimate master of the country, and his aim was to command it without sharing power. In short, he was as his fathers and grandfathers, *maatigi, mugutigi ni jitigi,* "master of men, powder and water."[21] Besides, the French had a history of not responding when villages were raided except when it was in their interest. Additionally, Archinard instructed the Resident, Underberg, to note all the damages inflicted by the Fama without discussion of it so that the French would have a reason to replace him with the Massassis at the right moment. Archinard insisted that the Bamana of Segu were incapable of ruling a state, a view which he had decided long before this moment and one which he had written previously in two letters. He wrote to Underberg, "The revolution ... should be rapid and indisputable. It will be next year."[22]

Archinard accused Mari Jara of not holding to any commitment mentioned in the palaver of April 11, 1890 when the latter agreed to assure the order and tranquility within the state. Instead, Mari Jara's sofas disrupted the country. Furthermore, Mari Jara took care to hide all of his acts from the Resident, for the French wanted to know each and every decision taken by the Fama. Archinard ultimately wanted to reorganize Segu, and preferably end the Jara dynasty.[23]

According to one Bamana source,[24] some 'Umarians informed the French that the Bamana had retained guns in order to betray the French after the conquest of Segu. Dyara agrees that the Futa population found means to engender discord between the Bamana and the French.[25] Gatelet asserts that one of Underberg's agents, Baidi Jop, revealed the plot to the French. He and his wife were involved in getting the Bamana to speak freely of their plan. Since Baidi could not understand Bamana, his wife translated for him.[26] Consequently, the French arrested some people, but released them after a brief inquiry. However, one French report states that the secret of the plot was told to the French by a member of the Resident's domestic staff (the identity of this employee was not given). Bojan and Hourst were also informed.

Tension continued to mount between the Ngolosi and the French. The French wanted close co-operation between the two groups, but not on equal terms. However, the Ngolosi refused, saying that they could not give the French their slaves in order to work for them, and they could not work for the French because "a son of a king should not work for another king." The French were confident that Mari Jara wanted to get rid of them to free himself from their guardianship. The surprise attack by the sofas was to take place on the day of the full moon of June during the hour of the siesta.Eventually, Underberg called Mari Jara and twenty-three Bamana leaders to come and talk. Ntò was warned by his French friends to not be present.[27] An oral report suggests that Underberg told the leaders to come and share the gold which Ahmadu had left in Segu.[28] When the Bamana arrived, the French massacred them, and threw their bodies into the river.[29] Even in the French records no explanation was recorded for this act. Underberg decided to shoot the Fama and the counselors before the suspected plot could be enacted, and the tirailleurs killed Mari Jara. After announcing his death to the counselors, "none offered to avow his crime." The tirailleurs were ordered to shoot them, but they were dilatory and negligent, allowing the counselors time to attempt an escape. In the end, Doctor Graff killed the first, and the tirailleurs killed the others. The French installed Bojan as the "Fama" in Segu, a title he would carry in the eyes of the French, but few Bamana accepted him as "Fama" even if he was recognized as a political figure.

After the massacre, war erupted in and around Segu, eventually spreading to other areas as Bamana populations took arms against the murderers of their Fama and the Bamana counselors. Although some Bamana "were stubborn and fought with the French,"[30] many declined to aid the French just as they had done with al-Hajj 'Umar. This led to the third dispersal of the people of Segu. After the massacre, many feared further French retaliation and repression.[31]

After the murder of Mari Jara and the counselors, the Bamana royal family and loyal soldiers fled to Baninko, on the right bank of the Bani River. The two most influential leaders were Bafi Jara at Ngunina (Banyana) and Binake Kokeba Jara at Tuna who urged all the Bamana to fight against the French and Bojan, and re-establish complete Bamana power. The villages to the south of the Bani which had never submitted to anyone immediately responded to the call. The provinces between the Niger and the Bani, on the other hand, were hesitant, although many joined later. The war spread to Bèlèdugu and Segu and "taxed to the limit the small reserves of troops left to the Segu Resident." Roberts argues that the "rebellion" revealed the weaknesses of Archinard's efforts at "indirect rule."[32] More importantly, Archinard failed to adequately assess the political and economic forces in the Middle Niger. After making Bojan King of Segu in 1891, Archinard complained that the Segu kingdom was too

large and unstable for Africans to govern because "they constantly produced revolts."[33] As will be discussed below, the French colonial regime
faced rebellion, just as their predecessors did. The problem, however, was
much more complex than the simple, racially-motivated explanation
given by Archinard. Clearly Underberg's massacre of the leaders of
Bamana society produced the war, a fact that French administrators
acknowledged in their reports.[34] The people of Baninko did not oppose
African leadership per se, but did attack French overlordship and the
African intermediaries like Bojan who were not chosen by the segment of
the population in a position to contest it. Underberg, a Frenchman, and
Bojan, a Kaartan, were foreigners encroaching on the power base of the
Segu Bamana, and the old regime refused to simply fade.

On December 13 the Resident was informed that Baninko had assembled a column in order to attack Segu.[35] Reports were that Kinian would
march also. According to one report which was exaggerated, the "revolt"
was still far from being organized. Another report noted that Bokoba
Tangara, head of Tuna, had led part of Baninko to "revolt" after the massacre.[36] The Tònjòn of Zambala, Bafi Jara, a relative of Mari Jara, and two
Marabouts held a meeting at Damunu. However, the population was
divided. Some had a leader who made common cause with the war.
Others preferred to monitor the situation. Nevertheless, few villages
remained completely neutral and nearly all supported the war even
though some waited for the opportunity to declare it.

Bafi Jara and Nango Ba, both relatives of Mari Jara, were the principal
leaders of the war effort in Baninko. Nearly all the Ngolosiw played an
active role in the war. The Tònjòn provided the main soldiery, and some
Markas increased the ranks. Baba Jan, former counsellor of Mari Jara,
and Makakè de Nida were major recruiters.

In the middle of December, two leaders were executed by the French,
Ba Samba So and Bako. At that point the war had become widespread.
The Resident was forced to send troops to fight the insurgents in January
1891. Worried about the desertion of his sofas, Bojan sent Ba Samba So
in the middle of December to get information. He and his companions
were stopped at Nyamina by the leader of the village. Ahmidi, a Bamana,
executed them after Nango Ba demanded Ba Samba's head. Nango Ba
accused Ba Samba of having killed Nango Ba's brother the previous

year.[37]

By the middle of January the Resident thought it was imperative that he take measures of security. Lt. de Vaisseau Hourst, the only available officer, left Segu with ten tirailleurs and some laptots, and a contingent of 400 to 500 men. Two hundred and ninety men were added near Duguninkoro. Patrols were sent all along the Bani River to gather information and to give the order to the Sòmònò to go down with their canoes toward Fentiguila and Garo. On January 28 Hourst learned that Bamana troops were aligned on the left bank in front of Garo. That night, 500 men joined the troops at Garo. The Bamana lost twenty-five men and four horses in the ensuing battle.

The supreme effort of the war was concentrated in Jèna, composed of four villages (Sido, Dugutiguila, Nabugu and Zanguma). Believing the defenders were very numerous, Hourst decided to attack the village. The French-African unit and an African column[38] arrived before Jèna. Sido consented to receive the column, but Dugutiguila closed the gates and refused to enter into the fray. Added to Hourst's small troop of tirailleurs and laptots were 800 to 900 of Ntò's soldiers from Segu. The following struggles occurred between Dugutigila and Sido. Hourst and the African unit attacked Dugutiguila, and two were killed and thirteen wounded. However, the army was forced to retreat to Sido and wait for help. The French emphasized in the official report that the "small" column had to retreat, rather than admit that an army of almost 900 men with superior weapons was unable to subdue Jèna and enter the village. The episode also says much about the will of the Bamana to reject the overtures of the French.

A large column came to reinforce the defenders of Jèna under the orders of Ahmidu. All the villages except one welcomed him. The French were uncertain of the specific movements of the soldiers in Dugutigila. Finally, the forces under Hourst attacked the village. After a long bloody battle which the casualties documented, the French-African army entered the village, and the tirailleurs pursued those who escaped. Twelve Europeans (eight were officers) and 73 tirailleurs were killed and 130 wounded. More than 250 Bamana (including Tònjònw) were killed. The army burned some villages (an act which the French criticized Africans for doing), and received the submission some others. The Mahdi and some Tònjònw were dead, but Ahmidu escaped. The defeat of Jèna incited terror among the others.

A column uniquely composed of African auxiliaries was placed under the command of Mademba Sy who, from March to August 1891, was charged with pacifying the southwest area of the region. He then marched to Ngunina to stop Bafi Jara, and executed him.[39] The French sent Bojan to aid Sy in putting an end to the war. Profiting from the absence of Bojan, other centers revolted. Nevertheless, by October the French representatives had received the submission of nearly all the villages of the Baninko. However, the Bamana in general, and the Ngolosiw, in particular, only submitted at gunpoint.[40] As soon as the column left, the fighting continued, now led by a Saharan holy man, Mosadi, and his adopted brother, a Bamana named Amidu from Daumana. They attempted to recruit an army until Bojan and his troops were able to affect numerous Bamana desertions.

After pacifying much of the region, Bojan reorganized the Segu Kingdom, dividing the territory into provinces and cantons. He named a leader to head each province, with the approval of the Resident, and placed a tax collector in the region to levy taxes on caravans. These agents reported directly to Bojan, functioning independently of the provincial head.

Peace was short-lived in the area.[41] When Mademba Sy was installed in Sinzani, Kolodugu, under Cenble Kulubali's rule, resisted. The revolt spread to Kala, Sana and Moninpèbugu.[42] Sinzani was a strong center of resistance for two reasons. First, the different groups— Bamana, Maraka, Sòmònò and Bozo— united. Second, the success was based on Sinzani riches, permitting the creation of a large mercenary army, very handsomely paid. These riches had also been the fortune of the Famaw of Segu.[43]

Areas north of Sinzani also revolted. Two Marabouts who had studied at the school of Shaykh Bakkay Koroba at Timbuktu, Badi Mahmond and Baya[44] sent a column commanded by Onmarel Samba Dudel to aid the Bamana. In October, the Resident of Segu sent some reinforcements under Dugu, cousin of Bojan. However, Briquelot had to recall them to Segu on March 2, 1892 because the war in Baninko and Kaminiandugu was spreading. Meanwhile, al-Hajj Buguni was getting closer to Sinzani (by March 10) to attack with 600 to 700 fantassins and 400 cavaliers, but the artillery of Sinzani prevented his getting closer than 200 meters.

Mamadi Jan, the provincial leader (under French administration) also joined the fight against the Bamana. However, when the Bamana opened fire, the leader's soldiers took flight, and Jan was killed in combat. The inhabitants of Bla fled and a great number were taken by the Bamana and made captives. The Bamana repulsed the "small troops" of Captain Briquelot, yet the latter regrouped to recommence their incursion. The Bamana returned to attack Bla under the leadership of Duguolo Mamuru, and succeeded in seizing the village, which could only defend itself with the garrison of the "Fama" that Briquelot had left there, and who were ultimately killed.

The French assembled a column of African soldiers at Dugassu and Gassolu re-established order in Baninko, but after the last attack on Bla, the safety of this contingent was very precarious. The Resident preferred to lead the column toward Kaminiandugu where discontentment had been brewing for some time. The Bamana and the Fula Dembere of Kaminiandugu had said that the people of Minianka and Sinzani rose up, and it was necessary to do the same. They had sent a column to Ahmadu at Banjagara, and the remaining section occupied Kogne and the villages which had remained faithful.

Following the Baninko episode, the Ngolosiw, and their counsellors and followers departed en masse to Kaminiandugu on the right bank of the Bani River, which was a stronghold during the 'Umarian period. In French assessments the Tònjòn had no real attachment to the Fama, but were linked by their common economy of raids and extractions.[45] The Tònjònw and Jula were blamed for the war in Baninko because they were malcontent.[46] The French argued that for some, the object of their efforts was to re-establish the Jaras; however, for the immense majority it was an era of pillage. Regardless of their motivation, the Tònjòn played a central role in the war. The French claimed that the provocation of the "revolt" by the Tònjòn made the task of reorganizing Segu relatively easy by nullifying any rights they could claim. Since they were confined in their eighteen villages of Segu, they lost all their power and influence.[47] However, the Tònjòn continued to have immense influence in other regions of the state since they could and did convince others to oppose

French rule. After the seizure of Jèna, the Tònjònw and Jula returned to their villages, some sought refuge in Miniankala or among the Bozo. Others followed the Jara entourage to Kinian and Baninko. During the winter, they rallied in the villages on the right bank of the Bani River, eager to fight. Bojan and a contingent was sent to Kinian to determine the possibility of success. The communications between Segu and Kinian via Baninko was precarious because the partisans and/or couriers of Bojan were stopped; some were even put to death.

Bokoba Tangara, village head of Tuna, was one of the stronger supporters of the Ngolosiw. After the execution of Mari Jara and his counsellors, Tangara stirred up part of Baninko and could have succeeded in causing the French serious trouble if the fear of an energetic reprisal had not given them pause. When Mademba and his column of 2000 sofas from Segu arrived at Tuna, Tangara united a sizeable number of men.[48]

The French administration was convinced that the results of the battle would be profound. The villagers who had furnished contingents to the war moved southward. Key leaders like Kelessere Jara, Kirango Ba, Balajan, Nango Ba, and Duya Nko escaped; however, the latter two were later captured and executed. Moreover, at Ndula Koro forty Tònjònw were taken and executed. As a result, some village leaders came to make their submission at Bla.

Bojan, leading a column, went to Baninko in order to receive the submissions and the fines. He executed the village leaders taking part in the war. However, the village of Kentieri, consisting of Bamana and Marka villages, closed its gates toBojan's envoy.[49] Although the Markas and some Bamana eventually submitted, five Bamana villages closed their tatas, sending no one to submit to Bojan. Many of the Bamana soldiers of Baninko who refused to submit took refuge in Kaminiandugu.[50]

After the defeat of Jèna in 1891, most of the Tònjòn took refuge in Minianka and Bèndugu where they encouraged an unsubjugated population to fight. Therefore, Bojan decided to visit these provinces, and noticed a pervasive hostility. For instance, the village of Kentien refused to receive him, and killed one of his men. Later at Segu, the representative of Kentien accused the Tònjòn among them of committing the murder, a weak defense as far as the French were concerned, arguing that the village leader could have prevented the murder while facilitating the sub-

mission of the village. The people still refused to pay the fine of two horses. As a result, the French ordered some auxiliaries, led by Mimabla
Kelema, to occupy the villages and restrain the Bamana inside.[51]

The auxiliaries of Minianka withdrew to Dacumana at the beginning of
October (1891), spurring Kentien raids on neighboring villages of
Dacumana. Meanwhile, at a significant meeting held in Jacuruna, military
action was decided against Bojan and the French, forcing the Resident to
place another garrison of auxiliaries at Bla.[52] Zambala and Kanoro joined
forces over the issue of surplus *jaka* (tax), but the first attempt failed.
People in Segu joined the war efforts, but for them the jaka issue was secondary to the opportunity to create havoc in Segu. Those who fought had
the luxury of fleeing to Kaminiandugu, if necessary, near the Ngolosiw
where they could find refuge.

Although some villages had not participated in the war, they still
refused to send representatives to Segu to acknowledge the French or
Bojan. In fact, the villages of Sele, Koro and Say remained loyal to the
Jaras, and after the death of Mari Jara, they refused to send any representatives to Segu. Mademba suggested that "they" (he and the French) occupy those villages because of the continued hostility the people expressed
toward the French.[53]

The French assessed the situation in the following terms. The Bamana
fell into two camps. The old, and/or the more prudent, those with something to risk, preferred to wait since the French administration placed men
in Kinian. The younger, on the other hand, and the more ardent adhered
to the columns of the Tònjòn. Two principal Ngolosiw remained in spite
of French orders. One, Bekari, sought to participate in the war, but
refused, fearing harm would come to his relatives still in Segu. He retreated to Moribugu in Kaminiandugu. The other,[54] however, joined the war. It
appeared that the Tònjòn had some secret relations with their counterparts
in Segu. In addition, all of the villages between Kan and Tuguba, to
Kamame, were ready to fight. The principal leaders were Alassi Karba,
Nogologuru Kossa, Gani Sangunba, Baba Jan (a Marka and former coun-
selor of Mari Jara), Duga Ngi, Muba (Chief of War of Zambala), and others whose names are not listed in French reports.

The Resident wanted to use "tactical means" to handle the incursion,
and attack the forty or fifty villages and take all their captives, cattle, and

guns, "leaving them only their hands for work." He particularly wanted to smash the most insubordinate villages, Ntokarlo, Zambala, Tufula, Bla, Dakhramane, Ngonu, Kamona and Mpiena.[55]

In February 1892 the Bamana of Minianka revolted, marched to Bla, chased the French-recruited garrison, and killed the governor of Baninko. Yet the French official report asserted that the revolt was led against the authority of the "Fama," and that rebels remained in good relations with the French. However, after an attempt by the French to have talks with the leaders of Minianka, a French column marched to Bla. After a four-hour battle, the rebels retreated to neighboring village until nightfall when they evacuated the village. An estimated 80 to 100 rebels were killed or wounded. Consequently, an order was sent to the "Fama" of Segu to assemble a column in order to monitor the area of Baninko.[56]

By September 1892 the French believed that Ahmadu's prestige was almost nil.[57] However, this was far from reality. Some Bamana villages sent a delegation to Ahmadu during the spring of 1892 to form an alliance "to chase the whites from Segu", and Ahmadu accepted.[58] A man of the Fama, who had spent five months at Banjagara as a captive, provided information to the French administrator. He said that Ahmadu had not tried a serious operation against Segu since the beginning of 1892; yet on the request of the people of Seladugu, he gave the order to form a column, which made an about-face when they arrived near Sars, after hearing about the fall of Koila. Jenné furnished 240 men of which eighty were Futaka sofas. The others were Bamana of Tunjanre, Fiemani and Niansanone; captives from the houses of Jenné; and Markas, a number of which had never carried a gun. The man also noted that young men comprised most of the column, many from Masina and without possessions.[59]

Despite the defeats, some Bamana from time to time assembled columns to attack the French recruited garrisons. However, they could only maintain the campaigns for four or five days. The French lieutenant Cailleau wanted to go to Duguolo to "give the Bamana a good lesson for the future"[60] because he had remained at Bla for several days in order to give the Bamana time to offer their submission, but none from Duguola came to do so, as inhabitants from other villages had done. He met with the sons of the leader of the village of Jedala, Cèkora and Mommonke Songomba, telling them that the Bamana had only to do one thing to seek their pardon. In the end, Cailleau received permission to attack the village. The tirailleurs fought eight hours during the first attack, but were unable to penetrate the central tata, using most of the available ammunition and leaving three cases of cartridges and ten projectiles. It was only after the attack commenced that Cailleau realized that the men inside the tata had guns.[61] A column from Minianka marched on Bla; Cailleau, however, wrote to the captain in Segu that he was ready to resist them (with 110 men), but reiterated that he needed more ammunition. Cailleau's message never arrived because the courier coming from Segu became lost when the porter was wounded near Duguolo.[62]

Still by late 1892, fourteen villages on the southern frontier and other individual villages refused to submit. In Kansankasso, village head Taracani Kulibali unrelentingly incited the other villages to revolt. The former village leader of Minianka, Petiona, who had submitted to the French, had to take refuge at Kamuna, ceding his place to Gounieghe Kulibali who was very hostile to the French. In November the Bamana of Miniankala revolted.[63] Also, the villages of Ngolokuna (village head, Tiror Malle) and Fanakalla were averse to French authority, and the latter attacked Bla (February 11), taking 400 captives.

Numutie Kulibali, leader of Kentieri, was the heart and soul of the war effort against the French in that region. The French felt that the villages had an exaggerated confidence in their force because they never wanted to discuss submitting, instead declaring that they were ready to stand up to the French. Several Jara leaders, including those of Dabila and Kajala were hostile to the French. Moreover, one of the military leaders of Banan was a principal instigator of the revolt at Bla.[64]

Alliances in the Middle Niger were created and broken as the political climate changed. Obviously, the theme of a "common enemy" was a short-lived phenomenon. In addition, West Africans had not developed the idea of race solidarity since race was a European socio-political construct. Rulers searched for the political conditions conducive to specific goals. The depth of the Segu Bamana alliance with the French should not be exaggerated, for it was quite weak, indeed much weaker than the French ties with the Beledugu Bamana. The murder of Mari Jara and the counselors only confirmed the suspicions of the Segu Bamana regarding the French.[65]

Ahmadu sent representatives to al-Hajj Ansumura Kuribari in Sikasso in November 1891 to convince Cèba to stop fighting Samori Turè, who had already formed an alliance with Ahmadu between 1889 and 1890.[66] Cèba agreed and ceased the war against Samori, additionally refusing to fight with the French at Nagana and Gankura in November. Moreover, Cèba's son, Ntu, did not join the French as had been agreed upon in an expedition under Marchand against Samori.[67] Instead, Cèba's son took the route of Tengrela with all the columns abandoning Marchand on January 27, 1892.

Samori wrote to Ahmadu, "I am very happy about what you tell me about the alliance which should exist between Tieba and me. I will do what you indicated to me on the subject because we three united, the French would no longer be against us. The Prophet said: 'union makes force.'"[68]

After the Bamana war spread to Kaarta and the Bamana joined forces with Ahmadu, the sphere of French opposition enlarged, and for the first time many of the western Sudanic polities were united.[69] Oloruntimehin argues that the eventual alliance between Ahmadu, Samori and Cèba was evidence that Muslims belonging to different brotherhoods could work closely together without the strains introduced in the Sénégambia and Masina by 'Umar's revolution.[70] The alliances seemed to have less to do with the ability of Muslims of different brotherhoods to unite than with the politics of resistance to alien overrule. For instance, the non-Muslim Bamana of Segu and the Muslims of Masina formed an alliance to fight al-Hajj 'Umar, an alliance which had far more to do with the goal to safeguard their political power than with religion. Also, Samori and Cèba fought each other until the French goals became clear to Cèba. Finally, probably the oddest alliance was that between the Bamana and Ahmadu. These alliances proved that the leaders were motivated by a desire for independence, anti-colonial sentiments, and the preservation of their commercial interests. However, religious solidarity did appear to play a role among Islamic leaders in the early 1890s.

The Bamana spearheaded the coalition's military campaigns against the French in the Segu area between 1891 and 1892, and they participated actively in the campaigns in Masina between 1892 and 1893. When Ahmadu formed a column in 1892, many of the men were Bamana.[71] The coalition was strong until the death of Cèba in 1893 and the fall of the last semblance of the 'Umarian state around 1893.[72]

Once the war had ended, and most of the revolts supplanted, the Bamana and other groups found other means to express their discontent with alien rule. For instance, of the nine provinces of the Kingdom of Segu, the three provinces of the West, Bani, Banifing and Bagke, recognized the authority of the imposed Fama, Bojan, but not that of the tax collector. Some villages refused to pay any tax although they remained calm during the revolt in Gwènka. Each province had a governor, selected by the Bojan, and a tax collector, but the latter's authority was far from being complete. Instead, the people in the villages only obeyed their local leaders, Nagar, Doko and Beleko.

The three provinces east and south of the Bani, Bèndugu, Baninko, and Miniakala, all refused to receive any of Bojan's representatives, refused to pay taxes, and would not be ruled by any Kaartans. They declared that if Bojan, "the Fama," wanted them to obey, he would have to force them. Not only were they openly hostile to Bojan, they were just as much so to the French. After the operations of Bonnier, a good part of the provinces seemed to want to renounce open hostility except Miniakala, which continued its raid. The French administration sent a garrison of sofas to occupy two villages (Jèna and Dakumana). The Miniankes and other inhabitants went to seek help from the 'Umarians and from the people of Ahmadu Abdul in Fion.

The French learned that they had to compromise. For example, the Bamana of Gwènka still refused to accept a governor not of their own choosing. They elected Faduba Tomba, much to the chagrin of the French, to be their governor. Also, in the province of Bagoe, the rumors of an incipient revolt were reported to the commandant. This revolt, however, was to be against the Kaartankes, whom they would not obey, not against the "Fama" or the French. The commandant had an agent in the region, a representative of Bojan, attempting to conciliate the two sides. The commandant regretted that on this occasion, the Resident was unable to rule directly. Finally, he suggested that it would be necessary to permit the Bamana to choose a governor themselves, as had been done in Gwènka, in order to achieve tranquility in the region.

The submission of Kaminiandugu (mostly Bamana) was considered complete. After the fall of Koila, many Bamana spontaneously sent some representatives to Kaminiandugu to swear allegiance to the Bojan. However, when many of the villages submitted, they sent representatives to the meet Bojan, not the French commander, feeling that although they must submit, they would not humble themselves before the French.

One of Bojan's detachments, including fifty-five auxiliary tirailleurs, was stationed at Bla and two other areas. Nonetheless, the Miniankes attempted to bar the routes and raid the market vendors in protest. Moreover, the regular garrisons of Bojan had to protect the communication lines. The Resident believed that it was bad to wait, arguing that the best response to the "war of raids" was to wage a similar war, but the lack of bravery of the sofas did not permit such a strategy. He also wanted to establish a garrison at Niambasso (in Bèndugu) and have negotiations with the village leader (not wanting to oppose him), believing that a garrison would have a powerful effect on the recalcitrant and hostile villages, Duguolo in particular.[73]

The French on the ground continued to report to their supervisors that the political situation was quiet, but indications of various forms of war and resistance reveal that the people were not as quiescent, nor had they entirely submitted as the French wanted to believe. For example, one commandant stated in a report, "The Bamana were very satisfied with the current regime;"[74] Nevertheless, some villages complained against the agents of Bojan who had been charged with assuring the transport of millet (as tax). He wrote, "It is convenient to only listen to these complaints as they merit; they are generally exaggerated because the Bamana were against the Kaartankes sent to Segu."[75] He, like other administrators, was pleased when villages sent representatives to Bojan, but, as others wrote, often little faith could be placed in many of these submissions.

Part of the population of the province of Segu was composed of Tònjònw, many who remained partisans of Mari Jara, taking refuge on the right bank of the Bani and participating in the war in Baninko. After the defeat of Jèna, they returned to their villages around Segu, but the French remained suspicious of them. Yet the administrator wrote, "They seemed now to have accepted the new state of things."[76] The commandant received them with the approval of Bojan and with other segments of the population. He desired relations with them because he needed them to reach an agreement with the people of Bèndugu and aid in helping him arrange talks with the people of Nimiankala. The commandant disbelieved the sincerity of Bamana relations with Bojan, but he was confident that with French support, the organisation of the Kingdom of Segu would seem definitive to the Tònjòn.

"The province of Segu was completed submitted," according to a French report.[77] Nevertheless, the administrator complained that these villages proclaimed that Bojan and the French could do nothing for them, yet they sent representatives to Segu for help when they needed it. Some even closed their gates, refusing military contingents from the French.

The French believed that the complete pacification of Segu was on track, and had been obtained with "prudence and patience." The commandant advised that if it were to happen more rapidly, it would require constant vigilance to repress any revolt using Bojan's *sofas*, and support from troops in the French-African army. He also warned that it would be better not to try to establish a uniform regime for all the provinces, and to be very prudent regarding tax collecting, to exercise a great surveillance over Bojan's agents.[78]

Some reports revealed that things were not as "pacific" as the French may have liked. However, the commandant moved with much more caution than Archinard had done. Nevertheless, he made one similar mistake: he too placed foreigners in local positions, and the people generally resented this. Although the commandant realized that it would be better for the Bamana to choose their own local governors, the French colonial office was hesitant to agree. Perhaps there was fear of these leaders promoting insurrection, but it is also clear that the French administration preferred having governors who supported the French cause.

French reports seem to indicate that they regarded only full blown-revolt as a serious forms of resistance. Resistance took on many forms besides this. As has been discussed, some Bamana communities refused to pay taxes; others refused to send representatives to be presented to Bojan and/or the French, and others closed their gates when the French or Bojan sent their agents. Although some villages did not revolt, they wished to be left free to do as they please. As a result, they paid the tax, and they sent representatives to submit to French-appointed authorities in order to avoid any soldiers interfering with their daily activities. Therefore, the acts of "allegiance" were not necessarily testament to an implicit wish to have French rule.

During the late 1890s and early 1900s the Bamana reasserted their political system on the Middle Niger in several ways. The defeat of the Bamana (and the 'Umarians) by 1892 failed to constitute a complete conquest in the Middle Niger although many villages had "submitted." As was described, "The first impression that one receives of the general situation is that our authority is uncontested and seems well-established in the country situated between the Niger and Bani (Gwènka, Segu and Kaminiandugu)."[79] However, south of the Bani, the Bamana still escaped close supervision by the French, and Bojan's administration was very limited. The agents of the Resident reported that for a long time, the former inhabitants of Segu took refuge south of the Bani, "fleeing the new masters who came from the outside."[80] For the Segu Bamana, Bojan was considered an enemy.

In January 1893 some village leaders decided to manifest their displeasure with French reorganization, particularly the fact that political affairs were in the hands of Kaartankes. Since Bojan had been installed in Segu (three years) all the posts of consequence had gone to foreigners.[81] The people of Gwenka outlined their grievances against Bojan. Bojan had raised the tax in millet three times, confiscated some captives, and permitted his men to operate directly in the villages. The Resident advised Fadomba, the village leader, to go and see Bojan. Fadomba had refused to answer Bojan's order to come to Segu. It is important to note that Fadomba was a Bamana Tòn member whom the French really did not want to see administer the area. As a result, the French wanted to launch "effective and durable actions" south of the Bani; the colonial administration, however, found it necessary to dismiss the Bojan, and deal directly with the Africans in order to put all the country from Banifing to Bèndugu under the dependence of the French post.

The Resident sent a representative to Bagoe to invite Bamana leaders from the region between the Bani and the Bagoe to travel to Segu and talk to the French commandant. (This approach had been adopted for certain villages in the East.) Alternately, they were instructed to meet with Bojan instead of meeting with the French administrator.[82]

By 1894 some frontier villages continued to raid caravans and travel-

ers and refused to send any representatives to Segu at the demand of the
commandant of the Cercle (administrative unit). They were audacious
enough to tell the commandant's messengers that it was true, they raided,
they would not return anything, and they would not go to Segu. In addition, some villages, including Marella, Bandugu, Nientona, Geleku,
Kursudugu, Sala, Bugukurula, Bamendo, Jebe and Seguene, refused to
pay the jaka.[83]

Raiding caravans and refusing to respond to the call of the commandant or other administrators in the French system was a popular form of
resistance. For example, Tukror, a village in Gwenka, refused to attend a
meeting with the commandant of the region. Another form of resistance
was to fail to recognize the authority of leaders whom the French and/or
Bojan placed in the regions. For instance, the people of Tokoro ignored
the authority of the provincial head. Additionally, four villages on the left
bank of the Niger in the canton of Ntò refused to recognize the authority
of Ntò and that of the French, or accept any form of domination. The
commandant complained that the French had never presented themselves
in the cercle, and advised that it would be necessary to at least send an
officer with some tirailleurs and spahis to go around the cercle and visit
those villages causing the "light agitation."[84]

After the French had won the war against the Bamana in 1891 and subdued revolts between 1892 and 1893, several Bamana communities still
refused to submit except on their own terms. For instance, the Bamana of
Gwènka decided to submit, but insisted that the provincial leader had to
be replaced by a local. After a long discussion, the French named a canton head with the approval of the Bamana. In another instance, the people of Bèndugu submitted to French authority only with the aid of the
Tònjòn generals, Balajan and Biratoma.[85] In the end, the leaders of
Bèndugu would only submit to the French Resident, not to Bojan. Still
other villages in the region, including Kasso, remained hostile.

The village of Ntesoba also negotiated through the Tònjòn, but did not
press to conclude a settlement. On the other hand, nine neighboring villages remained openly hostile. Although some of the Tònjòn served as
intermediaries, others like Manson and Mamuru continued to maintain
relations with Ahmadu.[86] In short, the French administration wavered
between "direct" and "indirect" rule. At times, the commandant wanted

to have direct relationships with Africans, and at other times, he preferred to use intermediaries like the Tònjòn or Bojan. However, the Bamana had much to do with the decision-making process by insisting on submitting directly to a French official or only to Bojan. Thus, they submitted only on their terms, or remained hostile, requiring the French to develop new strategies.

Kaminiandugu and Bintugu continued to be havens for Bamana leaders. By 1896 many Bamana sofa leaders were still in both provinces. However, Kogne Ba, a brother of Mari Jara, and Kissima, leader of the Bamana Bintugu column, were the only major military leaders in the provinces although secondary military leaders were also found there. Other superior leaders lived at Sama near the General of the Bamana army. Five years after the death of Mari Jara, part of the Bamana army was still intact and organized.[87]

Fields in Segu-Sekòrò.
The Maksun Collection.

CHAPTER 7

BAMANA RESPONSE TO EARLY FRENCH COLONIALISM

What is sometimes ignored in the debates about the differences or similarities of colonial administrative philosophies and why those philosophies and policies changed, is the role played by the colonized in the administration which followed conquest. Bamana responses affected the administrative decision-making processes as well as how the Bamana were able to maintain their culture despite French efforts to change them. Our focus will be on the administrative structure of the colonial occupation, schools, ideology (Islam), judicial system, colonial service (e.g. military recruitment), and language.

"Assimilation" is a colonial doctrine associated with France which in Raymond Betts' interpretation meant that "the colony was to become an integral, if not contiguous, part of the mother country, with its society and population made over— to whatever extent possible— in her image."[1] The colonial philosophies of assimilation and the administrative system of "direct rule" are sufficiently known and need not be reviewed here.[2]

However, certain elements of French colonial administration are very important for understanding Bamana reactions to French occupation, and it is to those elements we will turn in a discussion of the Bamana under early colonial occupation.

Yves Guyot asserted;

In France we confuse assimilation and uniformity, we have still the old Platonic idea of universals. We want to make everyone in our own image, as if it had attained an absolute perfection, and as if all Frenchmen were alike.[3]

Although it was unclear how the philosophy of assimilation would be defined and implemented in the Western Sudan, assimilation was widely understood to be an objective of colonial rule.

While Fouillee saw republicanism as the obvious objective for France, many other Frenchmen, particularly the defenders of the new colonial empire, promoted the idea of a civilizing mission toward less-developed peoples. Charles Castre, one who promoted the new objective, wrote, "There lives in French hearts a spontaneous piety for the civilizing mission to which France has ever dedicated herself."[4] Betts summarized this form of "cultural imperialism" as the notion of the right of a "superior" society to dominate and instruct a "lesser" one. For the French, the "white man's burden" translated into the notion of "assimilation."

The doctrine of assimilation, however, quickly gave way to one of "association."

The true significance of "association" was the belief that the economic betterment of the region was to be undertaken by native and Frenchman within the general framework of native institutions. It was a policy based on the acceptance of mutual interests and on a sort of fraternity, but not equality.[5]

The doctrine of assimilation implied centralization, and although doctrines were modified or replaced, France attempted throughout the modern colonial era to control colonial administration from Paris. The necessity for flexibility, however, made the initial doctrine impractical and untenable. As a result, it was condemned, and the colonies came to be viewed not as a homogenous empire, but a series of unrelated possessions, demanding separate administration.[6]

Gann and Duignan observe:

The British were on the whole pragmatic and more respectful of established chieftain authority while the French were more legally minded, bound to the continental tradition of centralized administration. . . . They generally saw themselves as the new chiefs, and the French service produced a whole generation of *rois de la brousse* who governed their districts with an iron hand. . . .African chiefs were generally treated as subaltern rather than as partners in government. . . Many tribal heads were deposed, titles were discontinued; some titles disappeared altogether and tribal areas were regrouped into larger units.[7]

Paris was viewed as the legal base of the French colonial government, but French strategies and philosophy had to be transformed to fit local conditions. The so-called "iron hand" rule proved to be far more flexible than might be expected from French philosophy on colonialism. Often the mythical colonial seat of Paris was far from the reality of what happened on the ground in a provincial administrative cercle.

The local colonial administrators, far from the influence of volatile public opinion and the interference of the Chamber of Deputies, acted according to their personal judgment. Joseph Gallieni explained, "The administrative organization of a new country must be in perfect rapport with its resources, its geographic configurations, the mentality of its inhabitants, and the goal that one proposes to attain."[8]

The administrator in the field was generally ill-prepared for the type of job that faced him. Robert Delavignette explains,

> It was the physical environment of my first post which brought home to me the distinctive character of our colonial administration in its most characteristic form—that of a *Cercle Commandant*. . . I became aware of that agency of government which did not exist at Dakar and was never displayed on the blackboard of the School: the *Cercle*.[9]

That administrative institution developed a character of its own, perhaps through trial and error, but far from the restrictions of the French bureaucracy. It was the local administrator who had or could acquire the "beat" of the region. "The *Cercle* had eyes and ears: it was aware of a significance in the life of the people which eluded our world of papers."[10]

French rule in the Sudan was not simply "French;" the local population also participated in and influenced the administration, forcing the colonial administration to adapt to local situations regardless of their initial intentions. Delavignette gives a detailed explanation:

> There is no administrative problem, however well-conceived the
> departmental instructions on it, which does not change its nature
> when it comes down to earth somewhere. And that somewhere is a
> country with depth as well as extension. The administrative problem
> immediately raises a native problem, that is to say a human problem,
> which demands a solution not only according to the regulations but
> in the moral sphere. This at once brings into play the necessity for
> authority. A road to map out, a population to vaccinate, a school to
> open—just so many local and native questions; and the administra-
> tor, who is perfectly well aware that the country cannot be run by
> written reports, looks for men, the men he has to command in order
> to get this particular thing done.[11]

Although Delavignette emphasized the role of the commandant, he
also stressed, inadvertently perhaps, the role of the men and women on
whom the administrator was forced to rely, mostly Africans.

These Africans performed a myriad of functions;

> guards and orderlies, cooks and their scullions, boys with their
> 'small boys' who worked the punkahs; and women for our need,
> prostitutes for the night, orconcubines for a tour, sometimes servant-
> mistresses for a lifetime. For each threescore of Europeans, there
> were nearly three hundred servants.[12]

The French viewed all the canton heads as agents of the commandant.
One commandant admitted that the absence of all African functionaries
made the task of the commandant of the Cercle delicate and laborious.
Some of the canton heads had great influence in the organization of the
state. The French believed, however, that they undermined this influence
with the transformations under French colonial rule, and that it would
have been difficult, but not impossible, for the African leaders to return to
their former status.[13]

The provincial "chiefs," the canton "chiefs," and the village leaders
were vital to administrative functions. If a Commandant failed to realize
the importance of local authorities, it was a lesson soon learned. As a
result, it was essential that the French choose local rulers who were

"devoted to the French cause." Even this, though, created problems because the people wanted to elect their own rulers. If the choice of local populations failed to coincide with those of the French, the administrator had other complications which fell under the heading "native problems," which Delavignette explained. For example, Battus wrote in a report in 1916 that the Africans wanted leaders on the sole condition that they choose them following their customs. "All of the cantons elected as leaders those whom they considered as such despite their suppression in 1905."[14] Although the French removed some authorities from their ruling positions, many of the villages re-elected them.

The African leaders, numbering around 50,000 on the village level alone, acted as "cogwheels" between the colonial authority and the African peoples. French West Africa, with 15 million people, 118 cercles, 2200 cantons and 48,000 villages, was eight times larger than the area of France; therefore, the 50,000 African authorities and other African collaborators were absolutely necessary to the administration.[15]

In Bamana territory the "provincial chiefs" were named by the Fama and confirmed by the French resident. However, their positions were not hereditary, and they could always be removed.[16] The age of the potential or current leaders appeared to have been a major concern of the French, but it is difficult to determine why age was deemed important. The French administrators emphasized the age of the leaders or contenders in files kept on them. The younger candidates, perhaps because they were more likely to be hungry for power and/or wealth would be easier pawns in their quest to augment their position, and were normally preferred over older ones. The French wanted to replace the very old leaders by a member of the family who was "active, energetic and devoted to our cause." However, the French did observe Bamana customs.[17] Often, the French attributed many problems in the villages to the fact that the village leaders were generally "too old and had no energy," lacking authority.[18] This assumption, however, is exactly the opposite of the custom that prevailed among the Bamana who respected age. Furthermore, older rulers were more likely to have been elected before the arrival of the colonial state, and this created fear, or at least, anxiety in the administration who wanted to maintain tranquility.

Perhaps the ruler's age was important because the French preferred to appoint officers with no "traditional authority."[19] Although the colonial political units might have divided pre-colonial boundaries, as Crowder argues, smaller political units, the villages for example, still existed intact which meant that at this level African authority administered the same political units. Crowder was correct that the French wanted to replace pre-colonial rulers, except those who were tied to "the French cause."

The provincial chief carried out the orders of the Fama. In addition, they handled all judicial affairs and levied fines or corporal punishment. When the parties involved in a case belonged to two different provinces, the chief of the territory where the crime was noted made the ruling. Each provincial chief had a troop of 100 to 150 sofas for this purpose, maintained by revenues from the Fama. However, they did command the troops in time of war. The Fama placed a tax collector to collect the local import taxes from the caravans, from the guards and from the forwarding agents. In an early administrative report came the warning: "It is certain that this organization will meet some difficulties of application in the beginning."[20]

The nominations of the village leaders were made by the commandants of the region; however, the lieutenant governor made the nomination of the more important leaders (of the cantons and provinces). The French thought that controlling the selection would "minimize the personalities too weak or hostile to French influence." The regional administrators transmitted information on the African leaders to the governor in Sénégal. Trentenian, a French Commandant in Segu, wanted to be sure that certain information was included in the files on leaders or potential leaders, especially their religious affiliation. He warned local administrators, "Do not lose the view that politics and religion have always closely tied the distinguished Muslim leaders or Marabouts."[21]

The French effectively weeded out the Ngolosiw from major leadership positions. After the creation of the cercle of Segu by the French and nominations were made for "Chiefs of Canton," the Ngolosiw conferred and decided to refuse "fragments of a power which, entirely, was theirs."[22] However, they left to their military and Kafow leaders the option to occupy the "chiefdoms of the canton." That is how the son of Mabèrè Kanu, called Alase, became the head of the canton of Npeba. After that, no Ngolosi became the head of a village or Kafo at Segu. Nevertheless, the

Ngolosiw continued to be kept under surveillance by the French.[23]

The French assumed that each French-African victory inspired fear, or at least awe, in the African peoples. Often, administrators believed that it was important to utilize these impressions to further the French cause. In the late 1890s Trentinian wrote, "The establishment of a strong political and administrative organization in the Sudan is eminently proper to fortify in the Africans the sentiment which they already have of French power." He believed that the French authorities were preoccupied with the interest of their district, the major concern being "to assure the prosperity of the colony." He also felt that the "blacks hold to their customs and institutions," but they had "respect for their leaders and obey them willingly."[24]

Certain aspects of the Bamana political economy survived under French administration. For example, the French made minor changes to the tax system organized by the Bamana. The populations paid the colonial Fama the established taxes which had been paid to the former Bamana Famaw. In the regions which were protectorates, the Kingdom of Segu had the right to establish and collect the taxes on all the commercial products imported or in transit in the territory.

The tax of the *wussuru*, tax on the caravans, varied with the different powers of Segu, but the institution survived. Under the Bamana, it amounted to one-tenth of the imported merchandise. The 'Umarians had imposed that rate, but without restricting tax collectors from arbitrarily levying additional taxes on the Markas. When the tax collectors demanded it, the wussuru was no longer paid, but furnished in merchandise worth more than that which would have been paid.

Historically, three great commercial routes crossed Segu territory. The one from Nyamina which passed through Baroueli was considered the most important because of the grand market at Baroueli which that route supplied. Yet it was impossible for the French to evaluate, even approximately, how much traffic that route could yield, due to the fact that for the first eighteen months that the French were in Segu, commerce had practically ceased due to the trouble in the region. Eventually, the route was banned. The second route led from Saharan territory in the North, and even French commerce from Sénégal used it. But, it was also rarely used at the time of French occupation. For this reason, some of the caravans traveled with armed escorts. For six months in 1896, there was no European merchandise in the market of Segu. The Jula carrying salt frequented the third route which departed from Sinzani. Most trade during 1896 was done on this route, for it was continually open.[25]

Although commercial routes were constantly disrupted during 1896, the French were still storing products from the wussuru and river transportation despite an earlier report suggesting that the tax system produced little.[26] Even so, the revenues from taxes were seriously reduced when the French opened a campaign against Samori, since all the commercial routes of the Niger were closed up to Segu, making tax collection in certain villages like Fatne only nominal. There tax returns were approximately 700 to 800 francs per month, with half going to the Residence in barrels of salt, cowries, kola nuts, cloths, and karité. The French estimated that the tax would be 1000 francs a month once the routes were constantly opened.[27]

From the point of view of the inhabitants, M. Semakula Kiwanuka tells us that in the aftermath of the imposition of colonial rule, two types of Africans emerged: "the defeated," who were resigned to imperial rule and "the collaborators."[28] This is an oversimplification, particularly of the "defeated." Bamana responses to French colonialism, for instance, often mirrored their responses to 'Umarian rule, including resignation, resistance and collaboration.

A major problem when studying any oppressed group is that the oppressed are often recorded through the eyes of the oppressors, and then, only when the oppressed present problems. As a result, in the absence of revolt, it might be assumed that the oppressed population is resigned to the rule of the oppressors. This has been a recurring debate, for example, in the historiography of slavery in the United States as it relates to the extent of the slaves' passive acceptance of their servile condition. Revisionist historians have documented how many slaves reacted differently to the varying situations.[29]

Some French administrators assumed, at least in their reports, that all was well when there was no indication of an actual "revolt" among the African populations. But, as we shall see, other administrators (and sometimes even those administrators who held those assumptions) contradicted this view in subsequent reports. Careful analysis of French colonial records reveal that the Bamana responded on multiple levels to the changing situation, challenging the French doctrine of colonial rule, and implementing changes of their own. As Kiwanuka states, "...the response of each colonial power was conditioned by the extent of the challenge or the degree of collaboration by the Africans."[30]

Some French administrators quickly realized that the "submissions" made by village leaders were often far from what the French expected or wanted. One commandant explained, "The word 'submission' is absolutely improper," referring to the hostile villages in Minianka and Bendugu. One village had refused to obey the French or pay the required tax for two, perhaps three years.[31] This was the case in nearly all the areas on the right bank of the Bani and areas south of Gwenka. The collection of the tax at the time of harvest was how one French administrator distinguished the villages which had submitted. Some people in Segu told the French that those who came from Minianka under the pretext to salute the commandant, had only as a goal to come and see if the whites had prepared a column against them.[32]

Taxes and censuses were the motivating factors for many acts of resistance. Many Africans resented censuses because they were acts of intrusion. It was soon apparent that the French wanted to know the population of a village for tax, military conscription, public works, or other reasons. French captain Besancon wrote that the African attitude toward the census was not surprising because they were aware that each visit of a white man "in order to count them . . . translated into a higher tax."[33] In some villages the heads of household would not pay taxes to the village leaders. The commandant sent a notebook to the governor with the names, highlighted in red, of those who had stopped paying the tax, and indicated that he wanted to send troops to these Bamana villages.[34]

One French administrator stated that the Bamana of Beledugu had a well-established reputation of independence. "They hardly know the surrounding areas of their village, and many among them never went to centers like Bamako, Kati, Kulikoro, etc."[35]

Other archival reports reflect that the territory was not as peaceful as some administrators had painted it. For instance, in 1896 the commandant of the cercle of Kita wrote to the commandant in Bamako to warn him that some Bamana had avowed to not permit any white to enter their villages. In addition, the French believed that Bamana had no foundation for sending a type of millet which killed some mules of the French.[36] Another example involved the people of Negne Kulibali, a local ruler in Bèlèdugu who detested the French. One year, they made an attempt against a European lieutenant who came with some Tirailleurs in order to requisition some cattle. Furthermore, the French administrators would find some villages deserted after the villagers heard that a European was coming. The typical attitude in the village of Koni was, "If we had thought that the white men would come here today, he would have found no one in the village."[37] Early in 1899 the administrator believed that it was necessary to police the cercles where French authority was insufficient, where the inhabitants poorly received the political agents of the French, and find a thousand pretexts to not follow French orders, and refused to pay tax.[38]

French administrator Besancon became so frustrated with the state of things involving one Bamana village after another until he finally decided that different tactics had to be used. When the Bamana of Ngolobèlèdugu created problems for him, he thought that it was necessary to finish with the "undisciplined" Bamana who with "their proud air of warriors" failed to furnish a single tirailleur, and "it was necessary to hit them hard."[39] He emphasized that the region had always been recalcitrant since French occupation. Large cantons of Kumi, Massantola and Nonkho and independent villages of Niara, Sabugu and Ngolobèlèdugu refused to furnish any porters, saying, "They were used to making war, not making porters." Besancon wanted to make "a round in the area with a strong company of Tirailleurs and two 80mm mountain guns" because he did not believe that they would defend themselves or resist, if there were "sufficient force to intimidate them."[40]

Babemba had several successful campaigns against the French-African army to the degree that the Bamana of Bèlèdugu expected the French would fail when they faced Babemba in a campaign in late 1898. Thus, the Bamana of Bèlèdugu openly revolted against the authority of the commandant of the cercle. Joce Traore, the forty-one-year-old Military Chief of the Confederation of the Bamana Soldiers, preached to Bamana populations that the French intended to be their absolute masters.[41] It was only after the fall of Sikasso that the French could subdue the Bèlèdugu revolt and arrest the leaders, Joce Traore; Faleye Traore, his brother; and Samba

Jara, head of the Canton of Kumi. In September 1898 the three were imprisoned.[42]

Still other villages continued to express their animosity through various acts of resistance. For instance, when in March 1899 the commandant demanded tax in millet, "the quantities carried were absolutely pathetic." The village of Waro with 520 inhabitants sent merely 150 kilograms.[43]

By 1900 the Bamana were a "submissive race," according to another administrator, Bonnasses; only the villages of Jo and Jago, which had opposed a strong French column, exhibited any rebellious spirit.[44] Carbone also depicted the Bamana population as submissive in 1912, writing, "The Bamana of Gueniekalari are crude and dirty, but respectful of authority and very sympathetic."[45] Nevertheless, other reports gave different impressions. One administrator argued that the authority of the French was weak, and "recalcitrant and obstinate, the Bamana have no idea of social hierarchy."[46] Another report read, "The people of Baninko have still not completely accepted the state of things created by the French" and the "civilization" that the French attempted to impose.[47]

The populations often hid "facts" from the representatives of the French administration, especially when the agent was white. Moreover, it was difficult for the French administrators and representatives to persuade some village leaders to admit that a crime had been committed, and more difficult to force them to deliver the guilty party to the French. The Baninko area, in particular, continued to be a thorn in the French administration's side. For example, in 1907 the young people in the Bamana village of Degnekòrò (in Baninko) rebelled, "refusing to listen to notables who advised them to remained compliant."[48]

On May 8, 1915 the French received news of a revolt in the cantons southwest of the cercle of Gumbu. Some days later, news circulated among the African populations that the Bamana of Bèlèdugu had refused to furnish recruits as stipulated and had risen against French authority. After some Europeans arrived in Segu and confirmed the rumors, political agents were sent to all corners of the cercle, principally the cantons of the north. The administrator thought that the insurrections of Bèlèdugu and the Kagoro of Gumbu would have no repercussions in the central zone of the cercle of Segu. Almost two weeks later, however, the Resident of Baroueli arrested Namankoro Jan who revealed that a plot had taken place near the creek of Wolodo; three whites had been killed and a fourth had escaped. The leader of Nonko, Mamuru Jara, had warned the villages of the region that the escaped man should be captured and led to him, and any village failing to carry out that order would be torched. By May 29 the revolt had been crushed, and the rebels had submitted. Bernard, the administrator, downplayed the revolt, writing that he ignored it, and was later informed by a telegram that a column had put down the revolt.[49] But the revolt was more serious than he depicted, for 400 rebels assembled between Bojana and Sirakoro alone.[50]

Another form of resistance was to choose African leaders contrary to French approval. Even by 1916 the African populations insisted on leaders whom they themselves chose, following their own customs. Most of the cantons elected people as leaders despite the suppression of these individuals by the French. The elected leaders were all from old families which had long exercised power. One French administrator surmised, "The blacks hold firmly to their customs and institutions; they have respect for their leaders . . . . The blacks support the new leaders that we impose on them because we are stronger."[51] Moreover, African populations re-established pre-colonial territorial boundaries.[52]

Politically, African populations used several forms of resistance against the French administration. Where some leaders co-operated with the French to promote their own interest, others refuse to completely accept the yoke of French dominion. The range of resistance included refusal to pay tax, send men for military service, or work as porters for the French. As discussed, some took arms against the French. By World War I the French were still faced with administrative problems which would be reflected in their military draft system.

Schools

Once the French believed that they had subdued the populations in the Middle Niger, they embarked on an education policy to develop French influence and to propagate the French language.[53] However, French education efforts were meager during the early years of their administration. The Bamana were not easily influenced since few Bamana attended the schools set up by the French, and several Bamana leaders refused outright to send their sons to the French schools despite French demands.

A number of young students were placed under the direction of an African teacher in Segu, and these students were taught the French language at a school called the "School of the Sons of Chiefs." These children were, according to a French report, sons of African rulers. However, local historians argue that most of these students were not the sons of African leaders, but rather the sons of their slaves. The French sent letters to the "Chiefs of Cantons, ordering them to send fifty or sixty students to the school. Generally, these leaders sent slaves and sons of the poor."[54] When the French demanded that the rulers send their sons to French schools, the rulers of Kumi, Nanko and Massantola responded negatively. The French advised the African rulers that the only goal of the administration was to improve their status by instructing them, and, by choosing their sons; it was "a mark of favor and of distinction." The letter also stated that the children would return from the school each year for a two-month vacation. The French administrators believed that it was important to instruct the sons of African leaders who had showed "marked opposition" to French administration. Therefore, the inculcation of French ideas could spread among the population the principles of French civilization.[55]

Samba Jara, ruler of Massantola, still refused to send his son to the French school, proclaiming that "one does not give a child as a handful of peanuts."[56] But, after having learned that the son of the ruler of Kumi was going to the school in Kayes, and after talking with Joce Traore, he decided to permit his son to go to attend. The ruler of Nonko refused, even after a second summons. The School of the Sons of the Chiefs at Kayes was the oldest of the colony, founded by Gallieni in December 1886. The schools at Kita and Bafulabe were started in the same period. In 1890 Archinard closed all the schools because of financial problems except for the one at Kayes where the sons of the African rulers were placed, and the School of the (White) Fathers at Kita. In 1893 the school at Kita began to take on a greater importance.[57]

The commandant complained in 1903 that the students of the White Fathers were always on vacation. In addition, the inhabitants of Segu complained that the White Fathers stopped them from working in their fields on Sundays. The commandant promised to try his best to convince

the schoolmaster to be more tolerant on "the day of rest," especially during the period of the year when he recommended the Africans make use
of anytime to augment their cultivation.

In 1903 the School of the White Fathers in Segu had 110 to 120 day
students and about twenty boarding students. Some families, however,
stopped sending their children to the school because of the harsh treatment they received from the teachers. As a result, the administration
sought to make the White Fathers reform their program.[58]

Even by 1908, the program of French education among the local populations progressed slowly. In November 1908 fifty-one students of Segu
and Segukòrò were recruited to study at a primary school by a French
teacher.[59] The next month twenty-five students were added, and forty-six
adults as evening students.[60]

Ideology: Islamization of the Bamana during the Early Years of French Occupation

It is important to note that even when the Bamana converted to Islam,
it was a time-consuming process and that Islam failed to eradicate all
aspects of Bamana religion and religious culture. As so often happens, the
Bamana synthesized many aspects of their religion with Islam, adapting
Islam to fit their specific needs.[61] The 'Umarian regime had attempted to
force Islam upon the non-Muslim population, but with no success, for
many of the Bamana rituals remained intact. Many of these rituals and
customs were far more difficult to destroy than by simply eradicating the
"fetishes." The destruction of religious artifacts did little to destroy the
beliefs which were connected to them. In addition, these artifacts could
have easily been duplicated. It was easier to force some men to give up
some of their wives than to destroy the hidden elements of religious
beliefs. In many instances during the late nineteenth and early twentieth
centuries, Islam "did not seem to have profoundly modified the ancestral
custom"[62] of the Bamana. The Bamana masses still owned and purchased
amulets, talismans, and magic incantations although the elites in the Segu
region are reported to have displayed a certain skepticism of these customs.[63] In addition, many who had been forced to adopt Islam (as in the

southwest cantons of Karadugu, Seladugu, and Say-Sarro for instance) returned to the Bamana religion after the defeat of Ahmadu by the Bamana army and the French-African army.[64]

A report in 1897 claimed that non-Muslims were little susceptible to the precepts of the Qur'an. Another report in 1901 stated that only the Bamana remained un-Islamized although some of them had been converted.[65] These who were devoted to Islam were not "fanatics" because in the estimation of the French there were so few holy men (Marabouts and Almamys). By the closing years of the nineteenth century many who had been formerly converted by force no longer followed Islamic practices. Many Bamana appreciated that the French did not interfere in religious matters.[66] The very few Bamana who adhered to Islam followed the Tijani tariqa (the other sects that concerned the French were the Qadiriyya and Independents). The French, at least until 1920, believed that the Tijaniyya were the "enemy of the French in the Sudan."[67]

The two major means of Muslim proselytization were through the Islamic schools or by those who contacted the people through their travels in the region. Rarely did the Bamana send their children to Islamic schools.[68] Even some of those who sent their children to school remained unresponsive to the Islamic ones. Of course, some had converted before the arrival of the French. On the other hand, some of the Muslim population, according to Benoit, had ultimately begun to support the French presence. The marabouts of Segu, the qadi, and the influential people, all Tijanis, sent their children to the school of the White Fathers. "Not only did they support the Fathers, they held them in high esteem."[69]

In 1913 with little-organized propaganda the spread of Islam seemed to be halted. Perhaps that was due to the absence of very influential religious leaders. Some religious functionaries attempted to create a following, traveling in the cercle. For example, some marabouts arrived in the region to convert the Bamana in 1903, but the French were convinced that those who converted would, in a certain time, abandon Islam and return to their former religion. Only in the northern region, especially in the canton of Tuba, was Islam firmly established. However, the Bamana generally maintained their religion, and those among them who were introduced to the Qur'an and the propaganda of Islam "remained unaffected."[70] Not only were there few holy men, but few were well instructed.[71]

Every Islamic leader or potential leader was put under surveillance, and each French administrative political report included a section on the activities of these leaders, along with other information about Islam deemed important.[72] This was odd insofar as several reports stated that the spread of Islam among the non-Muslim populations was minimal. One administrator stated, however,

> If I judge by the archives, the Muslim question seems to have been considered in the cercle as negligible.... I think that it is necessary, on the contrary, to give great attention to this question. I was surprised, in addressing the Commandant of the Cercle of Bamako, noting that no service of intelligence existed, that the administration of the cercle lived in the most complete ignorance of what happens in the residences and at Bamako even.[73]

When teachers of the faith entered the state, including Suleyman Kamite and al-Hajj Buguni, the French kept them under surveillance, particularly the ones who seemed to be influential enough to convert the non-Muslims. For example, in 1916 administrative reports indicate the French put some marabouts under surveillance who were in the Bamana and Marka villages.[74] Earlier, a marabout, Musa Jirè, had been put in prison for fifteen days in September 14, 1907 for opening a Qur'anic school and building a small mosque at Songolo without authorization.[75] In 1909 Kassama Cisse, who claimed to be a marabout, collected alms among the Bamana. The French assumed that he was an imposter, who "exploited the public credulity."[76]

French reports regularly emphasized that large segments of the Bamana population adhered to their own religion. For example, of the 32,608 inhabitants in Banamba in 1914, 17,808 were non-Muslims, all Bamana. In addition, the 205 of the 345 Sòmònòw who were Muslims were recent converts.[77] In Baruele where the Markas and Bamana formed the major part of the population of the region, the majority of the Markas and the few Fulani were Muslims, but very few of Bamana practiced Islam. The report also stated, "True Muslims are rare," suggesting that some practices of those who professed to be Muslims were much like those of Batair.[78]

The results were similar in several areas. Between 1891 and 1904 conversion to Islam was slow. There were 57,117 Muslims versus 107,186 non-Muslims estimated living in Sinzani, Bèndugu and Segu. By 1904 there were reported 61,942 Muslims and 116,239 non-Muslims.[79] Furthermore, a census report of 1908 in Gwènka listed most of the Bamana as non-Muslims. Some Muslims, however, were in Korodimi, Nango and Sambela, but the group identity of these is imprecise in the records. A mosque was located in Cènabugu, but no indication was given if the Bamana attended it since some of the inhabitants were Muslim Markas.[80] In Kaminiandugu some Bamana Muslims lived in Konsania and Mururubugu. However, the greater part of the population practiced Batair and many of the Bamana had a Kònò in the house.[81] Two mosques existed in the area of the Baninko; one in Maba, a Marka village, and at Tongo, a Jula village. But even in those villages the practice of Islam was weak.[82] From 1903 to 1909 French colonial reports maintain that the Islamization process among the Bamana was negligible, as well as among other non-Muslim populations, and even the new converts conserved all their former customs.

By 1909 the Bamana of the southwest cantons (Karadugu, Seladugu and Say Sarro) in the cercle of Jenné remained non-Muslims. Yet some of the population of Seladugu had embraced Islam (through constant contact with the Markas) during the time of Ahmadu's reign. But they returned to their Bamana practices after the fall of Ahmadu. The cult of the *Gna* was the majority religion of the Bamana in the region.[83]

In addition, the Bamana conserved many of their religious practices (including the Kòmò), and continued to have confidence in their gris-gris. The Bamana of Kaminiandugu had in each village a Kòmò, made with resin and wax. Even the children had their special Kòmò.[84] In a census of the region, none of the Bamana in the sixty villages were listed as being Muslim.[85] Similar results were found in the census of 1912 where the Bamana population of the eleven villages in Gwènka practiced Bamana religion.[86] The same results existed for Baninko.[87] Islam, as a result, seemed to French observers to have made little impact.[88] The religious beliefs of the Bamana were so stable that the commandant suggested in 1905 that the Catholic Missions not start their work among the Muslims, but to focus on the Bamana non-Muslims instead who would be, in his opinion, more easily detached from their "gross superstitions which they began to abandon themselves."[89] According to Bamana oral sources, those who were abandoning the Bamana religion at this time were converting to Islam.

Bamana religious beliefs thrived even after the Bamana non-Muslim population began to convert, but now under the general umbrella of Islam. The Bamana synthesized various aspects of their religion with Islam. However, the Bamana concept of family continued to distinguish itself from Qur'anic precepts, and it was the family as an institution that was the "principal armature," that permitted Bamana religious institutions to survive. Proselytism was seriously hampered according to one adminis-trator, by the uncompromising, strict application of Qur'anic laws.[90] The strength of Bamana religion could be attested by the fact that of the four-teen chiefs of canton in 1917, only four were Muslims, and the non-Muslim population was still in the vast majority in the cercle. It is ironic, too, that outside of the European administrative centers, the Bamana reli-gion was virtually unchanged.[91] Because of this, neither of the French administrators, Rocache in 1913, nor Lasse in 1917, considered either Islam or Batair as dangerous in the cercle, and they were assured by the surveillance system which included Muslim police who were sent in the region to survey the situation. Lasse advised that the French administra-tion should not awaken fears or imaginary dangers which could transform the situation.

However modestly, Islam was, in fact, spreading, and this phenomenon worried the French administrators who were under strict instruction up to 1921 to be on the lookout for the conspiracies led by Muslim "fanatics." On the other hand, the Bamana religion produced little or no fear in the French. Perhaps, the fear was induced because Islam was seen as a uni-fying factor, an "always dangerous cohesion."[92] However, the Bamana religion served the same function for Bamana society; it too served and had served as a unifying factor. One French observer noted that the French knew little about the Bamana religion although "it solicits less our vigilance, it is not less a religion just as undying, if not more, than Islam."[93] At least this observer realized the vitality of the Batair, and that it was (and is) more than just a conglomerate of loosely-connected beliefs and practices, but a viable religion. The attitude of the French, guided by their prejudice against any religion which was "unorganized" (as well as any which came out of an African society), caused them to overlook the importance of the Bamana religion. Even with their inquiries, their descriptions of the religion were quite trite, merely discussing the most visible features of the religion instead of understanding these beliefs and practices with the more profound role the religion held in the lives of the Bamana people. Consequently, the Bamana were able to freely practice their religion.

Although some French sources strongly suggested that Islam was a minor factor in the Middle Niger among the Bamana, other records suggest that some advances had been made. During the 'Umarian period, the 'Umarians had built only two mosques. However, by 1913 several mosques had been built: twenty in the canton of Kèlèke, twenty-five in Kaminiandugu, twelve in Ntò, sixty-three in Gwènka, and twenty-one in Sinzani.[94]

The first four regions were predominantly populated by Bamana. The figures were reported by an African agent, and offered no detailed documentation, only an approximate number according to the report. The report, though, stressed the importance of Islamic religious buildings in comparison with the population of the cantons.

Population of Cantons		*Previous Number of Mosques*
Keleke	51,499	4
Kaminiandugu	32,822	8
Nto	19,544	6
Gueniekalari	35,483	17
Sansanding	18,154	10
Baninko	21,221[95]	

There were twenty-eight Islamic schools with 1508 students in 1900 in the cercle of Segu. Twenty-three of the instructors were followers of the Tijaniyya while nineteen followed the Qadiriyya. Followers of both taught at the schools in Barueli and Boaje.[96] The instruction in the schools, however, failed to considerably modify the character of those attending by undermining the Bamana religious institutions. Brévié explained that the nature of religious instruction that the non-Muslim Bamana received was inappropriate to transform their character.[97] The instruction, lasting five or six years, focused on memorization. After-

wards, the students learned to distinguish Arabic characters, but memorization was still important as students learned by heart the Qur'anic verses. Brévié assumed that the students learned the verses without understanding the meaning since the verses were not translated into the local
languages.

According to local historians, the Bamana masses began to convert to
Islam during the early colonial period. "When the whites arrived, the
Bamana saw that Islam was true. They left the Kòmò house, and the different practice of the Boli in order to adhere to Islam."[98] Why did a large
segment of the Bamana population begin to convert to Islam, a religion so
vehemently rejected for many years? Although of marginal interests within the scope of this work, there are elements of African conversion in this
period that had important social and political consequences.

The first important issue that local historians stress is that the
Islamization of the Bamana had nothing to do with the 'Umarians, nor did
it occur during the 'Umarian period. Few had converted before the arrival
of the 'Umarians. For instance, Kirango Ba Jara argues that the Muslim
Bamana among them had been Islamized before the arrival of the
'Umarians.[99] Rather, it was through the efforts of another marabout, Niaro
Karamòkò, during the colonial period that the main Bamana conversion
can be dated.

After circa 1895, several teachers taught the Qur'an in Segu, including
the students of Dilli and of Karamòkò Amadu. In addition, Baba Sosso
was one of the marabouts who was responsible for the conversion among
the Bamana.[100] But the leading figure was Niaro Karamòkò whom the
French deported to Côte d'Ivoire,[101] where he was confined to prison for
ten years. Karamòkò, a farmer, was instrumental in spreading Islam in the
Middle Niger not only to the Bamana, but to the Bozo as well. His students helped him farm in order to feed themselves. One version is that the
French arrested him because he had many followers and Fama Mademba
Sy told the French that Karamòkò was preparing for a jihad against the
French as had al-Hajj 'Umar. The French arrested him after he openly
declared that for anyone who looked at the French, their forty-days
prayers would never be granted, and anyone who approached a
Frenchman was a perverted kaffir. He added that he did not like the
French, nor those who worked for or with them, or acted like them. The

French did not allow such open declarations of hostility.[102] After the French released Karamòkò, he returned to Segu, and continued to teach the Qur'an. He was locally considered to be a saint and is reputed for his fearlessness. He was described as "one who gives because he fears only God and whose life is of his own sweat and says astonishing things that God reveals to him in dreams, and never depend on anyone except God the Almighty."[103]

If Islam made little impact during the early colonial period, then the influence of Christianity was virtually non-existent. There was a Catholic mission in Segu by 1904 with a staff of twenty Europeans. Of the fifty-eight children at the mission, seven were entrusted to the mission by the administration. The Sisters held thirty-two orphans, all girls, and the Fathers adopted four boys. The number of Christians in the area was minimal. The census of 1904 showed 143 Christians in the cercle, 127 in the city of Segu; however, it is unclear if these were Africans or Europeans, or both. There were few Muslims, and no Christians in the villages with large Bamana populations.[104] However, there were 103 Africans identified as Catholics in another report on the cercle for that year, but the specific identity of these were omitted.[105]

The Bamana created a state where their religion remained independent of their administration. Other groups were free to practice whatever religion they wished. Of course, Bamana socio-religious systems were crucial to Bamana communities, but the empire was based on commercial and political contracts. With the 'Umarians, Islam became an integral part of the socio-political system. This created problems for the 'Umarians since they were in a continual campaign to force Islam upon the non-Islamic populations. The French, on the other hand, operated between these two extremes. Christianity was not an essential and direct influence of the early colonial years as it had been for the 'Umarians. However, personal religious beliefs held by individuals affected their view of the Africans as well as their decision-making processes. Later, Christian missionaries, which one could argue formed an arm of the colonial state, would expand the role of their religion in the society.

Justice

During the early colonial period three judicial systems operated in Segu: the French (Napoleonic Code), the Islamic Code, and the Bamana Code (although Bamana litigants were required to appear before one of the other two). Each time a case was tried before a *qadi*, the Muslim judge continued to follow the *Arrissala*.[106] The Bamana very often avoided the influence of the Muslim Tribunal.[107] The French often sought the Muslims in Segu for information and judgments; however, the Tiam family, one of the Muslim families which had served as qadis prior to French occupation, completely refused to work with the French.[108]

One of the first colonial administrators placed in Segu, Charles Correnson, wrote an essay on the Bamana system of justice and how it was reflected in the customs of the populations.[109] He argued that there existed a great opposition between the Islamic precepts and the "ancestral customs" in Bamana society. Moreover, the syncretism of Islam and Batair was manifested in the judicial practice. Correnson asserted that the "fetish rites still had profound roots even among those who demanded Islamic statutes."[110] For example, many Bamana continued to take the "traditional religious" oath when testifying because this oath was fearsome and could lead to grave consequences for the faithless on the part of the Spirits. For the mass of the people, Correnson argued, the "fetish" had its own power. For the educated, this was not an idol, but only an image. For all, it was fearsome and its vengeance was implacable.[111]

Under Bamana custom old men, marabouts, notables or village heads were designated to render justice, handling all affairs. As a result, Archinard advised,

> The Commandant of Cercle should only judge in some very exceptional cases and more particularly when there will be cause not of particular interests, but interests of different villages or cantons or passing strangers. (As in other areas), there is cause, then, to study these customs in order to clarify its own religion and give to the Commandant of the Cercle the elements of appreciation which are necessary to them in the serious affairs or in the judgment on appeal.[112]

The various African customary legal systems were important to the judicial process under the colonial power. It was as late as April 1946 that a decree abolished, at least legally, the African penal law and placed all the inhabitants of the A.O.F. (French West Africa) under the jurisdiction of the French Code and French penal laws. But, prior to this time African law, or "customary law" as the French called it, was applicable to African "subjects."[113]

Robert Delavignette, a colonial administrator, explained:

"The administration of native customary law is a branch of native policy and of territorial administration.The tribunal is an observation post from which the administrative officer who presides over it may study the effects of his own administration and the reactions of the people he governs. The African world is revealed to him. Litigants in civil cases and those accused of crimes will make plain to him the character of the customs and social habits of the country."[114]

During the late nineteenth century, the French administrators judged cases with French concepts of "moral matters" which differed from local notions based on local customs or the Islamic Code. Those Bamana who were Muslims often "exploited" their double identity as Bamana and Muslim, and adhered to whichever set of rules which favored their cause. The prevailing judicial conditions were complex; "sometimes rendering a solution was very delicate."[115]

So many cases were argued before the French administrator that he was forced to use African leaders to assist in judicial matters. In addition, the Circulaire no. 5H6 (October 16, 1896) limited the rights of the commandants of the regions and of the cercles in judicial matters. The French created the Council of Notables to hold sessions. The Qadi's role as an agent of the French administration was to ensure that the judgments followed French directives. However, the authority of the Qadi was not accepted by all populations, especially the Bamana. This made it possible for certain local leaders to function as judges.[116]

The tribunal was composed of members whom the French believed presented all the possible guarantees of independence and impartiality for Muslims and non-Muslims. Nevertheless, the French asserted that

African leaders were often incapable of rendering justice, or were corrupt. As a result, the French administration attempted to eliminate the Chiefs of Cantons as judges, believing that the majority of them had neither influence nor authority.[117] The commandant felt that it was a waste of "precious time" to handle the many complaints put before him. Therefore, by 1896 the African populations "were free to choose between the village chief, the Chief of Canton, the Qadi, the Council of Notables or the Cercle to litigate their problems." The people most often consulted the Council of Notables. A Qadi, a functionary of the cercle, headed the council, but did not participate in the arguments. The French hoped to ensure consistency in judgments by placing a Qadi at the head of the council.[118]

By July 1897 the cases before the French authority in Segu had diminished and its relations with outlying villages were rarer. However, the Bamana continued to present matters before the French authority while other groups preferred to take other recourse.[119] The most frequent cases concerned successions, reclamations of captives (non-free), divorces and marriages. The commandant considered many of the matters to be trivial, but the French did consider cases involving the sale of arms, and problems between villages, especially villages of different populations, just as important.[120]

It was noted by one administrator in 1903 that the Bamana were not always satisfied with the judgment rendered at Segu, and preferred their "habitual magic" over holding to the solution given by the commandant of the cercle. For example, the Bamana refused sums which the commandant ruled that the village head of Fimana was to pay them. However, the report fails to include what measures the Bamana took to settle the issue.[121]

The previous commandant, Montquey, failed to explain why the Bamana or any others preferred to have the French commandant hear their cases. However, this commandant asserted that the Africans, including the Bamana, bypassed these intermediaries to voice their complaints because of the actions of these notables. Consequently, he dismissed the notables, claiming that they were pseudo-agents who were of little use to the administration. He replaced them with two tribunals, composed of ten members each; one to assist the Qadi, and the other to judge the Bamana.

Before appearing before the tribunal judges, the plaintiffs had to present their complaints to the commandant of the cercle who then issued a paper carrying a number which gave the plaintiff permission to have the case heard by the tribunal.[122]

In 1903 Seiba Jara (president), Simbara Dembele and Cèkura Kulibali headed the Bamana tribunal.[123] In 1903, for example, the Bamana tribunal heard cases involving physical aggression (mainly due to debts), questions of marriage, theft, succession, and murder. In 1904 both tribunals condemned eighteen persons to prison for corruption, breach of trust, theft and complicity of theft; fourteen for physical assault; seven for adultery and complicity of adultery; three for involuntary homicide; and two for assassination.[124]

The decree of November 10, 1903 instituted the village tribunals which recognized and accepted the principles of the Bamana customs. The village political leaders, or, more often, the notables delivered judgments. The sentences rendered were not binding since the parties could settle their differences before the Provincial Tribunal. This is the same practice that had continued throughout the 'Umarian period.[125] The Bamana made up the bulk of the cases before the "Native Tribunal," mainly concerning adultery, debt, and disagreements stemming from inheritance.[126] The French actually created problems for themselves in their attempt to impose their system, for the Bamana took up more time of the local authorities than other groups, causing one administrator to generalize that "the Bamana yield very willingly before a superior power which assures them the peaceful use of his property, but refuses to be subjected to all other constraints."[127]

The French administrators seemed surprised that the Bamana were "very attached to their customs and traditions," implying an administrative assumption that the Bamana would immediately relinquish their customs for a system which was (in the eyes of the French) superior. The village heads continued to judge minor disputes although important issues were submitted to the Commandant of the Cercle.[128] Naturally, the French assumed that the tribunal of the cercle was superior to the provincial tribunals, and the major function of the Tribunal of the Cercle was to correct the errors of the Provincial Tribunals in all matters, especially criminal cases. The "Fama" of Segu was equally reluctant to act in cases where death and mutilation could be applied.

The African tribunals met a "real need of the populations."[129] These tribunals replaced the justice system under the leaders of former times whom the French characterized as "unsound and partial," or influenced by the family and fortune of the litigants. Apparently, the French had little confidence in the legal system headed by elders.

The fact that the French administration found it necessary to institute a new judicial system which would facilitate the needs and the demands of the Bamana indicates how instrumental the Bamana were in affecting the decision-making process. Certain aspects of the former judicial system continued to be very important, and Bamana customary laws were often used to decide cases even in colonial tribunals. For example, Bamana custom was followed to solve a dispute between the family of a deceased man over the latter's son in 1909.[130] Nevertheless, by 1908 the French administrator reported that the Bamana generally used and had come to accept the judgments of the provincial tribunal.[131]

Although the Tribunal of the Cercle was considered superior

it had difficulty settling problems between villages, particularly when land was involved. Normally, the customary law relating to land tenure recognized above all the rights of the first occupants. However, the French felt that "vague notions" (of land occupancy) complicated matters.[132] For example, for many years the Bamana of Segu granted the Sòmònò permission to cultivate certain plots. When the original owners wanted to retake the land, the Sòmònò refused, alleging that for many years, they had cultivated the soil; therefore, they had rights to the land. Although the issue was argued before the Tribunal of the Cercle, the French concluded that the particulars in the issue should be put before the village leaders because only they were well-versed in matters of land rights. In this instance neither tribunal was adequate in resolving the issue, and the French were forced to seek the advice of the very people whom they accused of being partial and inconsistent.

On the other hand, some property issues were resolved. For instance, the people of Digani and those of Kala had a property dispute settled before the tribunal in 1912.[133] The French also found that among the Bamana, questions of family and of property and the transmission of goods were solved according to Bamana customary law, "rules to which they are very attached and which are very different from the Islamic precepts."[134]

The colonial justice system was based on the race, group identity and religion of those being judged; different rules existed for different populations. The Commandant of the Cercle of Kayes judged the cases involving a European or an African against a European. The commandant of the cercle was the chief of the jury in cases of a European against an African, particularly if the crime carried the death penalty. In cases involving an African against an African, the village leaders or provincial head rendered justice. If the village leader was recognized as a Qadi, he was expected to have all thye necessary information, and to consult its usage and laws of the country and the customs of the Africans.

Many Africans preferred to settle their own problems. The people of Baninko, for instance, preferred to settle their quarrels among themselves without the intervention of French judicial authority. If a problem arose between different villages, the population of these villages "armed themselves with bows and arrows."[135] According to one Bamana historian, the tribunal system did little for the Bamana. As a result, if the problems between the Bamana could not be solved locally, they finally presented the problems directly to the French as a last recourse.[136]

Colonial Service

One of the most, if not the most, important spheres for employment with the French was in the military. The French needed soldiers, porters, guides, interpreters, and servants during the years of conquest. This need continued during the colonial era. Not only were African soldiers pertinent to the conquest of the Western Sudan, they were also important for the subsequent wars fought by the French, in and outside of Africa.

The French military system had sought young African men from various groups to fight in their army and conquer the Western Sudan. These professional soldiers sold their services to the French. Just as the French argued that many soldiers were not tied to any ideology of the Bamana or of Ahmadu, likewise, most of these soldiers, particularly those from the region of Segu, had no allegiance to the French cause. They offered their services in exchange for pay, or more often, the booty to be gained after the defeat of the enemy. However, the French changed the rules of military service as soon as the wars of conquest had ceased, and in 1914, the French found it necessary to conscript young men for military duties. This involved services as porters, and interpreters, as well as soldiers, and simple laborers.

The French needed soldiers for various tasks prior to the commencement of World War I. Besides quelling revolts, these soldiers were expected to build forts, and perform other labors. Consequently, many young men of Segu and the neighboring villages left the Cercle of Segu to take refuge in developing towns, especially Kulikoro and Bamako to avoid military conscription. They hoped to hide within in the larger population centers, and thereby created a "floating population."[137]

Although the French customarily had a very low opinion of the Bamana in many aspects, the excellent reputation of the Bamana soldier continued to thrive in the colonial army. Although no statistics were kept on regional or other specific origins of recruits, Marceau claimed that more than two-thirds of the tirailleurs from the Niger region were Bamana.[138] Bamana soldiers were singled out for their military qualities, making "good average soldiers, with an average of all good qualities and furnished excellent grades."[139] According to one French report, the Bamana was "a brave warrior" with "indomitable pride and ferocious resistance."[140] However, even these accolades were accompanied by insults. For example, Hippolyte-Victor Marceau, a captain in the French army, considered the Bamana soldier "an uncouth fellow" who possessed "all the strong warrior's virtues," but who did not, "unfortunately, show a keen intelligence."[141] Such racist stereotypes were repeated by other officers, and long prevailed. However, Echenberg argues that because of their reputation as excellent soldiers, the Bamana (and Mossi) gained opportunities to move up in the rank of noncommissioned offices.[142]

African soldiers saw another major change during World War I— the draft. Previously, young men (except captives) chose the military as a profession. Members of the Tònjòn were willing members who joined by choice. Even the Bamana men who fought with the 'Umarians often chose to do so, selling their military skills. During the French move into the Sudan, the Bamana and other African soldiers could again market their professional skills. With the order of general mobilization of August 1, 1914, the situation changed dramatically.

The mobile commission began its operation on October 30, 1915 and engaged 27 young men for the war. The French administrator expected to get 200 to 250 men from Sinzani and Baninko. Bernard thought that Africans would have viewed the military recruitment favorably, but, many Africans felt differently. Bernard complained that the populations of the cercle manifested no enthusiasm for the new recruitment despite "the numerous advantages granted to the enlisted men and to their families." He assumed that it was due to the lack of information available to the recruits about the benefits of retirement.[143]

The administrators continually complained about the lack of enthusiasm regarding service among the populations. Although the people generally yielded to recruitment, they demonstrated discontentment. It became evident that most of the families preferred to safeguard their children for work in the fields. Casse asserted that the French occupation was responsible for this in that it created a "stabilization of the family" which continued to grow.[144]

Because of the recruitment, it was believed that an entente existed between the Muslims and non-Muslims.[145] The populations considered the recruitment as a new tax that the French imposed on them, exemplified by the French demand that provinces which had not given any tirailleurs the previous year furnish contingents in 1916.[146]

The French assumed that the pay was significant enough to attract young men and to obtain the co-operation of the families which were expected to recognize the benefits. However, families apparently saw greater benefit in maintaining their young within the agricultural sector than to lose them to the military. Myron Echenberg, who has done extensive research on French military recruitment in the Sudan, argues that the well-born families often wanted at least one of their sons to serve in the army.[147] Of course, the military remained one of the institutions whereby an individual could advance himself. Even Echenberg agrees that being a soldier in the French army lacked the same attraction for African soldiers as during pre-colonial times.[148]

In 1919 the French enacted a conscription law which guaranteed a standing army during peacetime; the law affected men who were twenty years old. Echenberg explains that prior to the enactment of the conscription law, the men of the *deuxième contingent*, second portion, could return to their villages. However, after the enactment of the law, they were assigned to public and private works. Particularly in the Sudan (today's Mali), the French designed the labor brigades to get "less-than-free" labor for public works projects.[149]

Often, one Bamana response to forced military duty was migration. Migration became a prevalent form of resistance against the French during World War I.[150] The French administration attempted to explain the high rates of absenteeism by arguing that many of the men were seasonal migrants, Jula traders or Fula herdsmen seeking work elsewhere during the time when the annual military levy was taken. However, Echenberg writes that although there is "a grain of truth" in the statements, they misrepresent the administrators' efforts to "explain away damaging evidence of their misrule." The seasonal migrants were normally away from home from May to October, and the conscription was deliberately timed from January to April before the migration season began.[151]

This is yet another indication that African societies had the will and power to circumvent the rules of the French administration. And not only did the family and/or the village guard their youths; the private sector and public officials often refused to turn a valuable employee over to the army.[152]

Language

One of the major indication of Bamana presence and influence in the Middle Niger even during the period of French colonization was the widespread use of the Bamana language. From the time that the Bamana effectively spread their political hegemony over the Middle Niger region, the Bamana language was the most profound Bamana cultural element diffused. As discussed in chapter one, other cultural elements were less likely to be adopted by other groups due to the manner in which the Bamana controlled their empire. Unlike the 'Umarian and French regimes which sought to forcibly push certain cultural aspects on other populations, the Bamana language was disseminated by contact.

Jean-Loup Amselle connects the "invention of the ethnic" group with the codification of the Bamana language in the form of a dictionary, collection of proverbs, tales and legends, and the creation of a press in Bamana, all tied to a functional alphabetization. More recently, Amselle also argues that because of radio and television, the Bamana language has become, in some sort, the second official language of Mali.[153]

This argument is problematic, considering the few people with access to radio and television, not to mention that when the Bamana language became the "second official language," neither radio, nor television existed. Furthermore, alphabetizing the Bamana language has done little to promote the language since courses are taught in French in most schools, and most speakers of Bamana do not read Bamana.[154]

If Bamana can be regarded as an "official language" of Mali, this status was achieved before the French language was regarded as such. As shall be argued, colonialism promoted the propagation of the Bamana language only in order to facilitate French administration.

French archival records give a strong indication of the dissemination of the Bamana language during the pre-colonial period. For example, it was noted in 1896 that the Sòmònò spoke "an idiom very close to Bamana," and that many of the "Bobo" also spoke Bamana.[155] Another report indicates that in Jenné, Bamana was the most widespread language. It was well known even in the north region because the Famas of Segu had formerly marched to Timbuktu.[156] The Bamana soldiers carried the language to corners of the state when they were stationed in those areas.

The proliferation of the Bamana language can also be attested by the counting system. One report explains:

> A proof of the vitality of the Bamana dialect rests in the persistence of acclimatization of the numeration in usage almost everywhere despite a certain difficulty originating from the value of a hundred fixed at eighty. In all the neighboring markets a hundred is expressed in Bamana as 800 cowries (640 francs français).[157]

Outside of the heart of Segu, Bamana was spoken in the cantons of Derray, Femay, Nyansamary, Teladugu, Sarro, Say and Karadugu. It was reported that in Sarro and Seladugu, the Fulas from Segu "had forgotten totally their language, and spoke Bamana."[158] In addition, the Fula of

Kamina, and the Markas of Gwènka spoke Bamana.[159]

In one French observer's estimation the Bamana language appeared to be one which adapted slowly and little to outside influences. "The Bamana people wanted to conserve the independence of their race and the purity of their language."[160]

Another major reason for the spread of the Bamana language was that it was the language of trade. The Jula traders spoke a language which became identified with the traders and called Jula. Nevertheless, Bamana and Jula are virtually the same language. Yaya Amadou Kulibali argues that "Bamana became one of the great languages of communication in West Africa." Utilized by the Julas, the language was propagated as far as Côte d'Ivoire and Burkina Faso.[161]

The Bamana language was so widely spoken by the time the French set up their administration, that some of the workers for the French were required to learn Bamana in an effort to enable them to implement their objectives in the Niger region. Even in the attempts to have the local populations learn French, it was important for the instructors to learn Bamana.

Bamana was even used in the Catholic Mission girls' school in Segu. By 1902 the school of Segu was teaching French, which was obligatory during all the repertoires except on Thursdays and Sundays. Marie Ursule, the administrator of the school, wrote to the regional administrator, "Our interns are learning Bamana; we do not teach them French. And we have obtained the result that many of our girls know to read in the Bamana books."[162]

Use of the Bamana language expanded under the French administration even though the French language was promoted. For example, the Bamana came to dominate the ranks and noncommissioned grades in the colonial army, and "the Bamana language became, alongside the 'petit-negre' French that the military insisted upon, the colonial army's vernacular language."[163] In fact, General Duboc explains that it was rare that the tirailleurs knew enough French to understand military orders.[164]

The Bamana influence in the early colonial administration was apparent in many areas. The African populations were key in determining many of the decisions the French administrators compelled to make. Although the colonial administrators in Paris had an agenda, the administrators in the field were forced to create and modify policies based on the responses of the local population. The Bamana, in particular, influenced local administrations through their various responses. Outside of Segu, the villagers attempted to live as much as possible on a course shaped by their own will. In addition, the Bamana populations began to slowly adapt to Islam although the French administration clearly targeted them to be converted to Christianity. They attempted to take advantage of the French judicial system when it was in their own interests while maintaining vestiges of the Bamana legal system. They attempted to circumvent the French administrators' education policies by refusing to send their sons to the French schools. Culturally, the Bamana culture was still influential. The Bamana language was already widely spoken in the Middle Niger Valley, and became an important language in the French colonial regime, especially in the military, to the dismay of the French. Generally, the lives of common folk seem to have been less affected than that of the upper class. The people continued to earn a living. Commerce, agriculture and fishing continued to flourish despite the vicissitudes of political life, and wars.[165] "The people could devote themselves to their daily preoccupations."[166]

Government building constructed by the French in Segu.
The Maksun Collection.

A weaver working in Segu in 1993 is using methods very similar
to that used in the 19th century.
The Maksun Collection.

CHAPTER 8

CONCLUSION

In conclusion, I will return to three major issues that are informed by this study. First, my Bamana informers often present their assessment of the Bamana view of the 'Umarian and French occupations by a method of comparison and contrast. Second, it is important to discuss the Bamana as an "ethnic" group. The problems of identity are discussed in terms of the meaning of the name *Bamana* the notion of space, and how social scientists have approached the issue. The third is tied to the first in a comparison of African and European rule, and how the vocabulary employed in the historiography of political hegemony suggests differences between African and European rules when, in fact, many similarities also exist.

Some Bamana Views of Foreign Occupation

How are the alien occupations and foreign administrations recorded in the oral historiography of the Bamana? The answer to this question as it relates to the French administration is far more complex than the oral accounts of the 'Umarian occupation for two reasons. One, the French regime was more devastating to the Bamana state, and lasted longer than 'Umarian rule. Two, because of the length of French rule, it is difficult to isolate the influence of the early colonial period from the entire colonial experience. Furthermore, when family historians and professional oral historians answer this question, they generally telescope both the French and 'Umarian regimes.

One of the major themes in oral accounts of the alien regimes in the Middle Niger is that of compensation for obligatory work. The difference between the 'Umarian and French occupation was that the French paid in some manner for work performed for them. Although the French forced all of the various populations to work for them, they did actually render payment. (Some were forced to work on the barges of Kulikoro to Gao; others were forced to cut wood for use on steamboats).

The 'Umarian soldiers took advantage of their position to "commit excess."[1] During the 'Umarian period, everyone suffered. "No one except them owned anything. And, the 'Umarians forcefully applied their own laws." However, unlike the French, the 'Umarians recognized no difference between the various populations. "For them, all were *kaffirs*, and they took much of the property of the *kaffirs*."[2] Daou adds that the 'Umarians mistreated the Bamana because the Bamana refused to convert to Islam.[3]

Tierno Sako, on the other hand, argues that when the French occupied the country, it was the blacks who were given the majority of the work to do, but the blacks never had command.[4]

Ibrahima Traore agrees with Sako about the forced labor for the French regime. He maintains that it was virtually slavery. The fact that the French paid a salary mattered little in his estimation because the money paid was almost nothing, but the work was hard.[5]

As seen in chapters three and seven, the tax issue was very important under both foreign regimes. In reality, the French changed nothing in the system since the habit of paying tax was already in place. They only continued the practice as others in power had done, but there was one difference: the tax which the French imposed was much higher.[6]

In addition, the French did not change the political units which existed in the pre-'Umarian period, but only installed political offices atop that structure, the *kafotigi* (chief of canton) and the *jamanatigi* (provincial chief). In addition, the French had some military men in the city of Segu, and each time they had a need to collect tax, recruit men for the military, or recruit work crews, they sent these soldiers to the villages and instructed the provincial or canton heads to send that which was needed.[7]

In was the installation of many of these functionaries which created additional problems for the Bamana and others in the Middle Niger. As we have seen in the French archival reports, the Bamana often complained because these functionaries were selected by the French, and not by the people; a similar complaint was made against the 'Umarians. According to oral testimony, some of these functionaries made life very difficult for the people. One characterizes the 'chiefs of cantons' as "wicked;" therefore, many of the guards and soldiers whom they commanded were also wicked. For instance, when the Africans who worked on the public work crews for the French fell ill, the guards and the adjoints would shove them or throw water on them and force them to continue working. As a result, some people who worked on the barges died, driven by the African guards working for the whites.[8]

Identity: A Question for Whom?

Doing a study on the Bamana (or any specific population) presents a potentially problem for the researcher: that of the group's self-definition in contrast to the social scientists' definition. Jean Amselle, for example, is one of the leading scholars to raise this question about the Bamana. He argues that Bamana as an "ethnic" identity was created by French colonialism.[9] Bazin adds to this his view that the various statements about the Bamana are not simply an opinion or belief, but a structure of scholarly discourse.[10]

What are the rules and methods of identity?[11] Why are these rules played out differently in relation to colonized groups, particularly Africans? These are also important questions, just as important as the question: Who are the Bamana?

First, it might be helpful to discuss the term *ethnic*. Although the term has become popular in social science literature, there are still grounds to reject it. Much of the same argument for not using the term *tribe* can be applied against the usage of the term *ethnic*. Coquery-Vidrovitch argues, that the world *ethnic* originally signified *pagan*. in opposition to Christian, in the early nineteenth century, describing the mores and language of exotic people who were supposed to be of a different nature of that of the civilized society, the culture of the Judeo-Christian West.[12]

Although meaning and usage of any term can change over time and/or by its use by a group, the term still carries the cultural baggage today as it did when the term was first used. But to a person who calls him/herself a Bamana, is this debate important? Do they see themselves as an *ethnic group*?[13]

Like so many other facets of the literature on African people, this is a debate carried on by scholars in the West.[14] The Bamana people have had no voice on the issue. As C. Tsehloane Keto states:

> African reality represents the long term effects of a system of deci-sion-making about culture, economies and politics, to name a few areas, in the hands of people based outside the continent itself from the colonial and neo-colonial contexts.[15]

One problem with the debate is that social scientists still cling to the notion that the experience born of contact with the West is an all-power-ful one.[16] As a result, the effects of "colonialism" are often exaggerated. Simultaneously, the so-called "traditional Africa" is often presented as being static. Often, an African society is seen in this dichotomy with cer-tain segments remaining completely unchanged and others being totally modified.[17] The 'modernization' of Africa through European colonialism is one which bridged two or more cultures. Another factor in this equa-tion is that Africans learned from other Africans as has been shown with the spread of the Bamana language. As researchers focus on the degree to which Africa has been affected by European and American cultures, many overlook what one African group has learned from another. In addition, researchers stress the effects of urbanization on the individual's sensibil-ity while often ignoring how aspects developed in village life affects the city. Cultural and material elements from the villages also enter urban domains.

It seems clear that a Bamana group and a Bamana identity existed before French colonialism, and that the French view of this identity was largely shaped by their experience in the Middle Niger although they did systematically and narrowly define groups based on their findings. The French did not create the name *Bamana* even though the French trans-formed it to *Bambara* the spelling one most often sees in the literature.

The issue of the origins of usage of *Bamana* stems from several factors. First, it should be noted that the source of the name "Bamana" is unknown. Researchers have developed theories such as Person's suggestion that perhaps it was the Markas who used the term to contemptuously signify "those who refused Islam."[18] It has been suggested that *Bamana* became synonymous with *pagan* or *kaffir* terms used by Christians and Muslims to describe the "other" in cultural and religious terms. Yet the name is also accepted as being a Bamana word. Therefore, the meanings have been periodically applied by outsiders, based on their religious and political agendas. If the meaning of *rrefuse* is used in translating *ban*, then it possibly follows that the Bamana have always been identified as a people who have refused something, i.e. political overlordship, Islam, Christianity, as these intrusions entered Bamana society. Perhaps it was the refusal of something else which caused them to migrate to Segu and Kaarta in the first place. It should be noted that the French did not systematically refer to all non-Muslims as Bamana, but as *fetishists*.

I also question the translation of the term. The translation, "those who refuse God," is convenient since *ban* means to refuse, and *ma* means God. However, these words have other meanings. For example, *ban* also carries the meaning "to finish." Even if the popular translation is accepted, it is in itself problematic. If *ma* means Supreme God, then the Bamana had a belief in a supreme God as represented in their language. They did not refuse their God, they just refused the "God" under the context of an outside religion.

A second possible factor determining Bamana identity is that of space. Europeans had a difficult time understanding "landownership" in the African context, hampered by their own limited legal and cultural concepts of landownership. I think the problem lies in the concept of "nations" and "nationalities." Perhaps this idea has been argued because of the absence of maps in pre-colonial West Africa, and the assertion that pre-colonial Africans had no concept of "nations;" therefore, no identity akin to "nationality" could emerge. However, I argue that a "nation" is just another form of space, of boundary, and pre-colonial Africans did have concepts of boundaries.[19] Even the French were able to draw maps of supposedly boundary-less peoples after completing their investigations. If the concept of boundaries had not existed, early European maps of pre-colonial states would not have been possible. In addition, many wars were fought over land occupation. Also, to understand the African ties to the land shows clearly that the concepts of space and boundaries were crucial, not only to identity, but also to land rights of the group. Jean Gallais argues that each "ethnic" group distinguished itself by its organization of space. On the village level there is a precise geographic space. It is on this level that institutional, religious and economic life is developed. One thus learns individual and familial rights and their limitations.[20] Roberts argues:

> Despite their small size and the restricted development of effective state institutions, these were states. They had more or less defined boundaries, more or less paramount control within those boundaries, and greater or lesser legitimacy in imposing their decision on the populations residing there.[21]

Frederick Barth adds:

> It is clear that boundaries persist despite a flow of personnel across them. In other words, categorical ethnic distinctions do not depend on an absence of mobility, contact and information, but do entail social processes of exclusion and incorporation whereby discrete categories are maintained despite changing participation and membership in the course of individual life histories.[22]

Jomo Kenyatta explains how (in Gikuyu society) the family circle, the village, and secret societies are an educational system for a child. He argues that the individual character is formed within the family circle and then within the local group, and within the whole organization through a course of initiation ceremonies.[23]

A person born into a family was automatically a part of the group. However, the group could be enlarged by other means just as is the case with the "modern nations." Each group had rules by which a stranger could become a member. That stranger was expected to follow all the social customs of the group as well as share its responsibilities. In addition, a group was enlarged by captives, marriages, etc. Assimilation and adaptation were fundamental in African societies before the arrival of Europeans. Gallais refers to adaptation (due to colonialism) as "ethnic mutation," and is signified by abandoning of techniques in the of exploitation of nature, or conversion in religion, or urbanization. But, he explains, even with this "mutation," the basic elements are still vibrant. For example, even after urbanization, Africans maintained strong ties with their villages.[24]

One of the original questions we have posed was: What are the rules of identity? The Bamana could be identified in pre-colonial times in terms of language, religion, customs, historic traditions, and space. Each of these elements helped to create a cohesion despite migrations and the introduction of other populations. Person argues that the Bamana identity has survived despite colonialism, not because of it, since the French wanted to replace their culture and their identity with French civilization. Nevertheless, their community values continued to be vibrant. "The collective identity, fruit of a secular work of self-creation, has not been in this case, broken by ethnocide."[25] Gallais adds, "It is evident that there would not be any Bamana if the group does not consider themselves as Bamana."[26]

The Bamana and other groups had no difficulty in distinguishing themselves from other groups. It was not necessary for the French administrators to define their parameters. What is generally forgotten in the so-called "French construction of an ethnicity" is that much of the formation was based on information acquired through inquiry by the French in the field. And the local people told the French only what they wanted them to know. As Bazin asserts, it is difficult for an outsider to decide who is and who is not a Bamana.[27]

As a result, the determination of who is Bamana must be left to the people themselves. Keto argues:

> The Africa-centered paradigm is the original paradigm which Africans used to create knowledge about themselves for themselves and about the physical and social milieu in which they found themselves.[28]

I would recommend that a Bamana-centric approach be taken to discuss the issue of Bamana-ness, but not within the context of Western scholarly discourse Western constructs. Thandika Mkandawire argues that social scientists participate in "faddish theorizing" and "ephemeral debates" which are external to the African voice or "due consideration of the historical specificities of the African condition."[29]

A Re-examination of Political Hegemony

The Bamana rule could be described as "indirect rule" if one accepts the description of that terminology in colonial historiography. Amselle uses it to describe the relationship between Segu and Jitumu.[30] Roland Oliver and Brian Fagan argue that the usual method of state development in Africa was to "leave the conquered units intact, taking tribute and hostages, but otherwise simply adding a new tier of authority, making an empire out of subordinate states."[31] Initially, the Bamana Tònjòn forced local free villages to pay tribute. Eventually the sphere of influence would include smaller polities and states. Masina was exemplary of a smaller state that paid tribute to a larger one, but seized the opportunity to rebel against the major state when the latter showed signs of weakness and/or an internal element created a level of consciousness to produce a successful revolution.

Other smaller polities on the periphery were far more difficult to control due to distance. As a result, these units paid tribute and recognized the power of the Fama. Furthermore, the Fama did not require all smaller polities or other populations to supply young men to the professional army. Generally, smaller polities remained intact so that they could continue their local institutions. The Bamana did not impose their religion or culture on other populations (that is not to say that cultural exchanges did not occur), but provided security and cohesion so that the economy could flourish. For 148 years, the Bamana were able to control the state through a system of contracts with other populations in the region.

Unlike the Bamana, the 'Umarians attempted to force their religion upon the non-Islamic populations, with varying success and failure. But, outside of the nucleus, the 'Umarian control was precarious, and in certain provinces it was non-existent. The 'Umarians were unable to develop a theocratic state. Nonetheless, they attempted to use direct control and to force a cultural ideology (Islam) on populations which followed other religious beliefs, and impose a particular Islamic theology over other

Islamic populations with differing ones.

The French attempted to use what scholars have called both "direct" and "indirect" rule. After the Bamana removed the 'Umarians, the French attempted to impose themselves atop an administration which existed in the Bamana era. However, this "indirect" model was unsuccessful because the French, ultimately, wanted to have direct influences in certain spheres. Using more direct methods, the French attempted to impose their religion and culture as the 'Umarians had. In essence, the French administration on the ground was indirect although colonial policies were described as being "direct."

The three occupations had the same main objective: to control the flourishing commerce of the Middle Niger Valley. Even though the objective was the same, the description of their rules have been presented differently in the historiography of political hegemony. The French regime has been historically described as "imperialism." Yet, the African regimes have been described differently. It is ironic that African polities have been called "empires," but rarely have their rules been labeled "imperial. " However, Robin Law has written a work on the Oyo Empire and has referred to the regime as one of imperialism and colonialism. Law describes the varying degrees and different ways the Oyo controlled the empire. However, Law fails to explain why this terminology was used.[32]

The application of different terminology suggests a political difference between an African regime over African populations and that of a European regime over African populations[33] despite the many similarities. It is ironic that certain terminologies have been applied to African regimes while others are not. For instance, *king, queen, empire, state* have been used to describe pre-colonial African regimes although words exist in the local languages to describe these elements. Yet "imperialism" has not generally been applied. This suggest that historically, "imperialism" has been seen as a European, not a universal phenomenon. Does this suggest that non-Europeans are not capable of imperialistic endeavors? Or, does it mean that political hegemony since the fifteenth century is viewed in terms of race (and culture), specifically whites over non-whites?

An important question is whether Africans see a difference between foreign regimes. The case of the Bamana demonstrates that a people will fight any foreign regime to maintain its independence. The Bamana conquered other groups and asserted their rule over the Middle Niger, and fought the 'Umarians and the French to maintain political sovereignty. Alliances were made based on the political needs of the Bamana at a given point. As a result, alliances were made between groups regardless of color, religion, or occupation. Instead, the Bamana made or broke alliances based on strategies to promote their political agenda. African populations did not accept the rule of other African groups based on a glorious notion of African rule which exists in some American Afrocentric belie; nor, were empires created by a brutal savagery of Eurocentric thought. Either the group fought any intruding regime, like the Bamana, or they accepted a regime which permitted them to prosper in their normal occupations, like the Sòmònò or the Markas. But even the latter protected their economic interests when a regime encroached upon their livelihood. Empires were created by conquests, and the Bamana, 'Umarians, and French were able to occupy Segu because of a superior army and/or superior weaponry. While some of the Middle Niger welcomed the rule of any one of the three, others opposed any which threatened certain protective freedoms.

For more than a thousand years, the Western Sudan had been the scene of migrations, merging of peoples, political surgings and conflicts.[34] The Bamana emerged as a power at a time when the surrounding populations were being Islamized. In addition, they created a powerful polity at a time when other major polities were Islamic, or Islam was credited as being the force behind the stability and growth of the state. The Bamana, however, used other institutions to achieve cohesion.

As stated earlier, the goal of each of the occupations was to control the commerce in the Middle Niger. However, it was the 'Umarians and French who attempted to justify their expansions with carefully written treatises. The 'Umarians fought in the name of religious reform, and the French did so under another "civilizing" mission. Nevertheless, the Bamana presence was a constant factor in the political, social and economic activities in the Middle Niger. The Bamana serve as an example of an oppressed population who used any and all means to enhance their individual or group agenda within available latitudes.

APPENDIX A

CHRONOLOGY[1]

1559	Bamana presence in the region of Jenné is noted
1600	Bamana mercernaries fight with Prince of Masina against the Moroccans
1645	Bamana of Segu fight Marka leaders Bamana of Chibla destroyed the town and migrated to Sarro
1650	The Bamana Kulibali family migrated to Segu under Kalajan Kulibali.
c. 1689	Bitòn Kulubali came from Bèndugu to settle in Segu
1712	The Bamana Fanga emerge in Segu
1755	Bitòn Kulubali died
1757-1765	Three Tòn leaders ruled Segu
1766	Ngolo Jara comes to power
1782-1808	The Bamana Fanga reached its zenith (rule of Mònzòn)
c. 1839	Bamana detained 'Umar in Segu
1855	Bamana of Segu aided the Bamana of Kaarta against 'Umar

1860-1890   Bamana waged war against the 'Umarians

1860   Bamana faced 'Umarians at Watala 'Umar entered
        Sinzani

1861   'Umar marched on Segu Ali Jara takes refuge in Masina
        Kènyè Mari assumed the leadership of the Bamana
        army

1863-1889   Karamòkò Jara reigned as Fama

1863   Bamana army twice defeated 'Umarians at Sinzani

1864   Mari Jara attacked Dugassu

1868-1870   Bamana army defeated by Ahmadu

1890   The Bamana army chase Madani from Segu to Nioro
        Mari Jara returned to Segu

1891-1892   The Bamana waged war against the French

1891   The Battle at Mael (January 1) The French massacre
        Mari Jara and 23 Bamana leaders

1892   The Bamana army face the French at Garo The Bamana
        of Miniankala revolted and killed the governor of
        Baninko The Bamana formed an alliance with Ahmadu
        who had already allied himself with Samori and Cèba

APPENDIX B

BAMANA FAMAW

Dyara\Sauvageot	*1D55-2*	
Biton Kulubali	Biton	1685-1725
Ndyékoro	Dekoro	1725-1744
Bakari	Bakary	1744-1744
Kanoubanyouman	Tomassa	1744-1747
Ton-massa	Kegneba Noums	1747-1750
Kafadyougou	Kafa-Diougou	1750-1753
Ngolo Dyara	Ngolo	1753-1790
Monzon	Mienankoro	
Da	did not reign	1790-1808
Tyéfolo	Tiefolo	1827-1839
Bén de Kirango	Nienem	1839-1841
Démba de Massala	Kecango-Bin	1841-1849
Béma de Nalo	Malinkouma	1849-1851
Mari de Torokoro	Massali Demba	1851-1854
Ali de Wéta	Torocoro Mari	1854-1859
Mari de Kényé	Ali	1859-1863
Kamourou	Kegne-Mari	1863-1873
Nyénéma	Nienemba	1873-1876
l'homonyme de Monzon	Mansa Toma	1876-1879
Karamoko	Karamoko	1879-1889

Dyara\Sauvageot (cont.)	*1D55-2*	
Bina Mori[1]	Mari	(13 août 1889)
	Oikala Ba	n.d.
	Sai Ba	n.d.[2]

SUSOKO

The Kulubali:

Kalajan Kulubali	1652-1682
Danfasara	1682-1697
Suma	1697-1712
Mamari	1712-1755
Dekòrò	1755-1757
Bakari	1757-1757

The Tònden:

Tòn Masa	1757-1760
Kanyuba Nyuman	1760-1763
Kafa Jugu	1763-1766

The Jara:

Nolo Jara	1766-1790
Mònsòn	1790-1808
Fama Daa	1808-1827
Cèfòlò	1827-1839
Nyènènba	1839-1841
Keranga Ba	1841-1849
Naloma Nkuman	1849-1851
Masala Denba	1851-1854
Torokòrò Mari	1854-1856
Ali	1856-1861

APPENDIX C

GLOSSARY OF BAMANA TERMS

Balanza. Acacia albida. A tree considered to have powerful forces.

Boli. A ritual object which possesses extraordinary spiritual power. The four great Boliw were Bakungoba, Nangoloko, Kantara, and Binye-jugu. Person states that they were madeof wood in the form of animals like the buffalo, warthog and hippopotamus.

Denkundi. Child-naming ceremony.

Disi. Chest. Term used in the description of Bamana military formation.

Dòlò. Millet beer.

Fama. One who holds power. The title of the ruler of the Bamana of Segu.

Fanga. Strength, power, authority.

Furu. Marriage.

Jaka. Tax.

Jeli. Griot, bard.

Jenfa. A priest of the four great Boliw.

Jidi. A soldier serving in an administrative capacity in the village.

Jòn. Slave. Also a metaphor for "servant of God."

Kafo. An administrative district.

Kèlèbolo. Arms of war (in a military formation).

Kèlètigi. A general in the Bamana army.

Kèlèwelefin. Tribute to assure the food for the soldiers during a campaign.

Kòmò. A Bamana secret society.

Korokoro. A kind of beer.

Kuntigi. A Tònjòn leader of a military unit (Kèlèbolo).

Lisòngò. Honey price. A tribute which later became nisòngò.

Ngòyò. A bitter vegetable which resembles a bitter tomato on the outside and between a tomato and an egg plant on theinside.

Nisòngò. Soul price. See lisòngò.

Sèmè. A hatchet which (in this study) was used by soldiers to break the *tata* of the village under attack.

Sofa. A mounted soldier.

Sokala. A large place in the village.

Sudon. Funeral.

Tata. A great wall surrounding the city or village for protection.

Tòn. Association which formed the base of power for the Famaw of Segu.

Tònjòn. A slave of the Tòn; a Tòn member.

Tòntigi. A leader of the association.

APPENDIX D

GLOSSARY OF ARABIC TERMS

Almami. A variation of *imam*, a prayer leader.

Amir al-mu'minin. Commander of the Faithful, a leader in a jihad and in spiritual and temporal matters.

Awliya. Holy men.

Jihad. Jihad fi sabil Allah. An effort in Allah's way or forAllah's sake, or to convert infidels.

Mahdi. In Muslim eschatology one who is guided by Allah. One who is expected at the end of the world who will engage himself in jihad, and will be responsible for the final triumph of Islam over infidelity.

Mithqal. A measure of weight theorectically fixed in relation to the gold *dirham* (equaled 4.50 grams).

Qadi. An Islamic judge.

Qadiriyya. Sufi order associated with 'Abd al-Qadir al-Jilani (470/1077-8—561/1166) from Baghdad.

Risala. (A message). The Epistle on dogma and law of Islam, written by Abi Zayd al-Qayrawani (310/922-386/996).

Shaykh. A leading person amongst his people.

Talaba. (Singular-talib) Those who follow a Sufi Shaykh. Talibe is a variation.

Ta'rikh. A history.

Wird. The litany of a religious brotherhood.

APPENDIX E

GLOSSARY OF FRENCH TERMS

Fantassin. Infantry.

Spahi. (Turkish word) Calvaryman belonging to a corps created in1834 in Algeria, principally with a local recruitment.

Tirailleur. A *fantassin* recruited among the local populations in French territories overseas. Sometimestranslated as "sharpshooters."

APPENDIX F

GLOSSARY OF FULA TERM

Futa. The word which signifies "country."

Notes

Spelling Conventions and Caveats, p. ix

1. See glossary in the appendices for the meaning of these terms.
2. Name unknown.
3. Claude Welch Jr., "Warrior, Rebel, Guerrilla, and Putschist," Ali A. Mazrui, ed. The Warrior Tradition in Modern Africa (Leiden: E. J. Brill, 1977), p. 83.

Introduction, pp. 1-8

1. Susan K. and Roderick J. McIntosh, *Prehistoric Investigations in the Region of Jenné, Mali: A Study in the Development of Urbanism in the Sahel* (Oxford: BAR International, 1980). See also, Roland Oliver and Brian Fagan, *Africa in the Iron Age* (Cambridge: Cambridge University, 1975), p. 15.
2. Téréba Togola, "Archeological Investigations on Iron Age Sites in Méma, Mali," (Unpublished Ph. D. dissertation, Rice University, 1992), p. 13.
3. It is important to note that although the Bamana are generally described as farmers, hunters and artisans have been important in Bamana communities.
4. Richard Roberts, *Warriors, Merchants and Slaves* (Stanford: Stanford University, 1987), p. 11.
5. This group includes several occupation groups like the *jeliw*, griots; *numuw,* blacksmiths; *gesedalaw*, weavers; *garankew*, cobblers, etc.
6. Extended explanations of each stratum can be found in several ethnographies on the Bamana.
7. For a discussion of African religions see E. Bolaji Idowu, *African Traditional Religion, a Definition* (Maryknoll: Orbis, 1975); for the Bamana in particular see Charles Monteil, *Les Bambara de Ségou et du Kaarta* (Paris: Larosse, 1924); Louis Tauxier, *La Religion Bambara* (Paris: Librarie: Orientaliste Paul Geuthner, 1927); and, Germaine Dierterlen, *Essai sur la region Bambara* (Paris: Presses Universitaire de France, 1951).
8. Banbera's history of the Bamana has also been aired on Radio Mali (June 3, 1980).
9. C. Tsehloane Keto, "The Challenge of the Afrocentric Paradigm in the Reconstruction of Historical Knowledge about Africa," Paper for the Conference on Reconstructing the Study and Meaning of Africa, University of Illinois, April 8, 1994.

INTRODUCTION, PP. 1-8 (CONTINUED)

10. See Jan Vansina, "Use of Oral Tradition in Culture History," and Alan P. Merriam, "Use of Music in Reconstructing Culture History," in *Reconstructing African Culture History*, Creighton Gabel and Norman R. Bennett, eds. (Boston: Boston University, 1967) for discussions of the importance of these traditions.

Chapter 1, pp. 9-25

1. Togola, pp. 13-14.
2. ANM 1D 55-1 Notice sur le Royaume Bambara de Ségou- Mage-Barth à Farako 1889.
3. ANM 1D 55-2 Notice historique du Royaume et du Cercle de Ségou- 2° partie-Fondation de l'état Bambara de Ségou-Quelques notes sur l'histoire de cet état 1896.
4. Es-Sa'di, *Tarikh Es-Soudan*, O. Houdas, trans. (Paris: Adrien-Maisonneuve, 1964). See also Mahmoud Kati b. El-Hadj El-Motaouakkel Kati, *Tarikh El-Fettach*, O. Houdas and M. Delafosse, trans. (Paris: Adrien-Maisonneuve, 1964), pp. 20, 86, and 107.
5. Es-Sa'di, p. 172.
6. Ibid, p. 274.
7. Ibid, pp. 223, 274, and 276.
8. Ibid, p. 418.
9. Es-Sa'di, pp. 418, 420; and Yves Person, "Ngolo Jara ou la force de Segou," in *Les Africaines*, Charles André Julien, ed. vol 10, (Paris: Éditions J. A., 1978), p. 279.
10. Person, "Ngolo," p. 280.
11. It is said that a Bozo family already lived in Sikòrò; however, Banbera argues that the first inhabitants were Sòmònò. Tayiru Banbera, *A State of Intrigue, The Epic of Bamana Segou*, David C. Conrad, ed. and trans., (London: Oxford University, 1990), p. 103; Mariyan-Madi Susoko, *Wagadu Fo Sudan* (Bamako: Éditions Jamana, 1988), p. 27; and Tairou Bembera, "Biton Kulibali ka Masala," Mamadou Boidié Diarra, transcriber, Lilyan Kesteloot, trans., *Bulletin de l'Institut Fondamental d'Afrique Noire* 40(1978), pp. 616-7; see also Robert Pageard, "Note sur les Sòmònò," *Notes Africaines*, 98(1961), p. 17. The Sòmònò Jirè family is one which has been very important to the history of Segu through the period of French occupation. Mage asserts that the Sòmònò are of Soninke origin (pp. 373-4), but an archival report asserts that the Sòmònòs were a different branch of Bamana people; see ANM 1D 55-1 Notice sur le Royaume et le Cercle de Ségou.
12. The two were teachers together.
13. Banbera (Conrad), p. 103; see also Bembera (Kesteloot), pp. 616-7, and 1D55-2 Notice historique 2° partie.
14. Banbera (Conrad), p. 49; Dyara, p. 23. Markadugu consisted of nine villages, and Dodugu, twelve villages.
15. Later, when the Tòn succeeded in a campaign, Bitòn would leave a *jidi*, a person to warn the people of all that happened in the country, and to receive strangers. Interviews with Dramane Jara, "L'Histoire Bamana à la colonisation," Segu, 19 mai

1993, and Sunkalo Jara, "L'Histoire de Bamana," Soninkura, 9 juillet 1993.

16. Person, "Ngolo," p. 286.

17. Lilyan Kesteloot, "Le mythe et l'histoire dans la formation de l'empire de Ségou," *Bulletin de l'Institut de Fondamental d'Afrique Noire* 40(Juillet, 1978), p. 581.

18. C. Monteil, *Les Bambara*, p. 23.

19. Yaya Wane, "Reflexions sur la dimension sacrole chez les Toucouleurs," *Bulletin d'Institut Fondamental d'Afrique Noire*, ser. b 39(1977), pp. 386-404.

20. Kulibali means "(to cross the river) without a boat." It is unclear if the name was adapted after crossing the Niger. Interview: Buba Kulibali, Bamako, July 5, 1993. An oral tradition, translated by Robert Pageard, presents the Kulibali as a branch of the Keïta, the dynastic family of the Empire of Mali. *Notes sur l'histoire de Bambara de Ségou* (Clichy: Chez l'auteur, 1957), p. 7.

21. Interview: Sunkalo Jara. ANM 1D 55-2 Notice Historique, 2° Partie. See also C. Monteil, pp. 13-14 for another version. The names are different, but the events are very similar. See also Amadou Ba, *Histoire du Sahel Occidental Malien* (Bamako: Éditions Jamana, 1989), p. 103.

22. Age-grades were the primary vehicle for socialization and discipline. Bamana society had give grades: ages 0-6, 6-10, 10-15 bachelors and married adults. See Richard Roberts, *Warriors, Merchants and Slaves*, (Stanford: Stanford University, 1987), p. 31; and, Viviana Paques, *Les Bambara*, (Paris: Presses Universitaires de France, 1954). See also, J. B. Webster, A. A. Boahen and M. Tidy, *The Revolutionary Years, West Africa since 1800*, (Essex, England: Longman, 1980), p. 104.

23. Kesteloot, "Myth," p. 580.

24. Most versions include the river spirit. See also Germaine Dietelen; and Youssau Cisse, *Les Fondements de la société d'initiation du Komo* (Paris: Mouton, 1973).

25. See ANM 1D 55-2 2° partie; and, Person, p. 286. Mariyan-Madi Susoko argues that three Kulubali ruled in Segu before Bitòn: Kalajan Kulubali (1652-1682), Danfasari (1682-1697), and Suma (1697-1712). See *Wagadu Fo Sudan* (Bamako: Éditions Jamana, 1988), p. 28.

26. Person, p. 628-9. Many towns were located by the Niger and Bani Rivers, including Segu. For a discussion of the development of pre-colonial towns and cities see Richard C. Hull, *African Cities and Towns before the European Conquest* (New York: W. W. Norton, 1976).

27. C. Monteil (p. 39) argues that the name "Mamari" for the Bamana is the equivalent of Mahomet.

28. See Kesteloot's article, "Mythe," pp. 578-681. Even if the father is in the historical record, the role can be such that the child is made an orphan, often by exile. Compare with Sunjata, Chaka, etc. Also compare Bitòn's rise to power with Ngolo Jara's emergence during Bitòn's reign.

29. C. Monteil, pp. 29-32.

30. This legend has been repeated in several works. For discussion of the gold dinar see, Marion Johnson, "The Nineteenth Century Gold 'Mithqal' in West and North Africa," *Journal of African History*, 9(1968), 547-69; an Raymond Mauney, "Monnaies anciennes d'afrique occidentale," *Notes Africaines* 42 (avril, 1949), pp. 60-61.

31. Person, "Ngolo," p. 282.

32. C. Monteil, pp. 29-30, 32-38.

CHAPTER 1, PP. 9-25 (CONTINUED)

33. Banbera (Conrad), p. 95; Dyara, pp. 165-9; and C. Monteil, p. 29.
34. See Gaoussou Dyara, "Contribution a l'histoire du Royaume Bambara de Ségou," Complementary thesis by Serge Sauvageot, trans. Faculte des Lettres et Sciences Humaines de Dakar. Dakar, Sénégal, 1965, pp. 165-9 for detailed events.
35. Banbera (Conrad), p. 98. See also, Bazoumana Sissoko, Radio Television Mali Library, Bamako. Sissoko was also interviewed by Seydou Theiro.
36. Jean Bazin, "Recherches sur les formations socio-politiques anciennes en pays Bambara," *Études Maliennes*, no. 1(1970), p. 33.
37. ANM 1D 55-1 Notice Historique du Royaume de Ségou, 2° partie 1896 "Bambara et Tondions." Also 1D 55-2 Quelques notes.
38. Person, p. 285.
39. ANM 1D 55-1 2° partie, "Bambara et Tondions."
40. G. N. Uzoigwe, "The Warrior and the State in Pre-Colonial Africa," *The Warrior Tradition in Modern Africa*, Ali A. Mazrui, ed., (Leiden: E. J. Brill, 1977), p. 23.
41. See G. Dumestre, *La Geste de Ségou: Textes des Griots Bambaras* (Abidjan: Universite d'Abidjan, 1974), p. 264; and Person, "Ngolo," p. 304 for the sacrifice of Ngolo so that his family would never cease to rule Segu.
42. Uzoigwe, pp. 24, 28; and Bazin, p. 38.
43. Uzoigwe, pp. 34-5.
44. Ibid, p. 285.
45. Ibid, p. 286.
46. Ibramhima B. Kaké, *Les Armées traditionelles de l'Afrique noire* (Libreville: Éditions du Lion, 1980), p. 78.
47. Monteil, p. 313.
48. Conrad (Banbera), p. 61. The flintlock muskets (*ntuloma*) and the percussion cap (*konkon*) and pistols are still manufactured by local blacksmiths. Patrick R. McNaughton, "Bamana Blacksmiths," *African Arts*, 12 (February, 1979), pp. 35-6.
49. Interview: Dramane Jara.
50. Dyara, p. 28.
51. Ibid, p. 17
52. There exist estimates of the wealth garnered by the Famaw, but no clear information is available. The French attempted to evaluate it, but some of the treasure had already been removed by the 'Umarians. For records of what the French removed from the Segu treasure see ANM 1N 63 Procès Verbal de classification et d'embattage des objets et matières d'or provenant de la prise de Ségou et destinés à ∏tre envoyés en France, Année 1890.
53. Roberts, p. 19.
54. Ibid, p. 18. He argues that Bamana slaves constituted only a fraction of the total of slave export from the Senegambia and Sierra Leone. No clear distinction is made between captives of the Bamana army sold as slaves, and slaves who were Bamana. The Bamana is one of the groups listed as slaves exported to the Americas. For example, see John Blassingame, *The Slave Community* (London: Oxford University, 1972), p. 2; and Albert J. Raboteau, *Slave Religion* (London: Oxford University, 1978), p. 5.
55. Ibid., p. 38.

56. Person, pp. 291-5. Banbera (Conrad), p. 14; Cheikh Moussa Kamara, "La plus savoreuse des sciences et la plus agreable des informations concernant la vie du Maitre Cheikh El Hadj Omar," Amar Samb, trans. *Bulletin d'Institut Fondamental d'Afrique Noire* 32(1970), p. 468; Louis Tauxier, "Chronologie des Rois Bambara," *Cahiers d'Outremer*, 2(1930), p. 263; Abon Eugene Mage, *Voyage dans le Soudan Occidental* (Paris: Hachette, 1968), pp. 398-9. C. Monteil, pp. 53-4; and Dyara, p. 41 assert that Bitòn was succeeded by Cèkòrò and then Bakara, but Djiré claims the reverse. Mamadu Kulibali discusses four sons of Bitòn, Jekòrò, Birama, Fatoma Bira, and Bakarijan. Bitòn warned Jekòrò not to succeed him because the people would betray him. Interview with Mahmadou Kulibali, "Segu Bamana Fanga Maana ani al haji 'Umar ani Masina Fula ka Kèlè," Wèrèba 1989.

57. C. Monteil, p. 54; Banbera (Conrad), p. 14.

58. M. Abdourrahmane Djire, "Une Tradition musulmane relative à l'histoire de Ségou," Robert Pageard, ed. *Notes Africaines* 101(janvier 1964), p. 10. See also Conrad (Banbera), p. 16; Monteil, pp. 42, 53; Louis Tauxier, *Religion Bambara*, p. 82; Kesteloot, ed. *Da Monzon de Ségou épopée bambara* (Paris: Fernand Nathan, 1978), p. 5.

59. C. Monteil, p. 54. Kesteloot's version reports that he was killed while praying in a mosque he built. Some reports name the son who followed Bitòn as Jekòrò (probably a variation of Dekòrò or Cekòrò), and his brother as Ali. However, the events are similar in several versions about what happened to the second son, whether called Jekòrò or Ali. M. Abdourrahmane Djire, "Une tradition musulmane relative à l'histoire de Ségou," Robert Pageard, ed. *Notes Africaines* 101 (janvier 1964), p. 10. see also Conrad (Banbera), p. 16; Monteil, pp. 42, 53; Louis Tauxier, *Religion Bambara*, p. 82; Kesteloot, ed. *Da monzon de Ségou épopée bambara* (Paris: Fernand Nathan, 1978), p. 5.

60. Dyara (Sauvageot), pp. 136-9; ANM 1D 55-2 Notice Historique, 2° partie "Fondation de l'état;" Djire (Pageard), "Une tradition," p. 24; and Tauxier, pp. 84-8.

61. Interview: Sunkalo Jara; Person, p. 291; and Monteil, p. 54.

62. Dyara (Sauvageot), p. 171. Another informer, Tamura Kore, asserts that the son was killed by an attack force sent by Tòn Mansa. Jònkolo is also identified elsewhere as a daughter. Mage (p. 402), and Tauxier (p. 82) assert that Ngolo saved two of Bitòn's daughters. Mamadu Kulibali argues that Ngolo married Jekòrò's widow, Makòrò, who was pregnant. Therefore, the oldest son of Ngolo was really the son of Jekòrò and the Kulibali line continued, but under the Jara family name.

63. Dyara (Sauvageot), pp. 173-5.

64. For this section, see Dyara (Sauvageot), pp. 173-5; Monteil, p. 66.

65. Dyara (Sauvageot), p. 35; Dumestre, p. 250; ANM 1D 55-2 Fondation de l'état. See also Kesteloot, *Da Monzon*, pp. 14-22. This version was told by Sissoko Kabèrè.

66. Person, p. 291.

67. In Dyara's version, Ngolo was taken from his mother. Banbera claims that Ngolo asked the tax collectors to wiat until his mother's return, but they refused.

68. In Dumestre's version, Bitòn entrusted a ring to Ngolo. In Dyara's version the children ate meat.

69. See Banbera for this version. See also Dumestre, p. 252; Dyara, p. 35; Dumestre, p.252; Person, "Ngolo," p. 298; and Monteil, pp. 46-8.

70. Dyara (Sauvageot), pp. 49.

CHAPTER 1, PP. 9-25 (CONTINUED)

71. Interview with an Almamy, recorded by Moussa Coulibaly.
72. Person, p. 300. In Person's collected version, the uncles betrayed Ngolo.
73. Dyara (Sauvageot), p. 57.
74. Conrad (Benbara), p. 143, ff; and Person, pp. 300-1.
75. Dyara (Sauvageot), p. 91. Kesteloot reports that Mònzòn could place 100,000 men on the battlefield. The army was 40,000-strong during Bitòn's reign; see *Da Monzon*, p. 5.
76. Dyara (Sauvageot), p. 151.
77. Ibid.
78. Interviews with Mamadu Kulubali; and Bamyama Kulibali, "Bamana Maana," Segukura, 10 juillet 1993. Also, ANM 1D 33 Enquête Politique Musulman, Cercle de Bamako, Résidence de Banamba, 31 mai 1914.
79. Person, "Ngolo," p. 286. See also ANM 2N 42 Notice sur les Peuhls (Fouloukas et Sambourous).
80. Person, "Ngolo," p. 306.
81. Dyara (Sauvageot), p. 25.
82. Sidi Mohamed Mahibou and Jean Louis Triaud, *Voila ce qui est arrive. Bayan ma Waqa a d'al-Hagg 'Umar al-Futi* (Paris: Éditions du Centre Nationale de la Recherche Scientifique, 1983), p. 47.
83. Dyara (Sauvageot), p. 25.
84. Seydou Camara, "La Tradition orale en question: Conservation et transmission des traditions historiques au Manden: Le Centre de Kela et l'histoire du Minijan." (Thèse inédité, École des Hautes-Études en Sciences Sociales, Paris, France, 1990), pp. 124-136.
85. This hegemony was in part based on the monopoly of the construction of canoes which could only be built with the permission of the ruler of Kaaba.
86. Interviews with Bala Tarawere, Mamadi Jabate, Sanunu Karmara, Jeli Mamadu Kone, and Hawa Manbi Keyita by Seydou Camara.
87. Interview with Nfali Berete, Kangaba, 1981. This explanation contradicts what is generally known about the geography of Segu. Present Segu has many Balanzan, see photo of the monument as you enter Segu.
88. Kaké, p. 85; Dyara (Sauvageot), p. 25. Although the French described the Bamana wars as "plunder," they too would attack villages "for political reasons" or just to teach them a lesson. See chapter 7.
89. Jean Bazin, "Recherches," pp. 34-5.
90. Roberts, p. 45
91. Ibid, p. 46.
92. Ibid, pp. 46, 68. *Sòmònò* is the Bamana term for fisherman, and represent an occupational category whereas *Bozo* is a specific group that tend to fish.
93. They were Daa, Cèfòlò, Ben, Kassum, Nyènèma, Bema, Demba, Sonzan, Mari (Torokòrò), Ali Zanfin and Mari (Kènyè). Dyara, p. 121. See Appendices for several chronologies.
94. Person, p. 306.

Chapter 2, pp. 27-53

1. Thomas Hodgkin, "Islam, History and Politics," *Journal of Modern African Studies*, 1(1963), p. 95.

2. All goals are generally favored in modern West Africa; Hodgkin and Ruth Schachter, *French Speaking West Africa in Transition* (New York: Carnegie Endowment for International Peace, 1961), pp. 380-1. See also John D. Hargreaves, "The Tokolor Empire of Segou and Its Relations with the French," in J. Butler, ed. *Boston University Papers on Africa*, (Boston: Boston University, 1966), p. 125.

3. Mouhammed Moustapha Hane, *Les Trois Grandes Figures de l'Islam en Afrique* (Dakar: Librairie Hilal, 1966), p. 5.

4. Yves Saint-Martin, "Un Fils d'El Hadj Omar: Aguibou, roi du Dinguiray et du Macina (1843?-1907)," *Cahiers d'Études Africaines*, 8(1968), p. 145. See also Mohamadu Aliou Tyam, who was with al-Hajj, *La vie d'el Hadj Omar, Qacida en Poular* Henri Gaden, trans, (Paris: Institut d'Ethnologie, 1935), p. 6; Hane, p. 4. Muhammad al-Hafiz places his birth in 1212/1797-8, see *Al-Hagg 'Umar, Sultan al-dawlat al-tiganiyya bi-garbi Ifriqiyya* (Al-Qahira 1383/1963-4), p. 20.

5. During the last quarter of the eighteenth century, Futa Toro experienced an Islamic reform movement, initiated by Sulayman Bal that triggered a series of political changes. His political ambitions were continued by Abd al-Qadir who ruled at the time of 'Umar's birth. Abd al-Qadir Kan became the first Imam of Futa Toro in 1190/1775-76.

6. See Hane, pp. 4-5; Camille Pietri, *Les Français au Niger, Voyages et Combats* (Paris: Librairie Hachette, 1885), p. 66.

7. Yves Marquet, "Des Ihwan Al-Safa al-Hagg 'Umar (b. Sa'id Tall) Marabout et Conquerant Toucouleur," *Arabica* 15 (1968), p. 17. Al-Tijani, the founder, said that the Tijaniyya brotherhood abrogated all the others.

8. Mahibou and Triaud, p. 26.

9. Kamara, p. 62. See also Tyam, p. 21.

10. Aliore Koné, "La Prise de Ségou et la fin d'el Hadj Omar," *Notes Africaines* (1978), p. 62. Kamara states that 'Umar lived in the home of the Fama's sister, p. 475.

11. David Robinson, "The Chronicle of the Succession: An Important Document for the Umarian State," *Journal of African History*, 31 (1990), p. 247.

12. Vincent Monteil, *L'Islam Noir* (Paris: Éditions du Seuil, 1964), p. 90; St. Martin, p. 150.

13. Ibid, p. 86. This was in 1268. It was soon after this that he formed his first army; see Mamadou Sissoko, "Chroniques d'el Hadj Oumar et du Cheikh Tidiani," *L'Education Africaine* 95(1936), p. 214.

14. Interview: Dramane Jara.

15. The litany of a religious brotherhood.

16. Faidherbe to Minister of Marine and Colonies, July 19, 1851, quoted in A. S. Kanya-Forstner, "Mali-Tukulor," in Michael Crowder, ed. *West African Resistance, the Military Response to Colonial Occupation* (New York: Africana, 1971), p. 57.

17. Mage, p.235; ANM ID-3, "Étude Historique," p. 5.

18. He used gold powder purchased from Bure, a well-known gold producing area, to buy the arms.

CHAPTER 2, PP. 27-53 (CONTINUED)

19. Mage, p. 235.
20. St. Martin, p. 155.
21. Mage, p. 236.
22. Region in West Africa around the Senegal and Gambia rivers.
23. Mervyn Hiskett, *The Development of Islam in West Africa* (London: Longman, 1984), p. 228.
24. ANM 1E 71 Rapport sur les delimitation des Cercle de Bammako et du Royaume de Sansanding.
25. The French also called the "mulatto" group of the Peulhs which mixed with local populations in Sénégal "Toucouleurs," see Pietri, p. 65. See also 'Umar al-Naqar, "Takruur, the history of a Name," *Journal of African History*, 10 (1969), 365-74.
26. A sufi brotherhood.
27. B. Olatunji Oloruntimehin, "Resistance Movements in the Tukulor Empire," *Cahiers Études Afriques*, 8(1968), p. 124-5.
28. John Hargreaves, ed. *France and West Africa* (London: MacMillan, 1969), p. 128 ff; Peter Clarke, *West Africa and Islam* (London: Edward Arnold, 1982), p. 133.
29. "Mali-Tukulor," p. 58. See also Amar Samb, "Sur el Hadj Omar (à propos d'un article d'Yves Saint-Martin)," *Bulletin de l'Institut Fondamental d'Afrique Noire* ser. b 35(1935), pp. 803-5.
30. Yaya Wane, "De Halwaar à Degembere, ou l'itinéraire Islamique de Shaykh Umar Taal," *Bulletin de l'Institut Fondamental d'Afrique Noire* ser b. 1(1969), p. 449. See also C. Monteil, p. 87.
31. Kanya-Forstner, p. 57.
32. Qu'ran XXII-40. For other information, see "La Vie d'al Hajj 'Omar, Traduction d'un manuscrit arabe de la Zaouia tidjaniya de Fez," Jules Salenc, Trans. *Bulletin du Comité d'Études Historiques et Scientifiques de l'Afrique Occidentale Française*, 1(1918), pp. 411-12.
33. Robinson, *Holy War*, pp. 46-51.
34. See Mahibou and Triaud, p. 62.
35. The meaning of this statement is unclear. ANM 1D 9 Notice historique sur la Région du Sahel par le Capitaine de Lartique 1896. This account reportedly was told to the French by a Kassonke blacksmith, named Kankuma, living in Koniakari in 1890 and who followed 'Umar to the end.
36. After invading Nioro, he found some Bamana, Saharan groups, and soldiers from Masina at Dongudji.
37. Amadou Ba, p. 133.
38. Mahibou and Triaud, p. 28.
39. Interview with Kirango Ba Jara, "Les Bamanas et les Tukuleurs avaient 21 ans a se combattre," Segu, 3 June 1993. Also, interview with Tierno Sako, "Al-Hajj 'Umar et les conquêtes de Segu et Masina," pt. 1, Segu 26 Mai 1993. According to Koné, the Fama's wife had an affair with his younger brother, and the Fama gorged out the lad's eyes (p. 62).
40. Mage, p. 154. There is disagreement on the year of the assassination and to the reign of Ali. Most report that Torokoro was killed 1856 when 'Umar sent the talibe. But,

Tauxier cites 1859 ("Chronologie des rois Bambaras," *Cahiers d'Outremer*. 2[1930], pp. 119-130, 255-266). See lists of Famas.

41. Interview: Sunkalo Jara.

42. Kone, p. 62.

43. Mage, p. 154.

44. Mage, p. 256.

45. Also spelled Madicouya, Marcoia, and Mercoia.

46. Sissoko, "Chroniques," 96-97(1937), p. 129; Dyara (Sauvageot), p. 135.

47. April 9, according to Gaden. See Sissoko, "Chroniques," p. 130.

48. Horses were highly valuable; to capture horses from the enemy was just as an important indication of the battle as the number of people killed or captured. Chronicles generally stressed when horses were captured.

49. Kamara, p. 91; Mage's 'Umarian sources cited 20,000 in the Seguvian army, p. 257; Robinson, *Holy War*, pp. 200-1. Watala is also spelled Waytala, Wuyta, Oieta, Wuytala, and Woitala. According to the Almamy, Tata warned his father to not fight 'Umar.

50. Hanson and Robinson, p. 66.

51. Jules Brévié, *Islamisme contre Naturisme au Soudan Français* (Paris: Ernest Leroux, 1923), p. 166; Sissoko,"Chroniques," p. 131. Only Bamana losses are normally highlighted in 'Umarian chronicles. The 35,000 men were said to have been armed with guns.

52. Interview with Mountaga Tiam, "Histoire de Segu: Règle Futaka à Segu," Segu, 5 June 1993.

53. Interview: Dramane Jara. The Bamana of Kaarta had purchased weapons from the Sénégambia although an embargo had been placed on sales to the Bamana. 'Umar wrote Njay Sur, a Muslim who headed operations of Maurel and Prom, complaining of the sales and wanting to know the position of the Sénégalese Muslims. See John Hanson and David Robinson, *After the Jihad: The Reign of Ahmad al-Kabir in the Western Sudan* (East Lansing: Michigan State University, 1991), p. 107.

54. Kamara, p. 91; Mage reports 15,000, p. 257; Sissoko, p. 131. 560 horses were also captured.

55. Robinson, "Chronicle," p. 259.

56. Interview: Sunkalo Jara.

57. Interview: Tierno Sako, pt. 2, Segu, 20 juin 1993.

58. Roberts, *Warriors*, p. 84; Louis Quinton, "Souvenirs d'un voyage de Sénégal au Niger, 1863-66," *Bulletin de la Société de Géographies de Paris*, 1 (1881), p. 531.

59. Mage, pp. 258, 369-70; Mademba, Bendaud, "La dernière étape d'un conqueront," *Bulletin de Comité d'Études Historiques et Scientifiques de l'Afrique Occidentale Française* 3(1921), p. 473-480.

60. Quinton, p. 531; Roberts, *Warriors*, p. 87.

61. Mahibu and Triaud, p. 57.

62. Ibid.

63. Ibid.

64. For more on Masina see Amadou Hampate Ba and Jacques Daget, *L'Empire Peul de Macina* (Paris: Mouton, 1962); and, Marion Johnson, "Economic Foundations of an Islamic Theocracy: The Case of Macina," *Journal of African History* 17(1976), pp.

CHAPTER 2, PP. 27-53 (CONTINUED)

481-495.

65. Sissoko, p.132; ANM 1D 35, Notice sur les états d'Aguibu 1896, Bandiagara, le 31 décembre 1896, Meurielle.

66. See AMN 1D 55-2, "Quelques Notes."

67. An archival report gives an account of how the army of Masina spooked some cows with a gunshot, and the cows charged on the battle field toward the Segu army, causing the soldiers to disperse. ANM 1D 55-2, "Notice Historique."

68. Ibid, p. 306. The war continued even after Ali became Fama because columns from Masina continued to raid villages in Minianka, Saro and provinces east of Segu. ANM 1D 55-2 Notice Historique, 2° Partie Fondation de l'état.

69. Roberts, p. 82; Oloruntimehin, *Segu-Tukulor*, pp. 127-8.

70. Brévié, p. 167. Ba Lobo was the son of the older brother of Ahmad I, Bokar Mammad, and cousin of Ahmadu Ahmadu, according to Mahibu and Triaud, pp. 169-70. However, he is also stated to be the uncle of Ahmadu Ahmadu.

71. ANM ID 55-2 Notice Historique du Royaume et du Cercle de Ségou-2° parte Fondation de l'état Bambara de Ségou—Quelques Notes sur l'histoire de cet état 1896, p. 6.

72. Ibid. Short-haired meant most solid and most rapid.

73. Robinson cites a total of 15,000 calvary and infantry, p. 265, but a French report asserts that there were 4000 cavaliers, ANM 1D 35 "États d'Aguibu."

74. ANM 1D 35, "états d'Aguibu," and ANM 1D 7, Notice sur le Soudan, Kayes, le 31 décembre, 1896, Trentinian.

75. Interview: Kiranga Ba Jara.

76. Information in this section is from an interview with Tierno Sako; Kamara, p. 477; and Sissoko, p. 134.

77. Tyam, p. 163. According to 'Abd Allah 'Ali, a recorder of the event, 'Umar camped near Segu on March 9 and entered on March 10 (Mahibou and Triaud) p. 230. Mage also cites March 10, at 9:30 a.m., p. 168.

78. See Paul Soleillet, *Voyage à Ségou 1878-1879* (Paris: 1881), p. 394 for description of 'Umar's arms. See also J. E. Inikore, "The Import of Firearms into West Africa: 1750-1807: A Quantitative Analysis," *Journal of African History* , 18 (1977) for trends in the trade in firearms.

79. For this section see Mage, p. 262; Roberts, p. 83; Brévié, p. 166; Clarke, pp. 130, 135; and Koné, p. 63.

80. 'Umar wrote about the *takfir*, apostasy of Masina. The work is translated by Mahibou and Triaud.

81. ANM 1D 55-5 "Renseignements," Marge-Barth à Farako 1889, p. 2.

82. 'Umar was advised to only attack Ahmadu Ahmadu by surprise; otherwise, he would fail. The first battle occurred between Jafarabè and Masina on a Tuesday, and 'Umar failed twice to conquer Masina. 'Umar was also advised to attack Jennè where the richness of Masina was kept. The rule of Jennè was Ahmadu Aziz. When the 'Umarians surrounded the city, two virgin men were given gris gris which allowed them to pass by the enemy troops without trouble. The two young men later informed Ahmadu Ahmadu of the 'Umarian plan. A strange man assured Ahmadu Ahmadu that

the would lose to 'Umar, but Ahmadu Ahmadu would kill many 'Umarian soldiers. Aziz refused to remained in the city as Ahmadu Ahmadu instructed. In addition, the women refused to take shelter. Aziz, instead, led a unit to face the 'Umarians and killed one hundred 'Umarians. When he returned the second time to face the 'Umarian forces, he was killed. His face, however, could not be caught and he returned to Hamdallaye (Checik Oumar Bah, "Al-Hajj 'Umar et les Bamana de Segou," Bamako, Mali, n.d.).

83. Anonymous, "L'Empire Toucouleur d'El Hadj 'Omar," *Bingo* 64 (May 1958), p. 11.

84. Kamara, pp. 112-3; see also Sissoko, p. 134.

85. Later, the talibes took everything identified with Batair and threw them in the river. Interview with Seku Kulubali, Banankoro, 23 novembre 1984. Kamara, p.113.

86. Sissoko, p. 134.

87. Interview with Cèkòrò Tangara, "Ngolo Jara ni Tona Dunanbake Tangara Kaje," Tuna, 25 septembre 1984.

88. This time Mohammadou Sidiyanke led the offense.

89. See Sissoko, p. 135 for more details, including 'Umar's reply and the battle which followed.

90. Interview: Tierno Sako.

91. "Étude Historique," p. 9.

92. Wane, p. 450; Koné, p. 63. The oral account translated by Koné include the exchange between Bina Ali and 'Umar concerning the gold that Ali was hiding in a belt. A *garanke* (weaver) betrayed Ali.

93. John Spencer Trimingham, *A History of Islam in West Africa* (Oxford: University Press, 1962), p. 163.

94. André B"me, *Ségou Vielle Capitale* (Angoulême: Imprimerie H. Corrignan et J. Lachanard, 1952), p. 33; Pietri, p. 68.

95. "Chroniques de Oualata et de Nema," Paul Marty, trans. *Revue des Etudes Islamiques*, 3 (1927), p. 367.

96. Hiskett, p. 72.

97. Roberts, "Production and Reproduction of Warrior States: Segu Bambara and Segu Tokolor," *International Journal of African Historical Studies*, 13 (1980), p. 414.

98. John Hanson, "Generational Conflict in the 'Umarian Movement after the Jihad: Perspectives from the Futanke Grain Trade at Medine," *Journal of African History* 31 (1990), pp. 199-200.

99. Roberts, "Production," p. 416.

100. Hargreaves, pp. 128-9.

101. Soleillet, pp. 379, 425-6.

102. See also Claude Meillassoux, "The Role of Slavery in Economic and Social History of Sahelio-Sudanic Africa," *Forced Migration*, J. G. Inikori, ed. (New York: Hutchinson, 1982), pp. 90, 293 ff.

103. Méniaud, pp. 127-134.

104. Hanson and Robinson, p. 7.

105. Interviews: Dramane Jara, Tierno Sako, and Soumaila Fanè, "Les règle d'Ahmadu et l'installation des Français à 1930," Tiserila, 31 mai 1993.

106. Robinson, pp. 259-60.

107. Ibid. See also Hanson and Robinson, pp. 35, 44 and 64. According to Muhammad

CHAPTER 2, PP. 27-53 (CONTINUED)

ibn Ibrahim, this occurred on Sunday, 26th of Rajab 1276/February 18, 1860, p. 261. Also, interviews with Tierno Sako, and Soumaila Fane; "Zaouia," p. 417; and Abdoul Aziz Diallo, "La siège de Nyoro et la mort de Muntaga Tall," *Études Maliennes*, no. 3 (1979), p. 7.

108. For these versions see Kamara, pp. 100-1; Tyam, p. 135; see also M. G. Adam, "Légendes Historiques du Pays de Nioro," *Revue Coloniale*, 3-4 (1903-04), pp. 118, 233.

109. Ba, p. 141. See pp. 141-4 for full discussion.

110. Oloruntimehin, *Segu-Tukulor*, p. 155; Hanson and Robinson, p. 7, and Pietri, pp. 100-1.

111. Hanson and Robinson, p. 44.

112. Ibid, p. 41.

113. In 1868 Ahmadu proclaimed himself to be Amir al-Muminin, Commander of the Faithful; see Kanya-Forstner, p. 61. Oloruntimehin states that he took the title in 1869; see p. 180; see also Jamil Abun-Nasr, *The Tijaniyya* (London: Oxford University, 1965), who asserts that he claimed the title in 1868 although other researchers argue that he did it in 1873.

114. See Mage, p. 226-7.

115. ANM B 67 #16 Situation générale, (à Monsieur le Gouverneur).

116. Pietri, pp.102-6; Oloruntimehin, p. 191.

117. For this section see Soleillet, pp. 375, 382-3; ASAOF, 15G109/1 (157), Le Commandant de Médine à Monsieur le Gouveneur de Sénégal et dépendances, Médine 8 novembre 1870, cited in Oloruntimehin, p. 181; St. Martin, "Un Fils," p. 151; Pietri, p. 104, and Joseph Gallieni, *Voyage au Soudan Français 1879-1881* (Paris: Hachette, 1885), p. 42.

118. ANM 1D 55-2 Notice Historique du Royaume de Ségou, 2° partie-1896, p. 8; 1D 9 Notice historique sur la region du Sahel par le Capitaine Lartique 1896, p. 4. These two notices were probably taken from the same source.

119. Mage, p. 279-80; Robinson, "Chronicle," p. 248.

120. Soleillet, pp. 375-7.

121. St. Martin argues that the original core of 'Umarian *sofas* were domestic slaves of the Talaba and grooms who became soldiers during the campaigns, see *L'Empire Toucouleur et la France* (Dakar: Dakar Université, 1967), p. 184.

122. Oloruntimehin, *Segu-Tukulor*, p. 168; Gallieni, p. 609.

123. See Joseph Smaldone, *Warfare in the Sokoto Caliphate: Historical and Sociological Perspectives* (Cambridge: Cambridge University, 1977) pp. 91-2.

124. This statement was made in reference to the war at Kejje in 1868, see Hanson and Robinson, p. 100.

125. ANM 1D 55-2 Notice Historique du Royaume de Ségou-2° partie, 1896, p. 8. John Hanson states that the oral traditions of Western Mali uniformly argue that the Holy War ended with 'Umar's "disappearance" in 1864. One informant, el-Hajj Maeyel Diako, conceded that 'Umar's sons continued the Holy War despite the legal cessation. The period between 'Umar's Holy War and the French conquest is called the *jaamanu al-diina*. See "'Umarian Kaarta (Mali, West Africa) during the Late

Nineteenth Century: Dissent and Revolt after 'Umar Tal's Holy War," (Unpublished dissertation, Michigan State University, 1989), pp. 21, 147.

126. ANM 1D 55-2 Royaume de Ségou, p. 8; Oloruntimehin, *Segu-Tukulor*, p. 169.

127. Gallieni, p. 609.

128. See chapter 3.

129. Lt. Jaime argues that some of Ahmadu's sofa troops conspired with Bamana soldiers to block his march to Nioro. *De Koulikoro à Tombouctou sur la cannonière "le Mage,"* (Paris: Libraries Associés, 1894), p. 150.

130. Interview: Soumaila Fanè. According to this version, the men raced their horses for amusement after the battle.

131. Oloruntimehin, *Seku-Tukulor*, p. 263; and, Méniaud, pp. 342-3. Daah escaped to Farabugu. Amidu and Muniru found asylum at French posts in Kita and Bamako before returning to Masina.

132. See Oloruntimehin, pp. 272-4, and "Muhammad Lamine in Franco-Tukulor Relations, 1885-87," *Journal of the Historical Society of Nigeria*, 4 (December, 1968); Roberts, *Warriors*, pp. 86-88.

133. Robinson, "Chronicles," p. 250.

134. Ibid.

135. See Pietri, pp.100-1. Hanson and Robinson (p. 90) argue that Ahmadu's struggle against the Bamana gave him credit in the eyes of many Muslims. In addition, the threat of the Bamana at Gemukuro (1872) was fortunate for him since he could mobilize the 'Umarians under the banner of a jihad. The 'Umarian texts continued to refer to the Bamana in the same terminology as in the earlier rhetorical writings of the jihad.

Chapter 3, pp. 55-82

1. See Oloruntimehin, "Resistance," p. 126.

2. Interview: Dramane Jara.

3. Zaouia, p. 413. Even a Paris travel journal publicized the war between Segu and 'Umar, calling Segu "that energetic center of resistance which idolatrous fetishism had yet opposed Islam in Western Sudan," in "Voyages et Expéditions au Sénégal et dans les Contres Voisines," *Tour du Monde*, (Première Séméstre, 1861), p .26.

4. Interview with Bamyama Kulubali, "Bamana Maana," Segukura, 10 July, 1993.

5. Interview: Mountaga Tiam.

6. Robinson, p. 26; Mage, p. 169

7. Smith, p. 173.

8. Interviews with Bamyama Kulubali, Tierno Sako (pt. II), and Mountaga Tiam form the basis for this section. See also Kanya-Forstner, "Mali-Tukulor," p. 62; and Brévié, p. 167.

9. V. Monteil, p. 56.

10. Interviews with Tierno Sako (pts. I and II), Kirango Ba Jara, and Soumaila Fanè.

11. ANM 1D 33 Enquête politique musulman cercle de Bamako, Résidence de Banamba, 31 mai 1914.

CHAPTER 3, PP. 55-82 (CONTINUED)

12. Mage, p. 295.
13. Brévié, p. 168. This might, in a crude manner, explain the situation with the 'Umarians, but later the Sudan would see that secular support was unnecessary for conversion.
14. Interview: Tierno Sako.
15. ANM 1D 55 De l'orientation de la justice et des moeurs chez les populations de la region de Ségou par Charles Correnson, Ségou, 5 septembre 1907.
16. Interviews with Tierno Sako, Mountaga Tiam and Bokary Daou, "Bamana et les occupations étrangères," Duguninkoro, 22 juin 1993. The *Samurudang d'Arrissala* is probably a variation of *Risala*. Although learned in Arabic, the Tiam family never functioned as judges because it could not work with the power of the government.
17. Interview: Sunkalo Jara.
18. Interview: Bamyama Kulubali.
19. Interview: Mountaga Tiam.
20. Interview: Bokary Daou.
21. Interview with Koké Kulubali, "Segu sous les occupations futakas et françaises," Masala, 1975.
22. Kanya-Forstner, "Mali-Tukulor," p. 63. See also Méniaud, p. 345.
23. The following section is based on an interview with Mountaga Tiam. Some people of other groups collaborated with 'Umar because they were Muslims prior to his arrival, and some, like the Daou family, were against the "Bamana infidels." Interview: Bokary Daou.
24. Interview: Soumaila Fanè.
25. Ibid.
26. Ibid.
27. Robinson, p. 269.
28. Interview: Mountaga Tiam.
29. Interview: Sunkalo Jara.
30. Mage, p. 272.
31. Oloruntimehin, p. 138.
32. According to one account, Ntò poisoned Karamòkò Jara (see chapter 5. For this section, see Oloruntimehin, p. 138; Méniaud, p. 304. The internal dispute among the forces because of Ntò will have far greater consequences when the Bamana challenge the French.
33. ANM 1D 55-1 Notices Historiques, "Bambaras et Tondions."
34. Mage, p. 272.
35. ANM 1D 55 Renseignements politiques Mage-Barth, p. 2.
36. Interviews: Tierno Sako, Soumaila Fanè and Kirango Ba Jara.
37. Interview: Dramane Jara.
38. Interview: Dramane Jara. As for the assassination, this is the version found in ANM 1D 55-2 "Fondation de l'état Bambara,", p. 5.
39. Interview: Cèkòrò Tangara. See also ANM 5D 45 Notes Année 1891.
40. Thiero, p. 85.
41. Manjè was the grandson, on the side of his mother, of Sidi Baba Kulubali of Shuala,

cousin of Bitòn.

42. Interviews with Cèkòrò Tangara; and Amadu Tangara, Kirango, 21 septembre 1984.

43. Interviews with Amadu Tangara; and, Seidu Ble Kulubali, Kirango, 23 septembre 1984.

44. Thiero, p. 85.

45. Roberts, *Warriors*, p. 98.

46. Interview: Tierno Sako; Mage pp. 215, 277, 306 and 464; Roberts, *Warriors*, p. 98.

47. For this section see Cheikh Moussa Kamara, "Histoire de Ségou," *Bulletin de l'Institut Fondamental d'Afrique Noire*, ser. b (1978), pp. 480-1, and Mage, pp. 269 and 281.

48. Mage, pp. 295, 300 and 308.

49. Sissoko, p. 71; Mage 197-201.

50. Interview: Cèkòrò Tangara.

51. Oloruntimehin, p. 128; Tauxier, pp. 164-8.

52. Interview: Seku Kulubali.

53. Interview with Sajo Jara, "Segu sous occupation française," Segu, novembre 1974.

54. They transformed leaves and bark into *cous-cous*, and even practiced anthropophagy.

55. Interview: Cèkòrò Tangara.

56. Hanson and Robinson, p. 80. A distinguished Moroccan visitor, Ahmadu, the son of Muhammad al-Ghali, blessed Ahmadu before the battle.

57. Dyara (Sauvegeot), p. 141.

58. The author of the 'Umarian chronicle gave a similar account of 'Umar's attack on Segu in 1861.

59. "Kagoro" also represented a subgroup of Bamana and a sub-region of Kaarta-Biné.

60. Ibid, p. 129.

61. Hanson and Robinson, p. 187.

62. Interview: Cèkòrò Tangara.

63. Thiero, p. 89.

64. Interviews with Sajo Jara; and Ismaila Fanè, "Histoire de Segu: Occupations Toucouleures et Françaises," Tiserila, 1975.

65. Theiro's analysis, p. 89. Also interview with Ismaila Fane; and, Mage, p. 233.

66. ANM 1E 220 #28 La Fama de Sansanding et Dépendances à Monsieur le Resident de Ségou, Sansanding, 3 juin 1891, based on oral testimony and contemporary observances.

67. ANM 1D 55 "Renseignements."

68. Ibid.

69. Interview: Soumaila Fanè; "Renseignements," p. 2.

70. "Renseignements," p. 2.

71. Interview with Bafin Jara, Kirango, 24 septembre 1984.

72. Interview: Soumaila Fanè.

73. Interview: Cèkòrò Tangara.

74. Interviews with Cèkòrò Tangara, Ismaila Fanè, and Cènan Kulubali; "Segu de l'occupation Toucouleure au début de l'occupation française," Dekala, 1975.

75. Interview: Cènan Kulubali.

76. Ahmadu used the title of "Sultan," and Delanneau considered his position as "a moral power more than an effective one," yet many villages rallied around him.

CHAPTER 3, PP. 55-82 (CONTINUED)

77. Interview with Bacèkòrò Kulubali, "Histoire de Karamoko et Mari Jara," Segu, novembre 1974. For another description of the Bamana military uniform see Kakè, pp. 79-81.
78. Ibid.
79. He died in the murderous assassination of Mari Jara and his leaders by the French. Interview: Seidu Blen Kulubali. This depiction of Kanu's loyalty differs from that given by Oloruntimehin and Méniaud (see p. 108).
80. Interviews: Ismaila Fanè, Sajo Jara and Seidou Kulubali.
81. Interview: Seku Kulubali.
82. ANM 2E 67 #20 Le Capitaine Loyer, Commandant de Cercle de Bammako à Monsieur Lieutenant Colonel Commandant Supèrieur du Soudan Français, 1 mai 1887.
83. Dyara (Sauvageot), p. 143.
84. ANM 1D 222 Mission Delanneau, pp. 2, 8, 14; Rapport Militaire de Chef d'Escadron Archinard, *Le Soudan Français en 1888-1889* (Paris: Imprimerie Nationale, 1890), p. 7.
85. ANM 2E 67 Le Commandant du Cercle de Bamako à Monsieur le Commandant Supèrieur de Soudan Français, 16 novembre 1887, Tautain.
86. ANM 2E 67 Rapport politique agricole et commerce juillet 1886 à août 1886, le Commandant du Cercle de Bamako à Monsieur le Commandant Supèrieur du Haute Fleuve.
87. ANM 1E 220 #25 Le Fama de Sansanding et Dépendances à Monsieur le Resident de Ségou, Sansanding, 6 juin 1891.
88. ANM 2E 67 Le Commandant du Cercle de Bamako à Monsieur le Commandant Supèrieur de Soudan Français, 4 juillet 1887, Tautain.
89. ANM 149 #1117 Commandant de Region NE à Gouverneur (Kayes), Ségou, 1 decembre 1886.
90. ANM 1E 18 #192 L'Administrateur de Cercle de Bamako à Monsieur le Lt. Commandant Supèrieur de Soudan Français, 1 fèvrier, 1888. In addition, communications with Cèba in Kènèdugu had become very difficult.
91. ANM 1E 18, Le Capitaine Brevété d'état-major Septans Commandant le Cercle de Bamako à Monsieur le Chef d'Escadron, Commandant Supèrieur du Soudan Français, 27 octobre 1888, pp. 4, 9, and Mission Delanneau, p. 9.
92. ANM 1E 18, Le Capitaine d'auxiliare Commandant le Cercle de Bamako à Monsieur le Commandant Supèrieur, p. i. Soudan Français, p. 3.
93. Racine, whose mother was Bamana but his father French, played an important role in the French African army.
94. ANM 1E 18, Le Capitaine d'auxiliare Commandant le Cercle de Bamako à Monsieur le Commandant Supèrieur, p.i. Soudan Français, p. 3.
95. Dyara (Sauvageot), pp. 143-5.
96. ANM 1E 18, "Soudan Français," pp. 7-8.
97. Dyara (Sauvageot), p. 145.
98. ANM 1E 18, "Soudan Français," p. 5 makes reference to Depêche #139, 22 juillet 1888; 27 octobre 1888. This statement had not been confirmed at the time of this report.

99. See Méniaud, p. 349; Saint Martin, "Relations," pp. 209-13.

100. Pietri, p. 112.

101. Saint Martin, "La France," p. 196; "Oualata," p. 375; and Gallieni, p. 414.

102. ANM 1D 222 Mission Delanneau, p. 5.

103. ANM 1D 33 Monographie de Cercle de Bamako 1880-1914, p. 4.

104. ANM 1E 11 Rapport d'ensemble sur la situation politique de la Region du Sahel circulaire 147 et 148, Nioro, 25 juin 1896. The *tata* of Digna was taken and retaken three times. A true crusade operated in Bèlèdugu for its rebuilding. All the villages joined to build a *tata* so solid and thick that it could defy any attack. It was adorned with small pyramids.

105. Gallieni, p. 38.

106. AS 15 G 109/7 (e) "Poste de Médine," Bulletin agricole, commercial et politique, mois de décembre 1875, cited in Oloruntimehin, "Resistance," p. 133.

107. ANSOM Sénégal I 61 b, "notes sur la situation générale de la colonie," V. Valière, Saint-Louis, 20 mai 1876.

108. Gallieni, p. 379.

109. Jean Bayal, "Voyages au pays de Bamako," *Bulletin de la Société de Géographie de Paris*, 2(1881), pp. 147-8; Pietri, p. 391.

110. Oloruntimehin, "Resistance," p. 136.

111. Méniaud, p. 341.

112. MFOM Sénégal IV 87, de la Porte au Gouverneur Sénégal Instructions, 20 octobre 1886, cited in Kanya-Forstner, p. 148.

113. ANM 1E 18 Laroux-paiz, Fort de Bammako, Le Capitaine Commandant le fort à Monsieur le Commandment Supèrieur du Haute Fleuve, 28 fèvrier 1885; #385 A. Pounane, same to same, 1 décembre 1885; #215, same to same, 1 avril 1885; A. Pounane #385 same to same 1 décembre 1885; same to same, 31 octobre 1885.

114. ANM 1E 18 Note du Capitaine, Commandant de Cercle, mai 1896, Le Commandant de Cercle.

115. ANM 2E 67 #17 Le Commandant de Cercle de Bamako au Commandant Supèrieur de Haute Fleuve, Avril 1886, à mai 1886.

116. ANM 2E 67 #26 Rapport politique agricole et commerce septembre 1886.

117. ANM 2E 67 Loyer, Le Capitaine Loyer au Lt. Colonel, Commandant Supèrieur du Soudan Français, 20 fèvrier 1887; #20 same to same.

118. ANM 2E 67 Rapport politique le mois de mars 1887.

119. Ibid, 5 août 1887.

120. ANM 1E 18 Underberg, Bulletin Politique de Commandant de Bamako, Campagne 1888-89, 3 novembre 1889, p. 6.

121. Archinard, p. 16.

122. Interview: Kirango Ba Jara.

123. See Roberts, "Production," p. 414.

124. Mage, p. 182.

125. Interviews: Mountaga Tiam, Bokary Daou, Cekòrò Tangara and Amadu Tangara.

126. Interviews with Mountaga Tiam, and Bokary Daou.

127. Thiero, p. 101.

Chapter 4, pp. 83-99

1. ANM 1E 18 #28 Rapport politique agricole et commerce, 1 novembre 1886, p. 3.
2. See among others Saint-Martin, "Les Relations Diplomatiques entre la France et l'Empire Toucouleur de 1860 à 1887," *Bulletin de l'Institut Fondamental d'Afrique Noire*, 27(1965), p. 183; and, Claudine Gerresch, "Jugements du Moniteur du Sénégal sur al-Hajj 'Umar de 1857 à 1864," *Bulletin de l'Institut Fondamental d'Afrique Noire*, ser. b 35(1935), p. 576.
3. Kanya-Forstner, *The Conquest of the Western Sudan* (Cambridge: University Press, 1969), p. 149; see also Saint-Martin, "Relations," p. 185.
4. Hargreaves, "Tukulor," p. 129; Carrère and Holle, p. 195. For 'Umar's early contacts with French see Mage, p. 279; for analysis of his jihad to French imperialist goals, see Clarke, p. 134; and, for the attack of French post of Matam, see Wane, p. 448.
5. See, for example, Sanche de Gramont, *The Strong Brown God, the Story of the Niger River* (Boston: Haughton Mifflin, 1975), p. 249; also, ANM 1E 18, Bulletin Politique de Cercle de Bamako, 3 novembre 1889, Capitaine Underberg, p. 9.
6. ANM 1E 18, Bulletin Politique de Cercle de Bamako, 3 novembre 1889, Capitaine Underberg.
7. Louis Faidherbe, *Le Sénégal, la France dans l'Afrique Occidentale* (Paris: Hachette, 1889), p. 140; Mage, pp. 240, 248.
8. Hiskett, p. 230. See page 161 for author's views.
9. Oloruntimehin argues that no definitive peace treaty emerged from the discussions, *Segu-Tukulor*, p. 225. See also Saint-Martin, *L'Empire Toucouleur 1848-1891* (Paris: Livre Africain, 1970), pp. 59, 61, and 112.
10. Interview: Dramane Jara.
11. Frédéric Carrère and Paul Holle, *De la Sénégambie française* (Paris: Didot, 1855).
12. Hiskett, *Development*, p. 213; Carrère and Holle, pp. 59-62. Duveyrier (1840-1892) is the author of *Les Touareg du Nord* (Nendeln: Kraus rpt., 1973).
13. Mage, p. 284.
14. For text of treaty see Mage, pp. 588-9.
15. Kanya-Forstner, *Mali-Tukulor*, p. 63; Oloruntimehin, *Segu-Tukulor*, p. 227; Saint-Martin, "Relations," p. 190; Hargreaves, *Tukulor*, p. 133; and Mage, pp. 607-9.
16. Saint-Martin, *L'Empire*, p. 115; "Relations," pp. 193, 196-7; Kanya-Forstner, *Mali-Tukulor*, p. 64. The French had drafted plans by 1880 to build a railway between the Sénégal and the Niger, which required political control of the area; see C. W. Newberry and Kanya-Forstner, "French Policy and the Origin of the Scramble for West Africa," *Journal of African History* 10 (1969), 253-276.
17. ANS, Sénégal III, H. I. M. Cooper to Amade Seyhou, King of Segou-Sikoro, Bathurst, Gambia, 13 May 1876, cited in Oloruntimehin, *Segu-Tukulor*, p. 230; Soleillet, p. 443; Saint-Martin, *L'Empire*, p. 117.
18. Christopher Fyfe, *A History of Sierra Leone* (Oxford: University Press, 1962), p. 414. See pp. 427-8 for discussion of British-French competition. Gallieni reported that clothing materials, arms and ammunition were traded. His information was based on data from Ahmadu and interviews with Seydou Jeyla.
19. ANS 1G 18 (Lettre) au Roi de Segu par M. Raffenel, Officier du Commissariat de la Marine en Mission en Afrique, le 18 fèvrier 1848.

20. ANM 1E 18 #99 Tautain, le Commandant du Cercle de Bammako à Monsieur le Commandant Supèrieur de Soudan Française, 5 octobre 1887, p. 7.

21. Gallieni, p. 209.

22. Gallieni, p. 211. See Kanya-Forstner, "Mali-Tukulor," p. 64. The attack on the convoy alarmed the French for in future instructions all precautions were to be taken when traveling in the territory. ANM B 165 Projet et instructions pour le Lt. Col. Commandant Supèrieur de Haut-Sénégal.

23. Interview with the Elders of the Village of Nango, 10 octobre, 1995.

24. This section is primarily based on Gallieni, pp. 364-461.

25. These provinces included Dinguiray, Bafing, Manding, Fuladugu, Kaarta-Binè, Bakhunu, Kaarta, Jafunu, Jombokho, Kaniareme, Jala, Segu, Masina, Bambuk, Bondu, Futa, Kamera and Guidimakha.

26. Interview: Dramane Jara.

27. See also ANM 1D 55-2 Fondation de l'état Bambara de Ségou-quelques notes sur l'histoire de cet état, 1896, p. 9.

28. Oral evidence at Segu, May 1965 taken by Oloruntimehin, *Segu-Tukulor*, p. 240.

29. ANM 1D 33, Borgnes-Desbordes, "Bamako Hier, Aujourd'hui et Demain," p. 19; see also Oloruntimehin, *Segu-Tukulor*, pp. 241-2, p. 242 fn.

30. Gallieni, p. 365.

31. Gallieni, pp. 452-453. It is unclear how he arrived at this conclusion.

32. ANM B 165 #227 Le Gouverneur du Sénégal et Dépendances à Monsieur le Colonel Supèrieur du Haute-Sénégal, St. Louis, 4 janvier 1885.

33. Ibid.

34. The French perceived the weaknesses in the 'Umarian state in 1883, and they hoped to exploit them. ANM B 165 #1405 Felix Faure à Monsieur le Gouverneur, Paris, 5 novembre 1883; #142 Le Ministre à Monsieur le Gouverneur du Sénégal et Dépendances, A. Rousseau, Paris, 4 juillet 1885, p. 10.

35. ANM B 67 Le Commandant Supèrieur à Ahmadu, Kayes, 22 novembre 1885.

36. ANM B 165 Télégramme #117 Peyron au Gouverneur Paris, 19 avril 1884. Lt. Col. Boilevé had sent a telegram to the Minister of Marine on 14 fèvrier 1884.

37. One of the major goals of the French in seeking a treaty was to operate steamboats on the Niger. ANM B 165 Lettre d'Ahmadu Cheikh, 22 septembre 1884.

38. For example, see Pierre Gourou, "Gallieni," in Charles Julien, ed. *Les Techniciens de la Colonisation* (Paris: Presses Universitaires de France, 1946), p. 95 and Pierre Montagnon, *La France Coloniale la Gloire de l'Empire* (Paris: Pygmalion/Gerard Watelet, 1988).

39. The French repeated this tactic in other "negotiations" with African emissaries.

40. ANS 1D 69 Rapport sur la Campagne de 1882-1883 dans le Soudan par B. Desbordes, Bamako, 20 mars 1883, p. 73, rpt. in Oloruntimehin *Segu-Tukulor*, p. 255; see also p. 256.

41. ANM B 165 #1405 Feliz Faure à Monsieur le Gouverneur, 5 novembre 1883.

42. B"me, p. 38.

43. For a discussion of the history of Bamako and the transition by the 'Umarian regime and Bamana rebel activities see Roberts *Warriors*, pp. 140-51.

44. ANM B 165 Télégramme #227, St. Louis, 4 janvier 1885.

45. ANM B 67 Télégramme #333, Frey au Gouverneur à St. Louis, 29 octobre 1885. The

CHAPTER 4, PP. 83-99 (CONTINUED)

French wanted Samori and Mahmadu Lamine to sign treaties which would facilitate commerce. Perhaps fear that Ahmadu would attack the French was augmented by the fact that his brothers told the French that he was making preparations to do so; see ANM B67 Télégramme #483 à Monsieur le Gouverneur, Niagassila, 28 janvier 1886; ANM 67 #16 Situation générale, p. 1; Le Commandant Supèrieur à Ahmadu Ségou, Kayes 12 novembre 1885 and 22 novembre 1885.

46. ANM 1D 222 Mission Delanneau.

47. ANM 1E 18 #101 Capitaine Commandant le fort de Bammako à Monsieur le Commandant Supèrieur de Haute-Fleuve.

48. ANM 1D 222 Le Capitaine Delanneau Commissaire du Gouverneur à bord du "Niger" Chef de Mission à Commandant Supèrieur du Haut-Sénégal Rapport Complementaire.

49. ANM 1E 18 #385 Le Capitaine Commandant le fort de Bammako à Monsieur le Commandant Supèrieur de Haut-Fleuve, and Le Capitaine Breveté d'état-major Septans, Commandant le Cercle de Bammako à Monsieur le Chef d'Escadrons, Commandant Supèrieur du Soudan Français, 27 octobre 1888.

50. ANM B 165 Felix Faure à Monsieur le Gouverneur, Paris, 5 juin 1884.

51. ANM 1E 18 Mamadu Racine, Capitaine Commandant le Cercle Nyamina à Monsieur le Chef de Bataillon Commandant Supèrieur, p.i., Kayes, septembre 1889.

52. ANM 1D 222 Mission Delanneau.

53. ANM B 67 Télégramme #54, Commandant Supèrieur à Commandant Bammako, 26 novembre 1885.

54. ANM B 67 Télégramme #106, à Monsieur le Gouverneur, 28 novembre 1885.

55. Gallieni, *Deux Campagnes au Soudan-Français 1886-1888* (Paris: Librarie Hachette, 1891), pp. 185-9.

56. Saint-Martin, *L'Empire*, pp. 107-119; "La Volonté de paix d'El Hadj Omar et d'Ahmadu dans leurs relations avec la France," *Bulletin de l'Institut Fondamental d'Afrique Noire*, ser. b, 30 (1968) pp. 785-805, especially pp. 795-7; "Relations," pp. 183-221. Amar Samb argues that Saint-Martin's assertion that 'Umar had no desire to fight the French is not convincing; "Sur El Hadj," pp. 803-4.

57. Kanya-Forstner, *Mali-Tukulor*, p. 66.

58. ANM B 67 #483 à Monsieur le Gouverneur, Niagassada, 28 janvier 1886; "Chroniques de Oualata," p. 375.

Chapter 5, pp. 101-118

1. Raymond Betts, *Assimilation and Association in French Colonial Theory 1890-1914* (New York: Columbia University, 1961), pp. 90, 94. See also Arthur Girault, *Principles de Colonisation et de legislation coloniale* (Paris: Recueil Sirey, 1895).

2. Roberts, *Warriors*, p. 135.

3. Dr. Colin, "Le Soudan Occidental," *Revue Maritime et Coloniale*, 78(1883), p. 8.

4. Ibid, p. 8, f.n. 1.

5. Roberts, *Warriors*, p. 143, and "Emergence," p. 43.

6. Roberts, *Warriors*, p. 148.
7. Ibid, p.9.
8. Roberts, *Warriors*, p. 148.
9. Colin, pp. 5-6.
10. Gallieni to Archinard, 3 August 1888, Archinard Papers, quoted in Kanya-Forstner, *Conquest*, p. 175.
11. ANM B 83 Le Chef Escadron Archinard Commandant Supèrieur du Soudan Français à Monsieur Gouverneur du Sénégal et Dépendances. St Louis, Kayes 9 janvier 1890. Archinard complained that because of the auxiliaries employed and the bad installation of the telegraphs, there was no guarantee of secrecy.
12. Ibid, p. 8.
13. Archinard, *Le Soudan Français*, p. 28.
14. Kanya-Forstner, *Conquest*, p. 178.
15. Archinard, p. 6.
16. St. Martin, "L'Empire," p. 146.
17. Archinard, p. 6; Kanya-Forstner, p. 182.
18. Archinard, p. 7.
19. Ibid, p. 11. See also p. 143.
20. Interview: Dramane Jara. The chair is in the possession of Madani Tal in Segu.
21. St. Martin, "Un Fils," pp. 165-6.
22. Aguibu was the only viable successor as a son of al-Hajj 'Umar since his brothers were dead or in weaker positions to claim the throne.
23. Archinard, pp. 16-7.
24. ASAOF 1G 115/I, Le sous-lieutenent Marchand à Monsieur le Capitaine Underberg, Nyamina, 10 septembre 1899, quoted in Oloruntimehin, *Tukulor*, p. 289.
25. Méniaud, vol. I, p.459.
26. Interviews: Sajo Jara, and Cèkòrò Tangara.
27. Saint Martin, *L'Empire*, p. 145.
28. Interview: Bacèkòrò Kulubali.
29. Méniaud, vol. l, p. 459; Roberts, p. 151.
30. ANM IN 96 #2326. Télégramme. Kayes à Commandant Supèrieur troupes, St. Louis, 17 juillet 1890.
31. Interview: Dramane Jara. St. Martin states that Archinard had two 80mm mountain guns, two 95 mm field artillery guns, and a 150mm mortar. See *L'Empire*, p. 149.
32. Interview: Soumaila Fanè.
33. Interview: Mountaga Tiam.
34. Muslim intellectuals frequently maintained a personal house (Tiam).
35. Interview: Soumaila Fanè.
36. After the seizure of Segu, Archinard reportedly stalled when Abdul asked about the promises. Later, Archinard told him to go to Kayes for his rewards. When he arrived, he gave the letter from Archinard to the French authority. The latter asked him what did the 'Umarian leader do for you in this situation. He said that each time he returned from war, the ruler gave him ten slaves and ten cows, and that he had a king's daughter as a wife. The French authority responded to him, "We don't keep slaves. We don't fight in order to raid, but in order to free, and our daughters don't love you. A king

CHAPTER 5, PP. 101-118 (CONTINUED)

who did all that for you, you dared to betray him, and the one who cannot give you that, you know that you will betray us also as you have betrayed your king who gave you all that." Abdul was killed by the French, but before dying, he said, "I have lost this world and I have lost the other because I betrayed the *diina* (religion)." (Soumaila Fanè).

37. Kanya-Forstner, "Mali-Tukulor," p.69.

38. Thiero, p. 108. Koda Cèro later became the "Chief of Canton" (Sòmònò Canton).

39. Interview: Bokary Daou.

40. Saint-Martin, "L'Empire," p. 150.

41. Certain objects from Segu decorated two windows of the Sénégal Pavilion at the Exposition of 1900. 74 k 832 of gold pieces and 157 k 225 of silver pieces were taken. 1N 63 Objets et matières d'or.

42. Interview: Bokary Daou.

43. Kanya-Forstner, "Mali-Tukulor," p. 70.

44. For events in this section see St. Martin, *L'Empire*, pp.154-5; Kanya-Forstner, "Mali-Tukulor," pp. 70-1; Oloruntimehin, *Tukulor*, pp. 298-303.

45. ANM 1N 96 à Gouverneur à Saint-Louis, 3 juin 1890, and 5 juin 1890.

46. Lt. Slvaset Lucciardi was wounded, two African Sphahis (cavalrymen) wounded, and about a dozen auxiliary men were lost. ANM IN 96 Télégramme Commandant Supèrieur à Gouverneur, St. Louis, Médine 18 juin 1890. According to one report, Moors from Bakel had joined Ahmadu in early May. ANM IN 96 Télégramme, Commandant Supèrieur à Gouverneur, St. Louis, 6 mai 1890.

47. In order that people would revolt, Archinard proclaimed several areas under French protection independent of Ahmadu. After the battle of Yuri, 15 talibes demanded to return to Futa Toro; some were very important military leaders. ANM 1E 284 Kayes de Bamako #635 Depot 28 #198 21 juillet 1891 Résident de Ségou à Commandant Supèrieur, Kayes.

48. "Oualata," p. 541.

49. Amdiata Sidibe, a Futaka of Dianghirte who gave this information reported that Ali Buri refused to continue east, and attempted to get Ahmadu to return toward the Futa. When Ahmadu declined, they separated.

50. ANM 1E 219 Le Resident de Ségou à Monsieur le Colonel Commandant Supèrieur de Soudan Français, Ségou, 15 octobre 1891. Included in Ahmadu's army: a garrison of 150 Sokola cavaliers; 2000 *sofas* of Alpha Moussa; 1000 Futaka of Masina; 700 émigrés of Kingui; and contingents of Fulani and Tombes.

51. Mohammadu Muniru had been referred to as Vice-King of Masina although he considered himself an independent monarch. He wanted to mobilize troops against Ahmadu, but the 'Umarian counsel refused to follow him. Therefore, he gave the secret gris-gris which al-Hajj had given him to Tijani. See Mademba, "La Dernière étape," pp. 473-4. Besides the gris-gris, Ahmadu reclaimed all which was his. See ANM 1E 219 Le Résident de Ségou à Monsieur le Colonel Commandant Supèrieur de Soudan Français, Ségou 15 octobre 1891, p. 6; 1E 220 La Fama de Sansanding et Dépendances à Monsieur le Résident de Ségou, Sansanding, 18 mars, 1891; and ANM B 150 Lettre de Guget, Nioro, 18 juillet 1891, and (lettre) à Résident de Ségou Kayes,

19 juillet, 1891.

52. See Robinson, *Chiefs and Clerics, Abdul Bokal Kan and Futa Toro 1853-1891* (Oxford: Clarendon Press, 1975), pp. 149-50 for a similar analysis.

53. See Mage-Barth, p. 2.

54. When he finally formed an alliance with the Bamana, it was far too late.

55. See also Bill Freud, *The Making of Contemporary Africa* (Bloomington: Indiana University, 1984), Chapter 5; Myron Echenberg, *Colonial Conscripts: The Tirailleurs Senegalais in French West Africa, 1857-1960* (Portsmouth: Heinemann Educational, 1991; and, Roberts, "Emergence," p. 41.

56. Roberts, p. 152. St. Martin reports 35 officers, 635 African soldiers and 72 Europeans. See *L'Empire*, p. 149.

57. Dramane Jara discusses the role of Africans in the French Army.

58. Examples include when the Bamana soldiers of Bèlèdugu were instrumental in holding Samori in check; Ntaro, a military leader in the Bamana army of Segu, blocked the 'Umarians who attempted to encircle the column of Marchand; and at Kita, auxiliary troops were emplaced to prevent Ahmadu from reaching Samori or his brother in Dinguiray. ANM 1D 9 Notice Historique sur la Région du Sahel par le Capitaine de Lartique 1896.

59. ANM 220 #71 Le Fama de Sansanding et Dépendances à Monsieur le Résident de Ségou, Sansanding, 28 décembre 1891.

60. Interviews: Bacèkòrò Kulubali and Sajo Jara.

61. Lt. Gatelet, *Histoire de la Conquête du Soudan Français 1878-1899* (Paris: Nancy, Berger-Levrault, et Cie, 1901), p. 15.

62. Interview: Dramane Jara.

Chapter 6, pp. 119-141

1. Mademba had been an employee at the Sénégalese Colonial Post since 1869, a soldier since 1879, and a political officer for Desbordes in 1882-83. He was also a French citizen.

2. Ibid.

3. Interview: Soumaila Fanè.

4. ANS 1G 172 Palavre avec Mari Jara.

5. Interview: Soumaila Fanè.

6. ANM 1D 55-1 "Redevances payées par les Sòmònòs," Notices Historique du Royaume de Ségou.

7. Mountaga Tiam. According to Tiam, the interpreters were sent to collect the fish. Although a large portion of the Futanke population had been chased from Segu, the interpreters were often Futankes such as Ahmadu Koumba Ketal, Kalamine Mamudu and Fama Mademba Sy. For quotation in French records, ANM B150 #31 au Capitaine Briquelet, 24 octobre 1891, p. 4.

8. The Arabic library of Ahmadu and Madani was seized and sent to France.

9. ANS 15 G 172 Palavre avec Mari Jara.

10. ANM 1D 55-1 "Situation Intérieure," Notice sur le Royaume Bambara de Ségou,

CHAPTER 6, PP. 119-141 (CONTINUED)

Mage-Barth et à Farako 1889.

11. ANM 1D 55-1, "Situation Intérieure."

12. Theiro, p. 99.

13. The information in the next two paragraphs is based on information provided by Bacèkòrò Kulubali. Ntò's father, Nkaro Nji, military leader in Bamana army, and Ntò's brother, Nianson were faithful to the Ngolosiw after the 'Umarian invasion.

14. ANM 2E 67 Fiche de renseignements concernant le nommé Nto, Chief de Cantons de Nto et de Sokoro, ouverte le 1ère janvier 1897. Ntò later allied with the French.

15. ANM ID 55 Notice sur le Royaume Bambara de Ségou-Mage-Barth et à Farako 1889, p. 17.

16. Ibid.

17. Thiero, p. 110. See also Bill Freud, pp. 87-90.

18. Thiero, p. 110.

19. Interviews: Bamyama Kulubali and Sajo Jara.

20. Much of this information is based on ANM ID 55-2 "Fondation de l'état Bambara de Ségou-quelques notes sur l'histoire de cet état 1896."

21. Thiero, p. 108.

22. These letters were written on the 15 and 16 of April, 1890.

23. See also ANM B 83 Le Chef Escadron Archinard Commandant Supèrieur du Sudan Français à Monsieur Gouverneur du Sénégal et Dépendances, St. Louis. Kayes, 9 janvier 1890. This report reflects Archinard's early intentions to keep Mari Jara's power and actions in check.

24. This section is based on oral testimony by Dramane Jara unless otherwise noted.

25. Dyara (Sauvageot), p. 147.

26. Lt. Gatelet, *Histoire de la conquête du Soudan Français 1878-1899* (Paris: Nancy, Berger-Levrault et Cie, 1901), pp. 151-2.

27. Theiro, p. 111.

28. Interview: Soumaila Fanè.

29. Interviews: Soumaila Fanè and Dramane Jara.

30. Interview: Dramane Jara.

31. Interview: Kiranga Ba.

32. Roberts, *Warriors*, p. 156.

33. Ibid, p. 157.

34. See for example, ANM 1E 71 Rapport sur la Situation Politique des territoires dépendants de la résidence de Ségou, Ségou, 1891, and ANM 1E-72 Rapport sur l'organisation de Cercle de Ségou, Ségou le 16 janvier 1918.

35. This section is primarily based on ANM 1E 71 Historique de la revolte du Baninko, Royaume de Ségou.

36. ANM 5D 45 Notes Année, 1891. He became one of the strongest supporters of the Ngolosiw in freeing themselves of the French and Bojan.

37. His brother, according to the French, had been executed by Mademba the previous year.

38. Separate armies operated to control the Middle Niger, the French-African army, and the armies of local leaders like Ntò, Bojan, and Mademba Sy, which were under the

orders of these leaders.

39. See Capitaine Abd-el Kader Mademba, *Au Sénégal et au Soudan Français* (Paris: Librairie Larosse, 1931), pp. 45-6; and, ANM 1D 55-2 Notice Historique, "La prise de Ségou par les Français.

40. Interview: Bacèkòrò Kulubali.

41. Problems surrounding the boundary between Segu and Kènèdugu made it more difficult for pacification of the region.

42. See Abd-el-Kabir Mademba, pp. 79-83; and Mage, p. 117.

43. Interview: Seidu Kulubali.

44. Both communicated with Ahmadu in Banjagara. Baya was a former Marabout of Mari Jara.

45. ANM 1E 71 Rapport sur la situation politique des territoires dépendant de la Résidence de Ségou, Ségou 1891.

46. ANM ID 55-1 Notices historique du Royaume de Ségou 2° parte 1896.

47. ANM ID 55-1 Organisation du Royaume de Ségou.

48. ANM 5D 45 Notes Année 1891.

49. The village leader was Marka, but all refused to recognize him.

50. ANM 1E 220 Le Fama de Sansanding et Dépendances à Monsieur le Résident de Ségou.

51. ANM 1E 229 1ère Partie 1893 Sur les événements de Minanko fèvrier 1891-juin 1892.

52. The French gave the title of "Fama" to Bojan and Mademba, but the Bamana, in general, refused to recognize them as such. The title ended when the last dynastic Fama, Mari Jara, was murdered.

53. ANM 1E 220 Le Fama de Sansanding et Dépendances à Monsieur le Résident de Ségou, 3 juin 1891.

54. Name not given.

55. ANM 1E 229 (une lettre) à Monsieur Underberg, Djenné, 14 fèvrier, 1891.

56. ANM IN 149 #94 Télégramme pour Kayes de Ségou, 29 fèvrier 1892.

57. Situation politique des Royaumes de Ségou et Sansanding, "III Macina," p. 29.

58. Ibid. Mountaga Tiam asserts that the Bamana had also attempted to form an alliance with Samori Turè.

59. Ibid.

60. ANM 1N 64 Le Lt. Cailleau à Monsieur le Capitaine Résident à Ségou, 7 octobre 1892.

61. ANM 1N 64 Le Lieutenant Cailleau à Monsieur le Capitaine Résident à Ségou, n.d.; same to same, n.d. (two reports).

62. ANM 1N 64 Bla, same to same, 7 octobre 1892; same to same, 9 octobre 1892.

63. 1N 149 Operations militaires tèlègrammes et supérieur au Lt. de Cercle de Ségou, 1892.

64. ANM 1E 229. Capitaine Résident Bonaccorci, Ségou, 5 mars 1893. Sur les événements du Minanka, fèvrier 1891 à juin 1892.

65. When Ahmadu was fleeing to Banjagara in March 1891, the Bamana of Toguerasa (near Jenné) welcomed him. ANM 1E 220 (lettre) le Fama de Sansanding à Monsieur le Résident de Ségou, 21 mars 1891.

66. Ahmadu also made an alliance with Abdul Bokar during the same period. ANM 1D 3

CHAPTER 6, PP. 119-141 (CONTINUED)

Études Historique.

67. ANS 1D 128/10, Instructions pour le Résident de Ségou par le Commandant Supèrieur, G. Humbert, Bissandugu, 27 mars 1892, pp. 55-6, quoted in Oloruntimehin, *Segu-Tukulor*, p. 309. See also ANM 1D 221, "V Kenedugu," Rapport sur la situation politique des territoires dépendant de la Résidence de Ségou, Ségou, 15 septembre 1891; and ANM 1N 149 Télégramme #71, pour Kayes de Ségou, 11 fèvrier 1892.

68. See St. Martin, *L'Empire*, p.160, and Méniaud, vol. II, p. 277. Ahmadu's brother, Muntaga, had been with Sarancene Mori, a son of Samori, since the fall of Segu to the Bamana in 1890. ANM 1N 149 Télégramme #1924 à Col. Lieutinent, 1895, Ségou.

69. The 'Fama' of Sinzani reported that the French could not even count on the Fula of Masina who hated the French as much as the 'Umarians. ANM 1E 220 #26 Le Fama de Sansanding et Dépendances a Monsieur le Résident de Ségou, Sansanding, 9 juin 1891.

70. Oloruntimehin, "Anti-French Coalition of African States and Groups in the Western Sudan 1889-1893," *ODU* (April 1970), p. 8.

71. A griot, Kaartanke, reported that Ahmadu was powerless, and that his Bamana, Fula, Bozo and Tuboko followers were waiting for an occasion to abandon him, Situation politique, "III Macina."

72. Cèba's brother, Babemba, and Samori Turè would continue to fight until 1898.

73. Duguolo had given asylum to Sambori and Daba Demba and their followers.

74. This section was based on ANM 1E 71 Rapport politique de Royaume de Ségou et Sansanding en septembre 1892; Rapport politique sur les Etats de Sansanding et Ségou, Ségou, 10 novembre 1892; and, various oral testimony.

75. Ibid.

76. Ibid.

77. Ibid.

78. Ibid.

79. ANM 1E 71 Rapport sur la situation des états de Ségou et de Sansanding du 19 octobre 1892 au janvier 1893, 5 janvier 1893.

80. Ibid.

81. ANM 1E 71, "Pays au nord du Bani," Bulletin politique et militaire, janvier 1893.

82. Ibid.

83. ANM 1E 71 Bulletin politique et militaire, fèvrier 1894, 27 fèvrier 1894.

84. ANM 1E 71 Bulletin politique et militaire mars 1894, 1 avril 1894.

85. Two of the villages, Natasso and Yankasso, commanded the most frequent routes which led to San.

86. ANM 1D 55-2 Notice Historique, "Prise de Ségou par les Français."

87. ANM 1D 55-1 "Situation Intérieure."

Chapter 7, pp. 143-175

1. Betts, p. 8.

2. For a more detailed discussion of the origin of the "assimilation" ideology and its development in French culture and eventually in French colonial administration, see Betts, pp. 10-32; Girault; and, A. Arnaud and H. Meray, *Les colonies francaises, organisation administrative, judiciare, politique et financiere* (Paris: Augustin Challamel, 1900).

3. Yves Guyot, *Lettres sur la politique coloniale* (Paris: C. Reinwald, 1885), p. 215.

4. Alfred Fouillee, "Le Caractère des races humaines et l'avenir de la race blanche," *Revue des Deux Mondes*, 74(July 1, 1894), p. 88; and Charles Castre, *Ideals of France* (New York: The Abingdon Press, 1922) p. 34; see also Gabriel Hanotaux *L'Énergie Française* (Paris: Flammarion, 1902), p. 365.

5. Betts, p. 120.

6. Betts, p. 107. See also Joseph Chailley-Bert, *Dix années de politique coloniale* (Paris: Armond Colin, 1902), pp. 1-2; and Eugène Etienne, "Protectorate et décentralisation," *Dépêche Coloniale,* (28 décembre 1902).

7. Lewis Gann and Peter Duignan, *Burden of Empire: An Appraisal of Western Colonialism in Africa South of the Sahara* (New York: 1959), pp. 217-8.

8. Joseph Gallieni, *Neuf ans à Madagascar* (Paris: Hachette, 1908), p. 325.

9. Delavignette, pp. 1-2.

10. Ibid, p. 6.

11. Ibid, p. 11.

12. Ibid, pp. 3-4. See also Louis Brenner, *West African Sufi* (Berkeley: University of California, 1984), p. 34.

13. ANM 1E 71 Rapport politique du mois de mars 1897.

14. ANM 1E 72 Rapport politique quatrième trimestre 1916, Ségou, 31 décembre 1916, Battus.

15. Ibid, pp. 71-2; Banbera (Conrad), p. 93.

16. I use "provincial chief" because this is the term used in French colonial records to describe the administration of the region and the administration unit. ANM 1E 55-1 "Notice Historique."

17. ANM 1E 18 Rapport politique pour le mois de juin 1900.

18. ANM B 150 #10 (Correspondence) 5 avril 1909.

19. Michael Crowder, "Indirect Rule: British and French Style," *Africa* 34 (1964) 197-205, and *West Africa under European Rule* (Evanston: Northwestern University, 1968).

20. ANM ID 55-1 Organisation du royaume de Ségou.

21. ANM A 12 Décision #270, Le Général Lt. Gouverneur le Colonel charge de l'expédition des affairs, Kayes, 5 avril 1899; and, Circulaire #778 Re: Fiches de Renseignements, Kayes, 10 fèvrier 1899, Trentenian.

22. Thiero, p. 116.

23. Interview: Seidou Kulubali, Kirango. The French even placed some 'Umarians in Bamana (and other) villages to administer those which were dependent on Segu. The Bamana village of Turella continued to have a Bamana ruler, but Gallieni stated that

CHAPTER 7, PP. 143-175 (CONTINUED)

the authority was "merely nominal, and his role was to transmit orders of the tax collectors to the people." Gallieni, pp. 341-2.

24. ANM A 12 Circulaire #37 à Monsieurs (sic) les Commandants de Régions de Cercles, Kayes, 12 janvier 1899, Trentinian; and, Circulaire #583 à tous les Commandants des Régions et des Cercles. See also 1E 11 Rapport politique HLN Région du Sahel 1896 where a Commandant wrote that a show of French force in Beledugu made the Bamana realize French power.

25. ANM 1D 55-1 Notice Historique, "Revenues de la Résidence."

26. ANM 1D 55-1 Notice Historique, "Administration des revenues."

27. Ibid.

28. M. Semakula Kiwanuka, "Colonial Policies and Administrations in Africa: The Myths of the Contrasts," *International Journal of African Historical Studies* 3(1970), p. 297.

29. See Blassingame; Frederick Douglass, *My Bondage and My Freedom* (New York: Miller, Orton and Mulligan, 1968 (1855)); Marion Russell, "American Slave Discontent in Records of the High Courts," *Journal of Negro History,* 31(October 1946), pp. 411-34; and Marion D. Kilson, "Towards Freedom: An Analysis of Slave Revolts in the United States," *Phylon,* 25 (Summer, 1964), pp. 175-87.

30. Kiwanuka, p. 296.

31. One village leader sent a notable to make a submission, offering a sheep, and demanding justice against other villages. The Commandant argued, "These people only came when they needed the French, not when the French needed them." ANM 1E 71 Bulletin politique et militaire, mois de septembre 1894, Segou, 1 octobre 1894.

32. Ibid.

33. ANM 1E 18 Rapport sur la tournée faite par le Capitaine Besancon, Commandant de Cercle de Bamako.

34. ANM B 150 #421 L'Administrateur de Cercle de Segou à Monsieur le Commis en Service à Barouele; #10 (Correspondence) 5 avril 1909; and #14 9 avril 1909.

35. ANM 1E Rapport du Lieutenant Calisti du 2° regiment de Tiraileurs Sénégalais, sur la tournée de police faite dans le nord du cercle, Kayes, 1 juillet 1900, Calisti.

36. ANM 1E 18 Rapport politique du mois de fevrier 1896.

37. ANM 1E 72 Rapport d'ensemble sur la tournée effectué dans la region du Baninko par l'adjoint des Affaires Indigenes, Correnson, du 21 avril au 8 mai 1907, Segou, le 13 mai 1907.

38. ANM A-12 Circulaire #650 à tous les Commandants de Regions de Cercles, Kayes, 1899.

39. ANM 1E 18 #90 Bulletin politique, 1898, 13 avril 1898, A. Besancon.

40. Ibid.

41. Besancon rejected the idea that a military confederation really existed, nor that Joce was more powerful than other leaders like Samba Jara or Niamante Dembele.

42. ANM 1E 18 #1 Rapport semestriel du Commandant du Cercle, 2° Semestre 1898, le 2 janvier 1899; Bulletin politique, mois d'aout, à septembre 1898; Rapport sur la tournée de Bèlèdugu, 26 juin 1898, Bamako, A. Besancon.

43. ANM 1E 18 #131 Bulletin politique, mars 1899, 3 avril 1899. The Commandant sent an agent, Tamba Diallo, to bring Bague Jara, the Head of the Canton, and his princi-

pal village heads and 400 porters with millet to Bamako.

44. ANM 1E 19 Rapport politique, mois de Mars 1903, Bamako, 31 mars 1903, Bonnasses.

45. ANM 1E 72 Rapport sur la tournée effective du 6 au 21 mai 1912, Carbone.

46. ANM 1E 18 #283 Rapport general du Capitaine d'artillerie de Marine Charnet Commandant le Cercle de Bamako du Colonel Lieutenant Gouveneur p.t. sur la politique du cercle pendant le 1o semestre 1899, Bamako, a juillet 1899.

47. ANM 1E 71 Rapport sur la tournée.

48. ANM 1E 72 Rapport de tournée (Baninko), Barouele, le 20 avril 1917.

49. ANM 1E 72 Rapport politique, mois de mais 1915, Segou, 2 avril 1915, P. Benard; Compte-rendu de la tournée effective dans le N'to par l'Administrateur du Cercle du 26 mars au 7 avril 1915, Segou, le 30 avril 1915, P. Bernard.

50. ANM 1N 8 Revolte du Beledugu, Instruction Journal, 1915. The French "paid" the Africans who repressed the revolt in the cantons south of the Cercle of Gumbu with a cow or a heifer depending on the number of battles in which they participated. They gave ten cows to the family of those killed in action. See ANM 1N 3 L'Administrateur des Colonies, J. Rocache à Monsieur le Gouverneur de Haut-Sénégal-Niger, Koulouba, 7 juillet 1915.

51. ANM A 12 Circulaire #583 à tous les Commandants du Regions et de Cercles.

52. ANM 1E 72 Rapport politique quatrième trimestre 1916, Segou, 31 decembre 1916, Battus; and, Rapport sur la politique generale du cercle #4476, Segou, le 6 juillet 1917, Casse.

53. ANM 1E 19 Rapport Politique, mars 1903, Bamako, 31 mars 1903.

54. Interview: Kirango Ba Jara. These students learned trades, agriculture, animal husbandry, and fishing.

55. ANM 1E 19 Rapport politique, septembre 1903, Bamako.

56. Ibid.

57. ANM 1E 11 Rapport sur l'organization politique et administration du Haut-Sénégal, novembre 1900-1903.

58. ANM 1E 19 Rapport politique, mars 1903, Ségou, 31 mais 1903.

59. ANM 1E 72 Rapport politique, mois de novembre 1908, Ségou, 1 décembre 1908, Relhie.

60. ANM 1E 72 Rapport politique, mois de decembre 1908. By comparison with the indigenous system of Qur'anic schooling, the census before 1903 revealed that 75 marabouts in the cercle taught the Qur'an to 2100 students. In the French estimation, the progress of these students was slow due to the weak instruction of the teachers. See p. 30 for an account of Muslim schools under early colonial occupation.

61. See ANM 4E 69 Rapport du Capitaine Perignon, Commandant du Cercle de Ségou, à Monsieur le Délégué Gouverneur Général, 26 septembre 1900.

62. ANM 1D 33 Enquête Politique Musulman de Cercle de Bamako, Residence de Banamba, 31 mai 1914.

63. Ibid.

64. ANM 1D 38 Études Générales Monographie du Cercle de Djenné 1909, Djenné, 20 novembre 1909.

65. ANM 1E 71 Rapport Politique du mois d'août 1901.

66. ANM 1E 71 B. 2950 Rapport Général sur la Situation du Cercle, 1 septembre 1897,

CHAPTER 7, PP. 143-175 (CONTINUED)

Ségou 15 aout 1897, le Commandant Montguers.

67. ANM 4E 69 Rapport du Capitaine Mayer, Commandant le Cercle de Ségou. Objet=Response au questionnaire du Gouveneur Général de l'Algerie (Curculaire #B 281), Ségou, 16 octobre 1896, Commandant de la Région, L. Benoit.

68. ANM 4E 69 Rapport de Capitaine Perignon, Commandant du Cercle de Ségou, à Monsieur le Délégué du Gouverneur Général, 26 septembre 1900. See also CEDRAB #140, Abdallay Jiri, "Tarikh Ségou," Ségou, aout 1976.

69. ANM 4E 69 Rapport Ségou 1894-1917, Ségou, le 16 octobre 1896, L. Benoit.

70. ANM 1E 19 Rapport politique, mois d'avril 1903, Koulikoro, 5 mai 1903; mois de mars 1903, Bamako, 31 mars 1903; and, mois de juillet 1903, Bamako, 18 août 1903, Brévié.

71. ANM 4E 69 Rapport sur l'Islamisme, Ségou 1913, J. Rocache.

72. The administration considered al-Hajj Buguni as the only serious candidate for the title of Shaykh; see ANM 4E 69 1896 Cercle du Ségou, Rapport du Capitaine Mayer, Commandant le Cercle de Ségou, Objet=Response au questionnaire du gouverneur général de l'Algerie (Circulaire #B 281). The administration compiled a religio-political profile of the direct descendants of the last shaykhs, al-Hajj 'Umar and Ahmadu Lobo. Mamadu Shaykh, son of al Hajj, 40, was considered insane. Nagniron, 34, was without valor, and kept at a distance. Maqui, son of Ahmadu, 28, was without great influence, but possessed an irreproachable character, and was the only one who held French interest.

73. ANM 1E 20 Rapport politique, 3e trimestre (1920?), Bolichon.

74. ANM 1E 72 Administrateur en Chef de Ire Classe à Monsieur l'Administrateur Commandant de Cercle de Ségou, 12 aout 1916.

75. ANM 1E 72 Rapport politique de mois de mai 1915, Ségou 12 avril 1915, P. Bernard.

76. ANM B 150 #21 (Correspondence) 26 octobre 1909.

77. ANM ID 33 Enquête politique Musulman Cercle de Bamako, résidence de Banamba, 31 mai, 1914.

78. ANM 5D 44 Rapport de l'adjoint des affaires Indigènes. A. Combe sur sa tournée de recensement dans la circonsereftions de Barouelé, Barouelé le 31 octobre 1912.

79. ANM 5D 45 Recensement de la Population, Cercle de Ségou, 20 août 1904. In 1891 2,413 were listed without religion compared to 2,660 in 1904. The French provided no reasons for those falling in this category. Many Sòmònò and Bozo were also non-Muslims in Sinzani.

80. ANM 1E 72 Rapport de tournée de l'administrateur, adjoint Spitz, Guenekalary, de 21 novembre au 7 décembre 1908. Twenty-five of the thirty-eight villages were totally or mostly Bamana.

81. ANM 1E 72 Tournée effectué par l'administrateur adjoint du Cercle de Ségou dans le Kaminiandugu 10 mars 1909 au 30 mars 1909, Relhie. It is unclear who took the census in the villages, African employees or the person whose name appears in the title of the reports.

82. ANM 1E 72 Rapport de tournée, Ségou, le 27 septembre 1912, Bastide.

83. ANM 1D 38 Études générales-Monographie du Cercle de Djenné 1909, VIIème section.

84. ANM 1E 72 Tournée effectué par l'administrateur adjoint du Cercle de Ségou dans le Kaminiandugu du 10 Mars 1909 au 30 mars 1909, carnet d'itenéraire, Relhie.

85. The report listed the religion of the people. Most of the Bamana were specifically indicated as "Fetishes," or Muslim. A few, however, were followed by no religious notation.

86. ANM 1E 72 Rapport sur la tournée effective du 6 au 21 mai 1912.

87. ANM 1E 72 Rapport de Tournée, Ségou, le 27 septembre 1912, Bartide.

88. ANM 1E 71 Rapport semestriel sur la situation du Cercle, 1e semestre, 1898.

89. ANM E 4 Cercle de Ségou, Rapport sur les Associations Catholiques et indigènes (télégramme no. 2481 de Monsieur Lt. Gouverneur du Haut-Sénégal-Niger), Ségou, 18 août 1905, le Commandant du Cercle.

90. ANM 4E 69 "Situation de l'Islamism," Rapport annual sur la question Musulman, Ségou, 4 juillet 1917, l'Administrateur du Cercle, Lasse; and, Pascal James Imperato, *African Folk Medicine, Practices and Beliefs of the Bambara and Other Peoples* (Baltimore: York, 1977), pp. 48-9.

91. Ibid.

92. Ibid.

93. Ibid.

94. ANM 4E 69 Ségou 1913 Rapport sur l'Islamisme.

95. Ibid. Baninko also had mosques, but a census had not been taken.

96. The independent schools of the Peulhs are also found in this report, but is omitted from this analysis. ANM 1D 55 Rapport du Capitaine Perignon, Commandant du Cercle de Ségou à Monsieur le Délégué de Gouveneur Général, 26 septembre 1900.

97. ANM 1E 19 Rapport Général de fin d'année sur la politique du Cercle, Brévié.

98. Interview: Soumaila Fanè.

99. Interview: Kirango Ba Jara.

100. Interview: Bokary Daou.

101. The dates of the deportation and release were not given.

102. Interviews: Soumaila Fanè, and Bokary Daou.

103. Ibid.

104. ANM 5D 45, Recensement de la population, 20 août 1904, and Enfants des Pères et des Soeurs, Ségou, le 11 mars 1904.

105. ANM 5D 45 Ségou, le 18 août 1904 à Monsieur Administrateur Kopp.

106. Interview: Bokari Daou. The *Arrissala* is the term the Bamana used for the *Risala* of Ibn Abi Zar al-Qayrawani (see glossary).

107. ANM 1E 19 Rapport général de fin d'année sur la politique du Cercle.

108. Interview: Bokary Daou.

109. ANM 1D 55 De l'orientation de la justice et des moeurs chez les populations de la region de Ségou par Charles Correnson, Ségou, 5 septembre 1907.

110. Ibid.

111. Ibid.

112. Lettre no. 149 du 23 avril 1891, cited in ANM 1D 16, Ière partie, Notice Ethnologique par le Lt. J. L. M. Moreau 1897.

113. While the French and Africans who met stringent educational criteria were "citizens," most Africans were determined "subjects."

114. Robert Delavignette, *Freedom and Authority in French West Africa,* (London: Oxford

CHAPTER 7, PP. 143-175 (CONTINUED)

U., 1950) (translation of *Service Africaine* (Paris: Gallimard, 1946)), p. 85.

115. ANM 1E 71 Rapport politique mois de janvier 1897, Ségou, le 5 fèvrier 1897.

116. ANM 1E 71 Rapport politique du mois de fèvrier 1897, Ségou, le 1 mars 1897, et du mois d'avril 1897, Ségou, le 13 mai 1897, le Commandant de Cercle, Montquey.

117. ANM 1E 71 Rapport politique du mois d'avril 1897, le 13 mai 1897, and du mois de mai 1897, Ségou, le 1 juin 1897, Le Commandant de Cercle, Montquey.

118. The use of the Qadi created a "special problem" in that the Islamic Code required that all called before the Qadi follow the penalty in the Islamic Code. ANM 1E 71 1ère Semestre Rapport Générale sur la situation du Cercle (B. 295), 9 fèvrier 1897.

119. In contrast, the Fula, Sòmònò, and especially the Markas, argued their cases before their local leaders or the Cadi. They did, however, consult the Commandant on important issues. ANM 1E 71 Rapport politique du mois de juillet, Ségou, le 10 août 1897.

120. ANM 1E 71 Rapport politique du mois d'avril 1898, Ségou, 10 mai 1898, and du mois de mai 1898, Le Commandant, (n.d.).

121. The village leader was fined for using the *korte* against the Bamana plaintiffs. The korte was a custom of throwing a powder composed of poison on the body of an adversary, causing incurable sickness or even death. ANM 1E 71 Rapport politique, juin 1903, le 30 juin 1903.

122. ANM 1E 71 Rapport annuel sur la politique du Cercle, année 1902, 31 décembre 1902.

123. ANM 2M 34 Extrait du registre des jugements rendus par le Tribunal Bambara, l'an 1903.

124. ANM 1E 71 Rapport politiques pour les mois d'avril 1903, mars 1903, mai 1903, juillet 1903, août 1903, décembre 1903 et Rapport général sur la situation du Cercle 1904.

125. ANM 1D 55 Correnson, pp. 7-8.

126. ANM 1E 19 Rapport politique mois de Mars 1903, Bamako, 31 Mars 1903.

127. 1E 19 Rapport général sur la situation politique du Cercle de Bamako pendant l'année 1906.

128. ANM 1E 19 Rapport général de fin d'année sur la Politique du Cercle.

129. ANM 1D 55 Correnson, "Devant la justice," p. 6.

130. ANM B 150 #13 (Correspondence) 7 avril, 1909.

131. ANM 1E 72 Rapport général sur l'administration du Cercle pendant l'année 1907, Ségou, 14 janvier 1908.

132. ANM 1D 55 Correnson, p. 20. African concepts of land ownership confounded European administrators, and this produced a wealth of literature whereby many Westerners and some Africans would try to explain African notions of land ownership. See, for example, E. S. R. Handy, "The Religious Significance of Lance," *African Affairs*, 38 (January, 1939), 114-23; C. M. N. White, "Terminological Confusion in African Land Tenure," *Journal of African Administration*, 10 (July, 1958), 124-30; and Hiroshi Akabane, "Traditional Patterns of Land Occupancy in Black Africa," *Developing Economies*, 8 (June, 1970), 161-79.

133. ANM 1E 72 rapport mensuel, mois de novembre 1912, J. Rocache.

134. ANM 1D 55 Correnson, p. 50.

135. ANM 1E 72 Rapport sur la tournée effective du 6 au 21 mai 1912, Carbone.

136. Interview: Sunkalo Jara.

137. ANM B 138 #407 (Correspondence) au Gouverneur, Koulouba, Ségou, 19 septembre 1912.

138. Hippolyte-Victor Marceau, *Le Tirailleur Soudanais* (Paris: Berger-Levrault, 1911), p. 3.

139. Shelby Cullum Davis, *Reservoirs of Men: A History of the Black Troops of French West Africa* (Westport: Negro Universities, 1970), p. 83; J. D. Hargreaves, *France and West Africa*, p. 99.

140. ANM 1D 30 Notice sur les resources naturelle du Sudan= population, ethnographie, religion et moeurs institutions et coutumes indigènes.

141. Marceau, p. 3. See also Général A. Duboc, *Les Sénégalais au Service de la France* (Paris: Edgar Malfere, 1939), p. 134.

142. Echenberg, p. 15; and, Duboc, p. 11.

143. ANM 1E 72 Rapport politique du mois d'octobre 1915, Ségou, le 31 octobre, 1915 P. Bernard; Rapport politique du mois de novembre 1915, Ségou, le 7 décembre 1915, Bernard, and Rapport politique du mois de décembre 1915, Ségou, le 31 décembre 1915, Marcel Valaheques.

144. ANM 1E 72 Rapport sur la politique générale du cercle #4476, Ségou, le 6 juillet 1917, Casse, and Rapport politique du mois de janvier 1916, Ségou, le 31 janvier 1916, Battus.

145. Ibid.

146. ANM 1E 72 Rapport Politique Quatrieme Trimestre 1916, Ségou, 31 décembre 1916, Battus.

147. Echenberg, p. 63; and R. Lassalle-Séré, *Le Recrutement de l'armée noire*, (Paris: Librairie Moderne de droit et jurisprudence, 1919), p. 148. How colonialism affected the role of the African youth, and what youths provided to the African family is outlined in Charles C. Stewart, "When Youth Concludes: Changes in Marriage and the Production of Youth since 1890 (in Mauritania)," in Helene Almeida'Topor, Odile Goerg, and Catherine Coquery-Vidrovitch, eds. *Les mouvements de jeunesse en Afrique Francophone au Xxe siècle* (Paris: Harmattan, 1993), pp. 238-253.

148. Echenberg, pp. 18-19.

149. Myron J. Echenberg, "Paying the Blood Tax: Military Conscription in French West Africa, 1914-1929," *Canadian Journal of African Studies,* 9 (1975) p. 172.

150. See A. I. Asiwaju, "Migrations as Revolt: The Example of the Ivory Coast and the Upper Volta before 1945," *Journal of African History* 17 (1976), 577-94.

151. Echenberg, *Conscripts*, p. 72.

152. Lassalle-Séré, pp. 150-1.

153. Jean-Loup Amselle. *Logiques Métisses. Anthropologie de l'identité en Afrique et ailleurs*, (Paris: Éditions Payot, 1990), p. 86. At least four Bamana-French dictionaries have been published from 1906 to 1981. Charles Bird and Mamadou Kanté have compiled a Bamana-English lexicon (Bloomington: Indiana University Linguistics Club, 1977).

154. In present-day Mali, Bamana is taught in Segu. However, in the capital of Bamako, the omission of Bamana from the curriculum has created some tension between the

CHAPTER 7, PP. 143-175 (CONTINUED)

student body and the administration. See also comments by V. Monteil, pp. 201-2.

155. ANM 1D 35 Notice sur les états d'Aguibou 1896, Bandiagara, le 31 décembre 1896, Meurielle; and, ANM 1D 47 études générales notice sur le Macina de Bandiagara 1896, Trentinian.

156. ANM 1D 38 Monographie de Djenné, Djenné, 20 novembre 1909.

157. ANM 1D 38 Monographie de Djenné.

158. Ibid.

159. ANM 1E 72 Rapport sur la tournée effective du 6 au 21 mai 1912, Carbone.

160. ANM 5D 45 Recensement de la population Ségou, 1904, Lt. Collet-adjoint au Commandant du Cercle de Ségou, 5 décembre 1895.

161. Yaya Amadou Coulibaly, "Les Bambaras: Formation de l'Homme, Art et Creations," *Études Maliennes,* (1972), p. 21; interview with Togola. See also Louis le Barbier, *Étude sur les populations Bambaras* (Paris: Dujarric, 1906).

162. ANM 3E 4 (Lettre) à Monsieur l'administrator, 17 janvier 1902, Marie Ursule.

163. Echenberg, *Conscripts,* p. 15.

164. Duboc, p. 125. Because of urban development before and after colonialism, many populations would be attracted to cities to find employment. Since Bamana had already become the major language of the western Sudan, they would learn Bamana as the language of communication, not French. Interviews: Men of the Dògòn Village of Hombiri March 21, 1993, and Sekou Bertè, Bamako, October 12, 1992.

165. Theiro, p. 76.

166. Interview: Sunkalo Jara.

Chapter 8, pp. 177-186

1. Interview: Saku Kulubali, Banankoro, 23 novembre 1984.

2. Interview: Kirango Ba Jara.

3. Interview: Bokary Daou.

4. Interview: Tierno Sako.

5. Interview with Ibrahima Traore, Segu, 10 juin 1993.

6. Interview: Soumaila Fanè.

7. Ibid.

8. Interview: Kirango Ba Jara.

9. See Jean Amselle, *Logiques Métisses.*

10. Jean Bazin, "A Chacun son Bambara," *Au Coeur de l'ethnie: ethnies, tribalisme et état en Afrique*, Jean Amselle and Elikia Bokolo, eds. (Paris: Éditions la Decouverte, 1985) p. 90.

11. See Fredrik Barth, "Introduction," *Ethnic Groups and Boundaries, the Social Organization of Cultural Difference*, Barth, ed. (Boston: Little, Brown and Co., 1969), pp. 10-14.

12. Catherine Coquery-Vidrovitch, "The Rise of a Francophone African Social Science. From Colonial Knowledge to Knowledge of African Contradiction and Misunder-

standing: De l'anthropologie a l'histoire de l'afrique, c. 1830-c. 1990." Paper given at "The Reconstructing the Study and Meaning of Africa" Conference. Urbana-Champaign, April 7-9, 1994. Meaning quoted from Dictionnaire Lettre 1860. See also Amselle, *Logiques*, p. 38; Amselle, "Ethnies et espaces: pour une anthropologie topologique," in Amselle and Elikia M'bokolo, eds., *Au coeur de l'ethnie: ethnies, tribalisme et état en Afrique* (Paris: Éditions la Découverte, 1985), pp. 14-5; and, Jean Gallais, "Signification du groupe ethnique du Mali," *Homme* 2 (1962), p. 106.

13. The term ethnograpnic appeared in 1823, and ethnographe in 1835. The first Society of Ethnology in France was founded in 1838.

14. See Stanislas Adotevi, "Ethnology and the Repossession of the World," *Discourse: Berkeley Journal for Theorectical Studies in Media and Culture* 11 (Spring-Summer, 1989), pp. 19-46; and Edward Said, "Representing the Colonized: Anthropology's Interlocutors," *Critical Inquiry* 15 (Winter, 1989), pp. 205-225.

15. C. Tsehloane Keto, p. 2.

16. See also H. F. C. Smith, "A Neglected Theme of West African History: The Islamic Revolutions of the Nineteenth Century," *Journal of the Historical Society of Nigeria*, 2 (1969), p. 169.

17. McNaughton, p. 66.

18. Person, "Ngolo," p. 279. See also Amselle, *Logiques*, p. 80 who argues that Muslim merchants of the towns used the term.

19. For a series of correspondence concerning the Masina boundary see "'Sokoto-Masina Correspondence' with Mallam A. Kani," *Research Bulletin of the Center of Arabic Documentation*, 11 (1975), pp. 1-12; and, "Frontier Disputes and Problems of Legitimation," *Journal of African History*, 15 (1976), pp. 497-514.

20. Gallais, p. 116.

21. Roberts, *Warriors*, p. 10. See also Barth, pp. 9-38, especially pp. 15-16.

22. Barth, pp.9-10.

23. Jomo Kenyatta, *Facing Mt. Kenya* (New York: Random House, 1965), pp. 95-6.

24. Gallais, "Chacun," p. 120, and "Signification," p. 108.

25. Person, "Ngolo," p. 308. See Un Bambara de Saint Louis, "La Colonie bambara de Ndioloffen et de Khor à Saint Louis," *Notes Africaines*, 40 (octobre 1948), pp. 18-20, for a discussion of how Bamana cultural identity has survived in a large quarter in Saint Louis.

26. Gallais, "Signification," p. 106.

27. Bazin, "Chacun," p. 102.

28. Keto, p. 7.

29. Thandika Mkandawire, "Problems and Prospects of the Social Sciences in Africa," *International Social Science Journal* 45 (1993), pp. 129-40.

30. Amselle, *Logique*, p. 164; and "Migration et société neo-traditionelle: le cas des Bambara du Jitumu (Mali)," *Cahiers d'Études Africaines* 18 (1978), pp. 481-502.

31. Roland Oliver and Brian M. Fagan, *Africa in the Iron Age, c. 500 B. C. to A. D. 1400* (Cambridge: Cambridge University, 1990), p. 209.

32. Robin Law, *The Oyo Empire c. 1600-c.1836, A West African Imperialism in the Era of the Atlantic Slave Trade* (Oxford: Clarendon, 1977). The Oyo Kingdom levied tribute on several neighboring kingdoms, but exercised control within the sphere of the empire. The territories were subjugated to the Alafin in different ways and varying

CHAPTER 8, PP. 177-186 (CONTINUED)

degrees (pp. 3, 83).

33. This is similar to other non-European cultures, e.g. the Aztecs, the Incas, etc. Also, Saint-Martin refers to the French and 'Umarian regimes as ". . .two imperialisms, one white and colonialist, the other black and (a) propagator of Islam," "La Volonté," p. 792.

34. Harold Courlander and Ousmane Sako, *The Heart of the Ngoni* (New York: Crow, 1982), p. 1.

Appendix A, pp. 187-188

1. This chronology is based on dates from this study; Alpha Oumar and Adam Ba Konare, *Grandes Dates du Mali* (Bamako: Éditions Imprimeries du Mali, 1983); and "Calendrier Historique de Segu" (author unknown).

Appendix B, pp. 189-190

1. Sauvageot's comparison chart on p. 4 from where the above information was taken, differs from the Dyara text in that Kassum of Sen is listed after Ben of Kirango, the rule of Bema of Nalo precedes that of Demba of Massala, and the later is followed by Sanzan of Nango, whose name is missing from p. 4. See pp. 121-22.

2. The chart lists Kaladian Courbari (variation of Kulubali) as the founding Coubari of Segu, but not as a ruler. This chart in the French records show two rulers after the massacre of Mari Jara. Also, another record show Bafi Jara, as a leader of the war against the French, but it is unclear of his relationship to Mari Jara or whether claimed to be the heir to power.

BIBLIOGRAPHY

Primary Sources

ORAL DATA

Maksun Collection

Daou, Bokary. "Bamana et les occupations étrangères." Duguninkoro, 22 juin 1993.

Elders of the village of Nango, 10 octobre 1995.

Fanè, Soumaila. "Le règle d'Ahmadu et l'installation des Français à 1930." Tiserila, 31 mai 1993.

Jara, Dramane. "Bamana Maana fo Faransitile," Segu, 19 mai 1993.

Jara, Kirango. "Bamanaw ani Futakaw ye nyògòn kèlè 21 sanw na." Segu, 3 juin 1993.

Jara, Sunkalo. "Bamana Maana," Soninkura 9 juillet 1993.

Konè, Mamadu. Segukura, 10 juillet 1993.

Kulubali, Babalian. Segukura, 10 juillet 1993.

Kulibali, Bamyama. "Bamana Maana," Segukura, 10 juillet 1993.

Kulibali, Buba. "Kulibaliw," Bamako, 5 juillet, 1993.

Kulibali, Mahmadou. "Segu Bamana Fanga Maana ani al haji 'Umar ani Masina Fula ka Kèlè." Wèrèba 1989.

Men of the Village of Hombiri, 21 mars 1993.

Sako, Tierno. "Al-Hajj 'Umar et les conquêtes de Segu et Masina." Segu, 26 mai 1993 and 10 juin 1993.

Tiam, Mountaga. "Histoire de Segu: Règle Futaka à Segu." Segu, 5 juin 1993.

Togola, Tèrèba. Bamako, 22 octubre 1992.

Traore, Ibrahima. Segu, 10 juin 1993.

Public Recordings

Bah, Cheick Oumar, "Al-Hajj 'Umar et les Bamana de Segou," Bamako, Mali, produced by Moussa Coulibaly, n.d.

Enregistrements de Tradition Orale au Niveau de l'audiotheque (Seydou Theiro Collection)

Fanè, Ismaila. "Histoire de Segu: Occupations Toucouleures et Françaises." Tiserila, 1975.

Jara, Bafin. Kirango, 24 septembre 1984.

Jara, Sajo. "Segu sous occupation française." Segu, novembre 1974.

Jirè, Abdulai Mori. "Tarik de Segu." Segu, 28 mai 1968.

Kanè, Mahmoud. "Histoire de Segu sous les occupations toucouleure et française." Segukòrò, novembre 1974.

Kulubali, Bacèkòrò. "Histoire de Karamòkò et Mari Jara." Segu, novembre 1974.

Kulubali, Cènan. "Segu de l'occupation toucouleure à debut l'occupation française." Dakala, 1975.

Kulubali, Kokè. "Segu sous les occupations futakas et françaises." Masala, 1975.

Kulubali, Seidu Ble. Kirango, 23 septembre 1984.

Kulubali, Saku. Banankoro, 23 novembre 1984.

Samake, Musa. Zezana, 1975.

Sisoko, Bazumana. "Histoire de Segu: Succession des Faamaw." Bamako, 10 decembre 1977.

Tangara, Amadu. Kirango, 21 septembre 1984.

Tangara, Cèkòrò. "Ngolo Jara ni Tona Dunanbake Tangara Kaje."

Tuna, 25 septembre 1984.

Sekou Berté Library, Bamako Mali

The Elders of the villages of Jalado, 25 septembre 1992.

Radio Television Mali Library

Diallo, Baba Daye, Bamako, Mali.

Sissoko, Bazoumana, Bamako, Mali.

PUBLISHED ORAL ACCOUNTS

Banbera, Tayiru. *A State of Intrique, The Epic of Bamana Segou.* David C. Conrad, ed. London: Oxford University, 1990.

Bembera, Tairou. "Biton Kulibali ka masala." Mamadou

Boidie Diarra, transcriber, Lilyan Kesteloot, trans. *Bulletin de l'Institut Fondamental d'Afrique Noire,* ser. b40 (1978), 612-81.

Djire, M. Abdourrahmane. "Une Tradition musulmane relative à l'histoire de Ségou." Robert Pageard, ed. *Notes Africaines.* 101 (janvier 1964), 24-6.

Dumestre, G. *La Geste de Ségou: Textes des Griots Bambaras.* Abidjan: Université d'Abidjan, 1974.

Kamara, Cheikh Moussa. "Histoire de Ségou." Moustapha

Ndiaye, trans. *Bulletin de l'Institut Fondamental d'Afrique Noire.* ser. b. 40 (1978), 458-88.

UNPUBLISHED ORAL ACCOUNTS

Dyara, Gaoussou. "Contribution a l'histoire du Royaume Bambara de Ségou." Complementary thesis by Serge Sauvageot, trans. Faculte des Lettres et Sciences Humaines de Dakar. Dakar, Sénégal, 1965.

TRANSLATIONS OF DOCUMENTS/CHRONICLES

"Chroniques de Oualata et de Nema." Paul Marty, trans. *Revue des Études Islamiques,* 3 and 4 (1927), 355-426, 531-75.

"La Vie d'Al Hadj 'Omar (Traduction d'un manuscrit arabe de la Zaoua tidjana de Fez)." Jules Salenc, trans. *Bulletin du Comité d'Études Historiques et Scientifiques de l'Afrique Occidentale Française,* 1 (1918), 405-35.

Mahibou, Sidi Mohamed and Jean Louis Triaud. *Voila ce qui est arrive.*

Bayan ma Waqa'a d'al-Hagg 'Umar al-Futi. Paris: Éditions du Centre Nationale de la Recherche Scientifique, 1983.

Muhammed, al-Hafiz. *Al-Hagg 'Umar, Sultan al-dawlat al-tiganiyya begarbi Ifriqiyya.* Al-Qahira, 1383/1963-4.

Musa, Muhammad ibn Ibrahim. "'The Chronicle of the Succession,' An Important Document for the Umarian State." David Robinson, trans. *Journal of African History,* 31 (1990), 245-62.

Sissoko, Mamadou. "Chroniques d'El Hadj Oumar et du Cheikh Tidiani." *L'Education Africaine,* 95 (1936), 242-255; 96-97(1937), 5-22, 127-148.

Tyam, Mohammadou Aliou. *La Vie d'el Hadj Omar, Qacida en Poular.* Henri Gaden, trans. Paris: Institute d'Ethnologie, 1935.

ARCHIVES NATIONALES DU MALI (ANM), KOULOUBA, MALI

A	12	Ordres Généraux pour Cercle de Ségou 1893-1899 (Circulaires)
B	67	Correspondance confidentielle du Lieutenant Colonel Frey du 20 novembre 1885 au 11 juin 1886
B	83	Correspondance confidentielle du Commandant Supérieur Archinard du Governeur du Sénégal 1890
B	138	Correspondance générale de Ségou 1910-1914
B	150	Cercle de Ségou Correspondance générale-Arrivée Commandant, Supèrieur et Divers 1891-1921
B	165	Administrative Correspondance,
1D	3	Etude sur l'organisation du Soudan Français
1D	9	Notice sur la region du Sahel, Capitaine Lartique
1D	30	Notice sur les resources naturelles du Soudan
1D	33	Notice sur le Cercle de Bamako, 1885, Dr. Collomb
1D	35	Monographies du Cercle de Bandiagara
1D	38	Monographies du Cercle de Djenné
1D	47	Renseignements Historiques sur le Macina, 1864-1875
1D	55	Notice sur le Royaume et Cercle de Ségou
	1°	Notice Géographique 1896

2° Notice Historique du Royaume de Ségou, 2° partie 1896

4° Note pour l'Instruction et les Covées des Sofas de Ségou 1891

5° Notice sur le Royaume Bamana de Ségou-Marge-Barth à Farako 1889

1D 206 Rapport sur les Coutumes et Institutions juridiques Cercle de Ségou 1909

1D 222 Mission Delanneau 1885

5D 45 Recensement de la Population Cercle de Ségou 1891-1905

1E 11 Rapport politique d'ensemble du Soudan 1896-1905

1E 18 Rapports politiques et Rapports de Tournées Bamako 1881-1900

1E 19 Rapports politiques et Rapports de Tournées Cercle de Bamako 1901-1910

1E 20 Rapports politiques et Rapports de Tournées Bamako 1920

1E 71 Rapports politiques Cercle de Ségou/Sansanding 1891-1905

1E 72 Rapports politiques et Rapports de Tournées Ségou 1906-1920

1E 219 Correspondance Ségou 1891-1909

1E 220 Correspondance avec la Fama de Sansanding Cercle de Ségou 1890-1917

1E 229 Rapports Bonaccordi et Briquelet sur les événements du Mianka-Mesures prises à l'égard du pays de Ségou 1891-1893

1E 284 Télégrammes des affaires politiques Cercle Ségou 1891-1908

2E 67 Politique Indigène-Notes et fiches de renseignments sur les chefs et notables cercle de Ségou 1897-1909

3E 4 Culte Ségou 1895-1908 Correspondance-Rapport Cercle de Ségou

4E 69 Politique musulmane Rapports sur l'Islam et les confrèries musulmanes-Cercle de Ségou 1894-1917

K 132 Travaux Publics Rapports sur les Travaux Cercle de Ségou 1903-1911

2M 34 Justice Indigene Correspondance Cercle de Ségou

1893-1917

1N   3   Révolte du Beledougou Correspondance rapports 1915
1N   42   Organisation militaire-Correspondance générale Cercle de
           Ségou 1892-1916
1N   63   Opérations militaires procés-verbal de visite et de
           classement des objets d'or et d'argent
1N   64   Opérations militaires-marche du Gallieni sur Dougourela
           Correspondance avec le Cercle de Ségou 1892
1N   96   Opérations militaires-Opérations contre Ahmadou
           1889-1890 (télégrammes)
1N   149 Opération militaries Ségou 1892-1899-Télégrammes
2N   42   Opération Militaire, Ségou 1892-1916
1R   69   Rapports agricoles et commerciaux Cercle de Ségou
           1893-1917

ARCHIVES NATIONALES DU SÉNÉGAL (ANS), DAKAR, SÉNÉGAL

15G   172 Rapport politique sur l'organisation du pays de Ségou

CENTRE AHMED BABA (CEDRAB), TIMBUKTU, MALI

#140 Abdallay Jiri, "Tarikh Ségou," Ségou, aout 1976.

FRENCH ADMINISTRATIVE PUBLICATIONS

Carrère, Frédéric and Paul Holle. *De la Sénégambie française.* Paris:
    Didot, 1855.
Colin, Dr. "Le Soudan Occidental." *Revue Maritime et Colonial,* 78
    (Juillet, 1883), 5-32.
Duboc, Général A. *Les Sénégalais au Service de la France.* Paris: Edgar
    Maltere, 1939.
Faidherbe, Louis. *Le Sénégal, la France dans l'Afrique Occidentale.*

Paris: Hachette, 1889.

Frey, Le Colonel Henri. *Campagne dans le Haut-Sénégal et le Haut-Niger (1885-1886)*. Paris: Librairie Plon, 1888.

Gallieni, Joseph. *Neuf ans à Madagascar*. Paris: Hachette, 1908.

———. *Deux Campagnes au Soudan Français 1886-1888*. Paris: Hachette, 1891.

———. *Voyage au Soudan Français 1879-1881*. Paris: Hachette, 1885.

Gatelet, Lt. *Histoire de la conquête du Soudan Français 1878-1899*. Paris: Nancy, Berger-Levrault et Cie, 1901.

Hourst, Lt. de Vau. *French Enterprise in Africa. The Personal Narrative of Lieutenant Hourst of his Exploration on the Niger*. Nancy D'Anvers Bell, trans. 2nd ed. New York: E. P. Dutton, 1899.

Jaime, Lt. J. Gilbert. *De Koulikoro à Tombouctou sur la canonniére "le Mage."* Paris: Libraries Associés, 1894.

Marceau, Hippolyte-Victor. *Le Tirailleur Soudanais*. Paris: Berger-Levrault, 1911.

Marmier, G. *La Mission du Genie au Soudan en 1891-1892*. Paris: Berger-Levrault, 1894.

Ministère de la Marine et des Colonies. *Sénégal et Niger, La France dans l'Afrique Occidentale, 1879-1883*. Paris: Challamel Aine, 1884.

Pietri, Camille. *Les Français au Niger, Voyages et combats* Paris: Hachette, 1885.

Rappport Militaire du Chef d'Escadron Archinard. *Le Soudan Français en 1888-1889*. Paris: Imprimerie Nationale, 1890.

TRAVEL ACCOUNTS

Bayal, Jean. "Voyages au pays de Bamako." *Bulletin de la Société de Géographie de Paris*, 2 (1881).

Dubois, Félix. "Tombouctou la Mystérieuse, "L'Illustration (1 aout 1896), 85–106.

Mage, Abon Eugene. *Voyage dans le Soudan Occidental*. Paris: Hachette, 1868.

Park, Mungo. *Travels in Africa*. London: J. M. Dent, 1954 (1799).

Quinton, Louis. "Souvenirs d'un voyage de Sénégal au Niger, 1863-

1866." *Bulletin de la Société de Géographies de Paris*, 1 (1881).

Soleillet, Paul. *Voyage à Ségou 1878-1879*. Paris: Challumel Aine, 1887.

"Voyages et expéditions au Sénégal et dans les contrées voisines." *Tour de Monde*, (Première Semestre, 1861), 17-32.

AUTOBIOGRAPHY

Douglass, Frederick. *My Bondage and My Freedom*. New York: Miller, Orton, Mulligan, 1968 (1855).

Secondary Sources

ARTICLES AND BOOKS

Abun-Nasr, Jamil. *The Tijaniyya: A Sufi Order in the Modern World*. London: Oxford University, 1965.

———. "Some Aspects of the 'Umari Branch of the Tijaniyya." *Journal of African History*, 3 (1962), 329-330.

Adam, M. G. "Legendes Historiques du Pays de Nioro." *Revue Coloniale*, 3-4 (1903-1904), 486-96.

Adotevi, Stanislas. "Ethnology and the Repossession of the World." *Discourse: Berkeley Journal for Theoretical Studies in Media and Culture,* 11 (Spring-Summer, 1989), 19-46.

Al-Nagar, 'Umar. "Takruur, the History of a Name." *Journal of African History*, 10 (1969), 365-374.

Amselle, Jean. *Logiques Métisses Anthropologie de l'Identité en Afrique et Ailleurs*. Paris: Éditions Payot, 1990.

———. "Ethnies et espaces: pour une anthropologie topologique," in Amselle and Elikia M'bokolo, eds. *Au coeur de l'ethnie: ethnies, tribalisme et état en Afrique*. Paris: Éditions la Decouverte 1985.

———. "Migration et société neo-traditionelle: le cas des Bambara du Jitumu (Mali)." *Cahiers d'Études Africaines*, 18 (1978), 481-502.

Anonymous. "L'Empire Toucouleur d'El-Hadj 'Omar." *Bingo*, no. 64

(Mai 1958), 11-12.

Arnaud, A. and Meray H. *Les Colonies Françaises, organisation,administrative, judiciare, politique et financière.* Paris: Augustin Challamel, 1900.

Asiwaju, A. I. "Migrations as Revolt: The Example of the Ivory Coast and the Upper Volta before 1945." *Journal of African History,* 17 (1976), 577-94.

Ba, Amadou. *Histoire du Sahel Occidental Malien.* Bamako: Éditions Jamana, 1989.

Ba, Amadou Hampate and Jacques Daget. *L'Empire Peul de Macina.* Paris: Mouton, 1962.

Barth, Fredrik, ed. *Ethnic Groups and Boundaries.* Boston: Little, Brown and Company, 1969.

Bazin, Jean. "A Chaque son Bambara." *Au Coeur de l'Ethnie: Ethnies, Tribalisme et État en Afrique.* Jean Amselle andElikia Bokolo, eds. Paris: Éditions la Decouverte, 1985.

——. "Recherches sur les formations socio-politiques anciennes en pays Bambara." *Études Maliennes,* (1970), 33-38.

——. "War and Servitude in Ségou." *L'Esclavage en Afrique Pre-coloniale.* Claude Meillassoux, ed. Paris: François Maspero, 1975.

Beier, H. U. "The Historical and Psychological Significance of Yoruba Myths." *ODU*, (January, 1955), 17-25.

Berenger-Feraud, Laurent J. B. *Les peuplades de la Sénégambie.* Paris: Ernest Leroux, 1879.

Betts, Raymond F. *Assimilation and Association in French Colonial Theory 1890-1914.* New York: Columbia University, 1961.

B"me, André. "Ségou-koro et le Biton Mamari." *Notes Africaines,* (1957), 92-95.

——. *Ségou vielle capitale.* Angoulême: Imprimerie H. Corrignan et J. Lachanard, 1952.

Biobaku, S. O. "Myths and Oral History." *ODU,* (January, 1955), 12-17.

Bird, Charles and Mamadou Kanté. *Bambara-English StudentLexicon.* Bloomington, Indiana University, 1977.

Blassingame, John W. *The Slave Community: Plantation Life in the Antebellum South.* New York: Oxford University, 1972.

Brenner, Louis. *West African Sufi.* Berkeley: University of California,

1984.

Brévié, Jules. *Islamisme contre naturisme au Soudan français.* Paris: Ernest Leroux, 1923.

Castre, Charles. *Ideals of France.* New York: Abingdon, 1922.

Chailley-Bert, Jospeh. *Dix années de politique coloniale.* Paris: Armond Colin, 1902.

Cissé, Youssau. *Les fondements de la société d'initiation du Kòmò.* Paris: Mouton, 1973.

Clarke, Peter B. *West Africa and Islam.* London: Edward Arnold, 1982.

Coulibaly, Yaya Amadou. "Les Bambaras: Formation de l'Homme art et creations." *Études Maliennes,* (1971), 21-32.

Courlander, Harold and Ousmane Sako. *The Heart of the Ngoni.* New York: Crow, 1982.

Crowder, Micheal. *West Africa under Colonial Rule.* Evanston: Northwestern University, 1968.

————. "Indirect Rule: British and French Style." *Africa,* 34 (1964) 197-205.

Davis, Shelby Cullum. *Reservoirs of Men: A History of the Black Troops of French West Africa.* Westport: Negro Universities, 1970.

Delavignette, Robert. *Freedom and Authority in French West Africa.* London: Oxford University, 1950. Translation of *Service Africaine.* Paris: Gallimard, 1946.

Diallo, Abdoul Aziz. "Le siège de Nyoro et la mort de Muntaga Tall." *Études Maliennes,* (1979), 4-16.

Dieterlen, Germaine. *Essai sur la religion Bambara.* Paris: Presses Universitaire de France, 1951.

Diop, Abdoulaye B. *Société Toucouleure et migration.* Dakar: University of Dakar, 1965.

La Division de La Recherche Linguistique et Padeagogique.*Lexique Bambara-Français, Bamana kan ni Tubabu kan Danyegate.* Bamako: Imprimerie DNAFLA, 1980.

Drewry, William Sidney. *Slave Insurrections in Virginia (1830-1865).* Washington: Neale, 1900.

Dumont, Fernand. *L'Anti-Sultan ou Al Hajj Omar du Fouta-Combatton de la foi.* Dakar-Abidjan: Nouvelles Éditions Africaines, 1974.

Duveyrier, Henri. *Les Touareg du Nord.* Nendeln: Kraus rpt., 1973.

Echenberg, Myron. *Colonial Conscripts: The Tirailleurs Senegalais in French West Africa, 1857-1960.* Portsmouth: Heinemann Educational, 1991.

———. "Paying the Blood Tax: Military Conscriptionin French West Africa, 1914-1929," *Canadian Journal of African History,* 9 (1975), 171-192.

"Eighteenth Century Slaves as Advertised by Their Masters." *Journal of Negro History,* 1 (April, 1916), 163-216.

Emily, J. "La fin d'Ahmadou Sheikou," *Communications de l'Academie des Sciences Coloniales,* 8 (1926-7), 225-37.

Es-Sa'di, Abderrahman ben Abdullah ben 'Imran ben 'Amir. *Tarikh Es-Soudan.* O. Houdas, trans. Paris: Adrien-Maissonneuve, 1964.

Etienne, Eugène. "Protectorat et décentralisation." *Dépêche Coloniale.* (December 28, 1901).

Fouillee, Alfred. "Le Caractère des races humaines et l'avenir de la race blanche." *Revue des deux Mondes,* 74 (July 1, 1894).

Freud, Bill. *The Making of Contemporary Africa.* Bloomington: Indiana University, 1984.

"Frontier Disputes and Problems of Legitimation." *Journal of African History.* 15 (1976), 73-93.

Fyfe, Christopher. *A History of Sierra Leone.* London: Oxford University, 1962.

Gallais, Jean. "Signification du groupe ethnique du Mali." *Homme,* 2 (1962), 106-129.

Gann, Lewis H. and Peter Duignon. *Burden of Empire: An Appraisal of Western Colonialism in Africa, South of the Sahara.* New York: F. A. Praeger, 1959.

Gerresch, Claudine. "Jugements du Moniteur du Sénégal sur al-Hajj 'Umar de 1857 à 1864." *Bulletin de l'Institut Fondamental d'Afrique Noire,* ser. b 35 (1973), 574-92.

Girault, Arthur. *Principes de colonisation et de legislation coloniale.* Paris: Recueil Sirey, 1895.

Gourou, Pierre. "Gallieni." *Les Techniciens de la colonisation.* Charles Julien, ed. Paris: Presses Universitaires, 1946.

Gramont, Sanche de. *The Strong Brown God, the Story of the Niger River.* Boston: Haughton Mifflin, 1975.

Greene, Lorenzo. "The New England Negro as Seen in Advertisements for Runaway Slaves." *Journal of Negro History,* 39 (April, 1944), 125-46.

Guyot, Yves. *Lettres sur la politique coloniale.* Paris: C. Reinwald, 1885.

Hane, Mouhammed Moustapha. *Les Trois Grandes Figures de l'Islam en Afrique.* Dakar: Libraire Hilal, 1966.

Hanotaux, Gabriel. *L'Énergie française.* Paris: Flammarion, 1902.

Hanson, John and David Robinson. *After the Jihad: The Reign of Ahmad al-Kabir in the Western Sudan.* East Lansing: Michigan State University, 1991.

Hargreaves, John D. "The Tokolor Empire of Segou and Its Relations with the French." *Boston University papers on Africa.* J. Butler, ed. Boston: Boston University 1966.

———. *France and West Africa.* London: MacMillan, 1969.

Henry, Abbé Joseph. *L'Ame d'un peuple africain, les Bambara.* Münster: Aschendorffshen Buchhandlung, 1910.

Henry, P. J. M. "Le Culte des esprits chez les Bambara." *Anthropos,* 4 (1908), 702-717.

Higginson, Thomas W. *Black Rebellion.* New York: Arno, 1969.

Hiskett, Mervyn. *The Development of Islam in West Africa.* London: Longman, 1984.

———. "An Islamic Tradition of Reform in the Western Sudan from the Sixteenth to the Eighteenth Century." *Bulletin SOAS,* 19 (1957).

Hodgkin, Thomas. "Islam, History and Politics." *Journal of Modern African Studies.* 1 (1963) 91-6.

——— and Ruth Schachter. *French-Speaking West Africa in Transition.* New York: Carnegie Endowment for International Peace, 1961.

Hourst, Emile A. L. *French Enterprise in Africa.* trans. of *Sur le Niger et au pays des Touaregs.* London: Chapman and Hall, 1899.

Hull, Richard C. *African Cities and Towns before the European Conquest.* New York: W. W. Norton, 1976.

Idowu, E. Bolaji. *African Traditional Religion, a Definition.* Maryknoll: Orbis, 1975.

Imperato, Pascal James. *African Folk Medicine, Practices and Beliefs of the Bambara and Other Peoples.* Baltimore: York, 1977.

Inikore, J. E. "The Import of Firearms into West Africa, 1750-1807: A

Quanitative Analysis." *Journal of African History*, 18 (1977), 339-368.

Johnson, Marion. "Economic Foundations of an Islamic Theocracy: The Case of Macina." *Journal of African History,* 17 (1976), 481-495.

———. "The Nineteenth Century Gold 'Mithqal' in West North Africa." *Journal of African History*, 9 (1968), 547-569.

Kaké, Ibrahima B. *Les Armées traditionnelles de l'Afrique noire.* Libreville: Éditions du Lion, 1980.

Kamara, Cheikh Moussa. "La Plus savoreuse des sciences et la plus agreable des informations concernant la vie du Maitre Cheikh El Hadj Omar." Amar Samb, trans. *Bulletin d'Institut Fondamental d'Afrique Noire,* ser. b. 32 (1970),44-135.

Kanya-Forstner, A. S. "Mali-Tukulor." *West African Resistance: The Military Response to Colonial Occupation.* New York: Africana, 1971.

———. *The Conquest of the Western Sudan.* London: Cambridge, 1969.

Kati, Mahmud b. El-Hadj El-Motaouakkel. *Tarikh el-Fettach.* O.Houdas and M. Delafosse, trans. Paris: Adrien-Maisonneuve, 1981.

Kenyatta, Jomo. *Facing Mt. Kenya.* New York: Random House, 1965.

Kesteloot, Lilyan. "Le Mythe et l'historie dans la formation de l'empire de Ségou." *Bulletin d'Institut Fondamental Afrique Noire,* ser. b 41 (1978), 578-681.

———. *Da Monzon de Ségou, Epopée Bambara.* Paris: Fernand Nathan, 1972.

Keto, C. Tsehloane. *Vision, Identity and Time: Afrocentric Paradigm and the Study of the Past.* Dubuque: Kendall-Hunt, 1994.

Kilson, Marion D. "Towards Freedom: An Analysis of Slave Revolts in the United States." *Phylon*, 25 (Summer, 1964), 175-87.

Kiwanuka, M. Semakula. "Colonial Policies and Administrations in Africa: The Myths of the Contrasts." *International Journal of African Historical Studies III*, (1970), 295-315.

Klein, Martin. "Social and Economic Factors in the Muslim Revolution in Senegambia." *Journal of African History,* 13 (1972), 419-441.

Konare, Alpha Oumar and Adam Ba Konare. *Grandes Dates du Mali.* Bamako: Éditions Imprimeries du Mali, 1983.

Koné, Aliore. "La Prise de Ségou et la fin d'el Hadj Omar." *Notes Africaines,* (1978), 61-5.

Lassalle-Séré, R. *Le Recrutement de l'Armée noire.* Paris: Librairie

Moderne de droit et jurisprudence, 1929.

Law, Robin. *The Oyo Empire c. 1600-c.1836, A West African Imperialism in the Era of the Atlantic Slave Trade.* Oxford: Clarendon, 1977.

Le Barbier, Louis. *Études sur les populations Bambaras de la Vallee du Niger.* Paris: Dujarric, 1906.

Lewis, Martin D. "One Hundred Million Frenchmen: The Assimilationist Theory in French Colonial Policy." *Comparative Studies in Society and History,* 4 (January, 1962), 129-53.

Leynard, Emile. "Fraternités d'age et sociétés de culture dans la Haute-Valée de Niger." *Cahiers d'Études Africaines,* 6 (1966), 41-68.

Loppinot, A. de. "Souvenirs d'Aguibu." *Bulletin du Comité d'Études Historiques et Scientifiques de l'Afrique Occidentale Française,* 2 (1919), 39-41.

Mademba, Abd-el-Kadir. "Au Sénégal et au Soudan français, le Fama Mademba." *Bulletin du Comité des Études Historiques et Scientifiques de l'Afrique Occidentale française,* 13 (1930), 107-216.

Mademba, Bendaud. "La Dernière étape d'un conqueront." *Bulletin du Comité d'Études Historiques et Scientifiques de l'Afrique Occidentale Française,* 3 (1921), 473-80.

Marquet, Yves. "Des Ihwan Al-Safa a Al-Hagg 'Umar (B. Sa'id Tall) Marabout et Conquerant Toucouleur." *Arabica,* 15 (1968), 6-47.

Mauny, Raymond. "Monnaies anciennes d'afrique occidentale." *Notes Africaines,* 42 (avril 1949), 60-61.

McIntosh, Susan K. and Roderick J. *Prehistoric Investigations in the Region of Jenne, Mali: A Study in the Development of Urbanism in the Sahel.* Oxford: BAR International, 1980.

McNaughton, Patrick R. "Bamana Blacksmiths." *African Arts,* 12 (February, 1979), 65-71.

Meillassoux, Claude. "The Role of Slavery in Economic and Social History of Sahelio-Sudanic Africa." *Forced Migration.* J. G. Inikori, ed. New York: Hutchinson, 1982.

Méniaud, Jacques. *Les Pionniers du Sudan avant, avec et après Archinard, 1879-1894.* Paris: Société des Publications Modernes, 1937.

Merriam, Alan P. "Use of Music in Reconstructing Culture History." *Reconstructing African Culture History.* Creighton Gabel and Norman

Bennett, eds. Boston: Boston University, 1967.

Mkandawire, Thandika. "Problems and Prospects of the Social Sciences in Africa." *International Social Science Journal*, 45 (1993), 129-140.

Montagnon, Pierre. *La France Coloniale la gloire de l'empire*. Paris: Pygmalion/Gerard Watelet, 1988.

Monteil, Charles. *Les Bambara de Ségou et du Kaarta*. Paris: Larosse, 1924.

——. "Fin de siècle à Médine (1897-1899)." Vincent Monteil, ed. *Bulletin de l'Institut Fondamental d'Afrique Noire,* ser. b 28 (1966), 82-172.

Monteil, Vincent. *L'Islam Noir*. Paris: Éditions du Seuil, 1964.

Newbury, C. W. and A. S. Kanya-Forstner. "French Policy and the Origins of the Scramble for West Africa." *Journal of African History,* 10 (1969), 253-76.

Oloruntimehin, B. Olatunji. *The Segu Tukulor Empire*. London: Longman, 1972.

——. "The Idea of Islamic Revolution and Tukulor Constitutional Evolution." *Bulletin de l'Institut Fondamental d'Afrique Noire,* ser. b. 33 (1971), 675-92.

——. "Anti-French Coalition of African States and Groups in the Western Sudan 1889-1893." *ODU*, (April, 1970), 3-21.

——. "Resistance Movements in the Tukulor Empire." *Cahiers d'É-tudes Afriques,* 8 (1968), 123-43.

——. "Muhammed Lamine in Franco-Tukulor Relations, 1885-1887." *Journal of the Historical Society of Nigeria,* 4 (December, 1968), 375-96.

——. "Abd al-Qadir's Mission as a factor Franco-Tukulor Relations 1883-1887." *Genève-Afrique,* 7 (1968), 33-50.

Ouane, Ibrahima Mamadou. *L'Islam et la Civilisation française*. Avignon: Les Presses Universelles, 1957.

Pageard, Robert. "Notes sur les Somono." *Notes Africaines,* 98 (1961), 17-18.

——. *Notes sur l'histoire de Bambara de Ségou*. Clichy: Chez l'auteur, 1957.

Paques, Viviana. *Les Bambara*. Paris: Presses Universitaires de France, 1954.

Person, Yves. "Ngolo Jara ou la force de Ségou." *Les Africains.* Charles André Julien, ed. Paris: Éditions J. A., 1978.

Raboteau, Albert J. *Slave Religion, the "Invisible Institution" in the Antebellum South.* London: Oxford University, 1978.

Roberts, Richard. *Warriors, Merchants and Slaves.* Stanford: Stanford University, 1987.

————. "Production and Reproduction of Warrior States: Segu Bambara and Segu Tokolor." *International Journal of Historical Studies,* 13 (1980), 389-419.

————. "The Emergence of the Grain Market in Bamako 1883-1908." *Canadian Journal of African Studies,* 14 (1980), 37-54.

Robinson, David. *The Holy War of Umar Tal.* Oxford: Clarendon, 1985.

————. *Chiefs and Clercs: Abdul Bokar Kan and Futa Toro 1853-1891.* Oxford: Clarendon, 1975.

————. "Abdul Qadir and Shaykh 'Umar: A Continuing Tradition of Islamic Leadership in Futa Toro." *African Historical Studies,* 6 (1973), 286-303.

Russell, Marion. "American Slave Discontent in Records of the High Courts." *Journal of Negro History,* 31 (October, 1946), 411-34.

Said, Edward. "Representing the Colonized: Anthropology's Interlocutors," *Critical Inquiry,* 15 (Winter, 1989), 205-225.

Saint-Martin, Yves. *L'Empire Toucouleur.* Paris: Le Livre Africaine, 1970.

————. *L'Empire Toucouleur et la France.* Dakar: Dakar Université, 1967.

————. "La Volonté de paix d'El Hadj Omar et d'Ahmadou dans leurs relations avec la France." *Bulletin de l'Institut Fondamental d'Afrique Noire,* ser b. 30 (1968), 785-802.

————. "Un Fils d'El Hadj Omar: Aguibou, roi du Dinguiray et du Macina (1843?-1907)." *Cahiers d'Études Africaines,* 8 (1968), 144-178.

————. "Les Relations diplomatique entre la France et l'empire Toucouleur de 1860 à 1864." *Bulletin del'Institut Fondamental d'Afrique Noire,* ser. b 27 (1965),183-222.

————. "L'Artillerie d'el Hadj Omar et d'Ahmadou." *Bulletin de l'Institut Fondamental d'Afrique Noire,* ser. b. 27 (Juillet, 1965), 560-

72.

Samb, Amar. "Sur el Hadj Omar (à propos d'un article d'Yves Saint-Martin)," *Bulletin de l'Institut d'Afrique Noire*, ser. b. 30 (1968), 803-05.

Sékéné-Moody, Cissoko. *Contribution à l'histoire politique du Khasso dans le Haut-Sénégal des Origines à 1854*. Paris: L'Harmattan, 1986.

Smaldone, Joseph. *Warfare in the Sokoto Caliphate: Historical and Sociological Perspectives*. Cambridge: Cambridge University, 1977.

Smith, H. F. C. "A Neglected Theme of West African History: the Islamic Revolutions of the Nineteenth Century." *Journal of the Historical Society of Nigeria,* 2 (1961), 169-85.

Smith, Robert. *Warfare and Diplomacy in Pre-Colonial West Africa*. Madison: University of Wisconsin, 1989. "Sokoto-Masina Correspondence" with Mallam A. Kani." *Research Bulletin of the Center of Arabic Documentation*. 11 (1975), 1-12.

Stewart, Charles C. "When Youth Concludes: Changes in Marriage and the Production of Youth since 1890 (in Mauritania)," in Helene Almeida-Topor, Odile Goerg and Catherine Coquery-Vidrovitch, eds. *Les mouvements de jeunesse en Afrique Francophone au XXe siecle*. Paris: Harmattan, 1993.

Susoko, Mariyan-Madi. *Wagadu Fo Sudan*. Bamako: Éditions Jamana, 1988.

Tauxier, Louis. "Chornologie des Rois Bambaras." *Cahiers d'Outremer*, 2 (1930), 119-130, 155-266.

———. *La Religion Bambara*. Paris: Librarie Orientaliste Paul Geuthner, 1927.

Toutain, L. "Notes sur les croyances et pratiques religieuses des Bamana." *Revue d'Ethnographie,* 3 (1884), 389-97.

Trimingham, J. Spencer. *Islam in West Africa*. London: Oxford, 1959.

———. *A History of Islam in West Africa*. London: Oxford University, 1962.

Un Bambara de Saint Louis. "La colonie Bambara de Ndioloffen et de Khor à Saint-Louis." *Notes Africaines*, 40 (octobre 1948), 18-20.

Uzoigwe, G. N. "The Warrior and the state in Pre-ColonialAfrica," *The Warrior Tradition in Modern Africa*. Ali A. Mazrui, ed. Leiden: E. J. Brill, 1977.

Vansina, Jan. "Use of Oral Tradition in Culture History." *Reconstructing African Culture History.* Creighton Gabel and Norman R. Bennett, eds. Boston: Boston University, 1967.

Wane, Yaya. "De Halwaar à Degembere, ou l'itineraire Islamique de Shaykh 'Umar Taal." *Bulletin de l'Institut Fondamental d'Afrique Noire,* ser. b 31 (1969), 445-51.

———. "Reflexions sur la dimensions sacrole chez les Toucouleurs." *Bulletin de l'Institut Fondamental d'Afrique Noire.* ser. b 39 (1977), 386-404.

Webster, J. B., A. A. Boahen, and M. Tidy. *The Revolutionary Years, West Africa since 1800.* Essex, England: Longman, 1980.

Welch, Claude E. Jr. "Warrior, Rebel, Guerilla, and Putschist." *The Warrior Tradition in Modern Africa.* Ali A. Mazrui, ed. Leiden: E. J. Brill, 1977.

Willis, John Ralph. "Introduction: Reflections on the Diffusion of Islam in West Africa." J. Willis, ed. *Studies in West African Islamic History.* vol. I. London: Frank Cass, 1979.

Wish, Harvey. "American Slave Insurrections before 1861." *Journal of Negro History*, 22 (July, 1937), 299-320.

UNPUBLISHED SOURCES

Camara, Seydou. "La Tradition orale en question: Conservation et transmission des traditions historiques au Manden: Le centre de Kela et l'histoire du Minijan." Thèse inédite. École des Haute Études en Sciences Sociales, 1990.

Coquery-Vidrovitch, Catherine. "The Rise of a Francophone African Social Science. From Colonial Knowledge to Knowledge of Africa, Contradition and Misunderstanding: De l'anthropologie à l'histoire de l'Afrique, c. 1830-c.1990." Paper at the Reconstructing the Study and Meaning of Africa Conference. Urbana-Champaign, April 7-9, 1994.

Hanson, John. "'Umarian Karta (Mali, West Africa) during the Late Nineteenth Century: Dissent and Revolt after 'Umar Tal's Holy War." Unpublished Dissertation. Michigan State University, 1989.

Keto, C. Tsehloane. "The Challenge of the Afrocentric Paradigm in the

Reconstruction of Historical Knowledge about Africa." Paper given at the Reconstructing the Study and Meaning of Africa Conference. Urbana-Champaign, April 7-9, 1994.

Sissoko, Abdourhamane Dramane. "Ségou sous l'occupation Toucouleure, 1860-1890." Thèse inédite. École Normale Supèrieure de Bamako, 1983.

Thiero, Seydou. "Les Ngolosiw et la décadence du Fanga de Ségou 1818-1893." Thèse inédite. École Normale Supèrieure de Bamako, 1985.

Togola, Téréba. "Archeological Investigations on Iron Age Cites in Méma, Mali." Unpublished dissertation. Rice University, 1992.